Policy Coordination in a Monetary Union

Springer
Berlin
Heidelberg
New York
Hong Kong
London
Milan
Paris
Tokyo

Michael Carlberg

Policy Coordination
in a Monetary Union

With 65 Tables

 Springer

Prof. Michael Carlberg
Department of Economics
Federal University of Hamburg
Holstenhofweg 85
22043 Hamburg
Germany
carlberg@unibw-hamburg.de

ISBN 3-540-00694-X Springer-Verlag Berlin Heidelberg New York

Cataloging-in-Publication Data applied for
A catalog record for this book is available from the Library of Congress.
Bibliographic information published by Die Deutsche Bibliothek
Die Deutsche Bibliothek lists this publication in the Deutsche Nationalbibliografie; detailed bibliographic
data is available in the Internet at <http://dnb.ddb.de>.

Springer-Verlag Berlin Heidelberg New York
a member of BertelsmannSpringer Science+Business Media GmbH

http://www.springer.de

© Springer-Verlag Berlin · Heidelberg 2003
Printed in Germany

SPIN 10917619   42/3130-5 4 3 2 1 0 – Printed on acid-free paper

Preface

This book studies the international coordination of economic policy in a monetary union. It carefully discusses the process of policy competition and the structure of policy cooperation. As to policy competition, the focus is on competition between the union central bank, the German government, and the French government. Similarly, as to policy cooperation, the focus is on cooperation between the union central bank, the German government, and the French government. The key questions are: Does the process of policy competition lead to full employment and price stability? Can these targets be achieved through policy cooperation? And is policy cooperation superior to policy competition? Another important issue is monetary competition / monetary cooperation between Europe and America.

The present book is part of a larger research project on monetary union, see Carlberg (1999, 2000, 2001, 2002). Some parts of this project were presented at the World Congress of the International Economic Association in Lisbon 2002. Other parts were presented at the Macro Study Group of the German Economic Association, at the Annual Conference of the German Economic Association, and at the Workshop on International Economics. Over the years, in working on this project, I have benefited from comments by Volker Clausen, Peter Flaschel, Wilfried Fuhrmann, Michael Funke, Franz X. Hof, Florence Huart, Jay H. Levin, Alfred Maußner, Hans G. Monissen, Manfred J. M. Neumann, Klaus Neusser, Franco Reither, Michael Schmid, Roberto Tamborini, Jürgen von Hagen, and Helmut Wagner. In addition, Michael Bräuninger and Alkis Otto carefully discussed with me all parts of the manuscript. Last but not least, Doris Ehrich did the secretarial work as excellently as ever. I would like to thank all of them.

January 2003   Michael Carlberg

Executive Summary

1) The monetary union of two countries, say Germany and France. First consider monetary policy in the union. The primary target of the union central bank is price stability in the union, and the secondary target is high employment in Germany and France. Now let there be unemployment in the union. More precisely, let unemployment in Germany exceed unemployment in France. Then monetary policy in the union can achieve full employment in France. Moreover, it can reduce unemployment in Germany. However, it cannot achieve full employment in Germany and France. Instead, let there be overemployment and hence inflation. More precisely, let overemployment in Germany exceed overemployment in France. Then monetary policy in the union can achieve price stability in the union. But it cannot achieve full employment in Germany and France.

Second consider fiscal competition between Germany and France. At the beginning there is unemployment in the union. More precisely, unemployment in Germany exceeds unemployment in France. As a result, the process of fiscal competition is unstable. In other words, fiscal competition does not lead to full employment in Germany and France. The reason is the large external effect of fiscal policy. There is a continuous increase in German government purchases, as there is in French government purchases. There are uniform oscillations in German output, as there are in French output. The German economy oscillates between high and low unemployment, as does the French economy. Third consider fiscal cooperation between Germany and France. As a result, there is no solution. In other words, fiscal cooperation cannot achieve full employment in Germany and France.

Fourth consider competition between the union central bank, the German government, and the French government. At the start there is unemployment in the union. Let unemployment in Germany exceed unemployment in France. As a result, the process of monetary and fiscal competition is unstable. In other words, monetary and fiscal competition does not lead to full employment in Germany and France. There is a one-time increase in union money supply. There is an

VIII

upward trend in German government purchases, as there is in French government purchases. There are uniform oscillations in German output, as there are in French output. The German economy oscillates between unemployment and full employment, as does the French economy. Fifth consider cooperation between the union central bank, the German government, and the French government. As a result, there is an infinite number of solutions. In other words, monetary and fiscal cooperation can achieve full employment in Germany and France.

2) The world of two monetary regions, say Europe and America. First consider monetary competition between Europe and America. At the beginning there is unemployment in the world. More precisely, unemployment in Europe exceeds unemployment in America. As a result, the process of monetary competition is stable. In other words, monetary competition leads to full employment in Europe and America. There is a continuous increase in European money supply, as there is in American money supply. And there is a continuous increase in European output, as there is in American output. Second consider monetary cooperation between Europe and America. As a result, there is a solution. In other words, monetary cooperation can achieve full employment in Europe and America.

Third consider fiscal competition between Europe and America. At the start there is unemployment in the world. Let unemployment in Europe exceed unemployment in America. As a result, the process of fiscal competition is unstable. In other words, fiscal competition does not lead to full employment in Europe and America. The reason is the large external effect of fiscal policy. There is an upward trend in European government purchases. By contrast, there is a downward trend in American government purchases. There are uniform oscillations in European output, as there are in American output. The European economy oscillates between unemployment and overemployment, as does the American economy. Fourth consider fiscal cooperation between Europe and America. As a result, there is no solution. In other words, fiscal cooperation cannot achieve full employment in Europe and America.

Contents in Brief

Contents

Introduction

1. Subject and Approach

This book studies the international coordination of economic policy in a monetary union. It carefully discusses the process of policy competition and the structure of policy cooperation. With respect to policy competition, the focus is on:

- fiscal competition between Germany and France
- competition between the union central bank,
  the German government, and the French government
- monetary competition between Europe and America
- fiscal competition between Europe and America.

With respect to policy cooperation, the focus is on:

- fiscal cooperation between Germany and France
- cooperation between the union central bank,
  the German government, and the French government
- monetary cooperation between Europe and America
- fiscal cooperation between Europe and America.

The primary target of the union central bank is price stability in the union. The secondary target of the union central bank is high employment in Germany and France. The target of the German government is full employment in Germany. And the target of the French government is full employment in France. Economic policy in one of the areas has a large external effect on the other area. For instance, an increase in German government purchases causes a decline in French output. An increase in European government purchases causes an increase in American output. And an increase in European money supply causes a decline in American output. The key questions are:

- Does the process of policy competition
  lead to full employment and price stability?
- Can policy cooperation
  achieve full employment and price stability?
- Is policy cooperation superior to policy competition?

This book takes new approaches that are firmly grounded on modern macroeconomics. The framework of analysis is as follows. The monetary union is defined as a group of countries that share a common currency. The monetary union is an open economy with international trade and capital mobility. The exchange rate between the monetary union and the rest of the world is flexible. A special feature of this book is the numerical estimation of shock and policy multipliers. There are numerical simulations of policy competition. There are numerical examples of policy cooperation. And there are lots of tables.

This book consists of four major parts:
- The Small Monetary Union of Two Countries
- The World of Two Monetary Regions
- The Large Monetary Union of Two Countries
- Rational Policy Expectations.

Now the approach will be presented in greater detail.

2. The Small Monetary Union of Two Countries

1) The basic model. The monetary union consists of two countries, say Germany and France. The exchange rate between the monetary union and the rest of the world is flexible. German goods and French goods are imperfect substitutes for each other. German output is determined by the demand for German goods. French output is determined by the demand for French goods. And union money demand equals union money supply. The monetary union is a small open economy with perfect capital mobility. For the small union, the world interest rate is given exogenously. Under perfect capital mobility, the union interest rate is determined by the world interest rate. Therefore the union interest rate is constant too. The union countries are the same size and have the same behavioural functions. In the short run, nominal wages and prices are rigid. This assumption will be relaxed below. Take for example an increase in German government purchases. Then what will be the effect of German output, and what

on French output? Correspondingly take an increase in union money supply. Again, what will be the effect on German output, and what on French output?

2) Monetary policy in the union. An increase in union money supply raises both German output and French output, to the same extent respectively. In the numerical example, a 1 percent increase in union money supply causes a 1 percent increase in German output and a 1 percent increase in French output. The primary target of the union central bank is price stability in the union, and the secondary target is high employment in Germany and France. The instrument of the union central bank is union money supply. It proves useful to consider two cases:

- unemployment in Germany and France
- inflation in Germany and France.

First consider unemployment in Germany and France. More precisely, let unemployment in Germany exceed unemployment in France. Then the specific target of the union central bank is full employment in France. Aiming at full employment in Germany would imply overemployment in France and, hence, inflation in France. Second consider inflation in Germany and France. Let there be overemployment in Germany and France, and let overemployment in Germany exceed overemployment in France. Then the specific target of the union central bank is full employment in Germany and, thus, price stability in Germany. Aiming at full employment in France would imply overemployment in Germany and, hence, inflation in Germany.

3) Fiscal competition between Germany and France. First consider the static model. An increase in German government purchases raises German output. On the other hand, it lowers French output. And what is more, the rise in German output is equal to the fall in French output. That is to say, union output does not change. Similarly, an increase in French government purchases raises French output. On the other hand, it lowers German output. And what is more, the rise in French output is equal to the fall in German output. Once again, union output does not change. In the numerical example, an increase in German government purchases of 100 causes an increase in German output of 74 and a decline in French output of equally 74. Likewise, an increase in French government purchases of 100 causes an increase in French output of 74 and a decline in

German output of equally 74. In a sense, the internal effect of fiscal policy is very small, while the external effect of fiscal policy is very large.

Second consider the dynamic model. At the beginning there is unemployment in both Germany and France. More precisely, unemployment in Germany exceeds unemployment in France. The target of the German government is full employment in Germany, and the instrument is German government purchases. The German government raises German government purchases so as to close the output gap in Germany. The target of the French government is full employment in France, and the instrument is French government purchases. The French government raises French government purchases so as to close the output gap in France. We assume that the German government and the French government decide simultaneously and independently. In addition there is an output lag. German output next period is determined by German government purchases this period as well as by French government purchases this period. In the same way, French output next period is determined by French government purchases this period as well as by German government purchases this period. The key questions are: Is there a steady state of fiscal competition? Is the steady state of fiscal competition stable? In other words, does fiscal competition lead to full employment in Germany and France? Besides, what are the dynamic characteristics of the policy process?

4) Fiscal cooperation between Germany and France. The targets are full employment in Germany and France. The instruments are German and French government purchases. So there are two targets and two instruments. Is there a solution to fiscal cooperation? And is fiscal cooperation superior to fiscal competition?

5) Competition between the union central bank, the German government, and the French government. At the start there is unemployment in both Germany and France. Let unemployment in Germany exceed unemployment in France. The primary target of the union central bank is price stability in the union, and the secondary target is high employment in Germany and France. The instrument of the union central bank is union money supply. The target of the German government is full employment in Germany, and the instrument is German government purchases. The target of the French government is full employment in France, and the instrument is French government purchases.

We assume that the central bank and the governments decide sequentially. First the central bank decides, and then the governments decide. In step 1, the union central bank decides. In step 2, the German government and the French government decide simultaneously and independently. In step 3, the union central bank decides. In step 4, the German government and the French government decide simultaneously and independently. And so on. The reasons for this stepwise procedure are: First, the inside lag of monetary policy is short, whereas the inside lag of fiscal policy is long. And second, the internal effect of monetary policy is very large, whereas the internal effect of fiscal policy is very small. Indeed, the effective multiplier of fiscal policy is zero. Now the key questions are: Does the process of monetary and fiscal competition lead to full employment in Germany and France? Moreover, is monetary and fiscal competition superior to fiscal competition?

6) Cooperation between the union central bank, the German government, and the French government. The targets are full employment in Germany and France. The instruments are union money supply, German government purchases, and French government purchases. So there are two targets and three instruments. Is there a solution to monetary and fiscal cooperation? Further, is monetary and fiscal cooperation superior to monetary and fiscal competition?

7) Competition between the German labour union and the French labour union. First consider the static model. An increase in German nominal wages lowers both German output and French output. Here the fall in German output exceeds the fall in French output. Correspondingly, an increase in French nominal wages lowers both French output and German output. Here the fall in French output exceeds the fall in German output. In the numerical example, a 1 percent increase in German nominal wages causes a 0.79 percent decline in German output and a 0.21 percent decline in French output. Similarly, a 1 percent increase in French nominal wages causes a 0.79 percent decline in French output and a 0.21 percent decline in German output. That means, the internal effect of wage policy is very large, and the external effect of wage policy is large.

Second consider the dynamic model. At the beginning there is unemployment in both Germany and France. More precisely, unemployment in Germany

6

exceeds unemployment in France. The target of the German labour union is full employment in Germany. The instrument of the German labour union is German nominal wages. The German labour union lowers German nominal wages so as to close the output gap in Germany. The target of the French labour union is full employment in France. The instrument of the French labour union is French nominal wages. The French labour union lowers French nominal wages so as to close the output gap in France. We assume that the German labour union and the French labour union decide simultaneously and independently. In addition there is an output lag. German output next period is determined by German nominal wages this period as well as by French nominal wages this period. In the same way, French output next period is determined by French nominal wages this period as well as by German nominal wages this period. The key questions are: Is there a stable steady state of wage policy competition? Put differently, does wage policy competition lead to full employment in Germany and France? Besides, is wage policy competition superior to fiscal competition?

8) Cooperation between the German labour union and the French labour union. The targets are full employment in Germany and France. The instruments are German and French nominal wages. So there are two targets and two instruments. Is there a solution to wage policy cooperation? And is wage policy cooperation superior to wage policy competition?

9) Competition between the central bank, the German labour union, and the French labour union. At the start there is unemployment in both Germany and France. Let unemployment in Germany exceed unemployment in France. The primary target of the union central bank is price stability in the union, and the secondary target is high employment in Germany and France. The instrument of the union central bank is union money supply. The target of the German labour union is full employment in Germany, and the instrument is German nominal wages. The target of the French labour union is full employment in France, and the instrument is French nominal wages. We assume that the central bank and the labour unions decide sequentially. First the central bank decides, and then the labour unions decide. In step 1, the central bank decides. In step 2, the German labour union and the French labour union decide simultaneously and independently. In step 3, the central bank decides. In step 4, the German labour union and the French labour union decide simultaneously and independently. And so on. The key questions are: Does the process of monetary and wage

competition lead to full employment in Germany and France? Moreover, is monetary and wage competition superior to wage competition?

10) Cooperation between the central bank, the German labour union, and the French labour union. The targets are full employment in Germany and France. The instruments are union money supply, German nominal wages, and French nominal wages. So there are two targets and three instruments. Is there a solution to monetary and wage cooperation? Further, is monetary and wage cooperation superior to monetary and wage competition?

3. The World of Two Monetary Regions

1) The basic model. The world consists of two monetary regions, say Europe and America. The exchange rate between Europe and America is flexible. European goods and American goods are imperfect substitutes for each other. European output is determined by the demand for European goods. American output is determined by the demand for American goods. European money demand equals European money supply. And American money demand equals American money supply. There is perfect capital mobility between Europe and America, so the European interest rate agrees with the American interest rate. The monetary regions are the same size and have the same behavioural functions. In the short run, nominal wages and prices are rigid. Take for example an increase in European money supply. Then what will be the effect on European output, and what on American output? Similarly, take an increase in European government purchases. Again, what will be the effect on European output, and what on American output?

2) Monetary competition between Europe and America. First consider the static model. An increase in European money supply raises European output. On the other hand, it lowers American output. Here the rise in European output exceeds the fall in American output. Correspondingly, an increase in American money supply raises American output. On the other hand, it lowers European

8

output. Here the rise in American output exceeds the fall in European output. In the numerical example, an increase in European money supply of 100 causes an increase in European output of 300 and a decline in American output of 100. Likewise, an increase in American money supply of 100 causes an increase in American output of 300 and a decline in European output of 100. That is to say, the internal effect of monetary policy is very large, and the external effect of monetary policy is large.

Second consider the dynamic model. At the beginning there is unemployment in both Europe and America. More precisely, unemployment in Europe exceeds unemployment in America. The target of the European central bank is full employment in Europe. The instrument of the European central bank is European money supply. The European central bank raises European money supply so as to close the output gap in Europe. The target of the American central bank is full employment in America. The instrument of the American central bank is American money supply. The American central bank raises American money supply so as to close the output gap in America. We assume that the European central bank and the American central bank decide simultaneously and independently. In addition there is an output lag. European output next period is determined by European money supply this period as well as by American money supply this period. In the same way, American output next period is determined by American money supply this period as well as by European money supply this period. The key questions are: Is there a steady state of monetary competition? Is the steady state of monetary competition stable? In other words, does monetary competition lead to full employment in Europe and America? And what are the dynamic characteristics of the policy process?

3) Monetary cooperation between Europe and America. The targets are full employment in Europe and America. The instruments are European and American money supply. So there are two targets and two instruments. Is there a solution to monetary cooperation? And is monetary cooperation superior to monetary competition?

4) Fiscal competition between Europe and America. First consider the static model. An increase in European government purchases raises both European output and American output. And what is more, the rise in European output is equal to the rise in American output. Similarly, an increase in American

government purchases raises both American output and European output. And what is more, the rise in American output is equal to the rise in European output. In the numerical example, an increase in European government purchases of 100 causes an increase in European output of 90 and an increase in American output of equally 90. Likewise, an increase in American government purchases of 100 causes an increase in American output of 90 and an increase in European output of equally 90. In a sense, the internal effect of fiscal policy is rather small, whereas the external effect of fiscal policy is quite large.

Second consider the dynamic model. At the start there is unemployment in both Europe and America. Let unemployment in Europe exceed unemployment in America. The target of the European government is full employment in Europe, and the instrument is European government purchases. The European government raises European government purchases so as to close the output gap in Europe. The target of the American government is full employment in America, and the instrument is American government purchases. The American government raises American government purchases so as to close the output gap in America. We assume that the European government and the American government decide simultaneously and independently. In addition there is an output lag. European output next period is determined by European government purchases this period as well as by American government purchases this period. In the same way, American output next period is determined by American government purchases this period as well as by European government purchases this period. The key questions are: Is there a stable steady state of fiscal competition? Put differently, does fiscal competition lead to full employment in Europe and America? Besides, is monetary competition superior to fiscal competition?

5) Fiscal cooperation between Europe and America. The targets are full employment in Europe and America. The instruments are European and American government purchases. So there are two targets and two instruments. Is there a solution to fiscal cooperation? And is fiscal cooperation superior to fiscal competition?

4. The Large Monetary Union of Two Countries

1) The basic model. The world consists of two monetary regions, say Europe and America. The exchange rate between Europe and America is flexible. Europe in turn consists of two countries, say Germany and France. So Germany and France form a monetary union. German goods, French goods and American goods are imperfect substitutes for each other. German output is determined by the demand for German goods. French output is determined by the demand for French goods. And American output is determined by the demand for American goods. European money demand equals European money supply. And American money demand equals American money supply. There is perfect capital mobility between Germany, France and America. Thus the German interest rate, the French interest rate, and the American interest rate are equalized. The monetary regions are the same size and have the same behavioural functions. The union countries are the same size and have the same behavioural functions. In the short run, nominal wages and prices are rigid. Take for example an increase in German government purchases. Then what will be the effect on German output, and what on French output?

2) Fiscal competition between Germany and France. First consider the static model. An increase in German government purchases raises German output. On the other hand, it lowers French output. Here the rise in German output exceeds the fall in French output. Correspondingly, an increase in French government purchases raises French output. On the other hand, it lowers German output. Here the rise in French output exceeds the fall in German output. In the numerical example, an increase in German government purchases of 100 causes an increase in German output of 141 and a decline in French output of 52. Correspondingly, an increase in French government purchases of 100 causes an increase in French output of 141 and a decline in German output of 52.

Second consider the dynamic model. At the beginning there is unemployment in both Germany and France. More precisely, unemployment in Germany exceeds unemployment in France. The target of the German government is full employment in Germany, and the instrument is German government purchases. The German government raises German government purchases so as to close the output gap in Germany. The target of the French government is full employment in France, and the instrument is French government purchases. The French government raises French government purchases so as to close the output gap in France. The key questions are: Is there a steady state of fiscal competition? Is the steady state of fiscal competition stable? In other words, does fiscal competition lead to full employment in Germany and France? And what are the dynamic characteristics of the policy process?

3) Fiscal cooperation between Germany and France. The targets are full employment in Germany and France. The instruments are German and French government purchases. So there are two targets and two instruments. Is there a solution to fiscal cooperation? And is fiscal cooperation superior to fiscal competition?

4) Competition between the European central bank, the German government, and the French government. First consider the static model. An increase in European money supply raises both German output and French output, to the same extent respectively. An increase in German government purchases raises German output. On the other hand, it lowers French output. Here the rise in German output exceeds the fall in French output. In the numerical example, an increase in European money supply of 100 causes an increase in German output of 150 and an increase in French output of equally 150. An increase in German government purchases of 100 causes an increase in German output of 141 and a decline in French output of 52.

Second consider the dynamic model. At the start there is unemployment in both Germany and France. Let unemployment in Germany exceed unemployment in France. The primary target of the European central bank is price stability in Europe, and the secondary target is high employment in Germany and France. The instrument of the European central bank is European money supply. The target of the German government is full employment in Germany, and the instrument is German government purchases. The target of the French government is full employment in France, and the instrument is French government purchases. We assume that the central bank and the governments decide sequentially. First the central bank decides, and then the governments decide. In step 1, the European central bank decides. In step 2, the German government and the French government decide simultaneously and independently. In step 3, the European central bank decides. In step 4, the German government and the French government decide simultaneously and independently. And so on. The key questions are: Does the process of monetary and fiscal competition lead to full employment in Germany and France? Is monetary and fiscal competition superior to fiscal competition?

5) Cooperation between the European central bank, the German government, and the French government. The targets are full employment in Germany and France. The instruments are European money supply, German government purchases, and French government purchases. So there are two targets and three instruments. Is there a solution to monetary and fiscal cooperation? Is monetary and fiscal cooperation superior to monetary and fiscal competition?

5. Rational Policy Expectations

1) The small monetary union of two countries. First consider fiscal competition between Germany and France. At the beginning there is unemployment in both Germany and France. More precisely, unemployment in Germany exceeds unemployment in France. The target of the German government is full employment in Germany, and the instrument is German government purchases. The target of the French government is full employment in France, and the instrument is French government purchases. The German government and the French government decide simultaneously and independently. The German government sets German government purchases, forming rational expectations of French government purchases. And the French government sets French government purchases, forming rational expectations of German government purchases. That is to say, the German government sets German government purchases, predicting French government purchases by means of the model. And the French government sets French government purchases, predicting German government purchases by means of the model. The key questions are: Under rational expectations, is there an equilibrium of fiscal competition? In other words, does fiscal competition lead to full employment?

Second consider competition between the union central bank, the German government, and the French government. The primary target of the union central bank is price stability in the union, and the secondary target is high employment in Germany and France. The instrument of the union central bank is union money supply. The target of the German government is full employment in Germany, and the instrument is German government purchases. The target of the French government is full employment in France, and the instrument is French government purchases. We assume that the union central bank, the German government, and the French government decide simultaneously and independently. The union central bank sets union money supply, forming rational expectations of German and French government purchases. The German government sets German government purchases, forming rational expectations of union money supply and French government purchases. And the French government sets French government purchases, forming rational expectations of union money supply and German government purchases. The key questions are: Under rational expectations, is there a unique equilibrium of monetary and fiscal competition? Put differently, does monetary and fiscal competition lead to full employment?

2) The world of two monetary regions. First consider monetary competition between Europe and America. At the start there is unemployment in Europe and America. Let unemployment in Europe exceed unemployment in America. The target of the European central bank is full employment in Europe, and the instrument is European money supply. The target of the American central bank is full employment in America, and the instrument is American money supply. We assume that the central banks decide simultaneously and independently. The European central bank sets European money supply, forming rational expectations of American money supply. And the American central bank sets American money supply, forming rational expectations of European money supply. That is to say, the European central bank sets European money supply, predicting American money supply by means of the model. And the American central bank sets American money supply, predicting European money supply by means of the model. The key questions are: Under rational expectations, is there an immediate equilibrium of monetary competition? In other words, does monetary competition lead to full employment immediately?

Second consider fiscal competition between Europe and America. The target of the European government is full employment in Europe, and the instrument is European government purchases. The target of the American government is full employment in America, and the instrument is American government purchases. We assume that the governments decide simultaneously and independently. The European government sets European government purchases, forming rational expectations of American government purchases. And the American government sets American government purchases, forming rational expectations of European government purchases. The key questions are: Under rational expectations, is there an equilibrium of fiscal competition? Put another way, does fiscal competition lead to full employment?

Part One

The Small Monetary Union
of Two Countries

Chapter 1
The Basic Model

1) Introduction. In this chapter we consider a monetary union of two countries, let us say Germany and France. The exchange rate between the monetary union and the rest of the world is flexible. Take for instance an increase in German government purchases. Then what will be the effect on German income, and what on French income? Alternatively, take an increase in union money supply. Again what will be the effect on German income, and what on French income?

In doing the analysis, we make the following assumptions. German goods and French goods are imperfect substitutes for each other. German output is determined by the demand for German goods. French output is determined by the demand for French goods. And union money demand equals union money supply. The monetary union is a small open economy with perfect capital mobility. For the small union, the world interest rate is given exogenously $r_f = const$. Under perfect capital mobility, the union interest rate is determined by the world interest rate $r = r_f$. Therefore the union interest rate is constant too. In the short run, nominal wages and prices are rigid. This assumption will be relaxed below, see Chapter 11. P_1 denotes the price of German goods, as measured in euros. And P_2 denotes the price of French goods, as measured in euros. To simplify notation, let be $P_1 = P_2 = 1$.

2) The market for German goods. The behavioural functions underlying the analysis are as follows:

$$C_1 = C_1(Y_1) \tag{1}$$

$$I_1 = I_1(r) \tag{2}$$

$$G_1 = const \tag{3}$$

$$X_{12} = X_{12}(Y_2) \tag{4}$$

$$X_{13} = X_{13}(e) \tag{5}$$

$$Q_1 = Q_1(Y_1) \tag{6}$$

Equation (1) is the consumption function of Germany. It states that German consumption is an increasing function of German income. Here C_1 denotes German consumption, and Y_1 is German income. Equation (2) is the investment function of Germany. It states that German investment is a decreasing function of the world interest rate. I_1 denotes German investment, and r is the world interest rate. According to equation (3), the German government fixes its purchases of goods and services. G_1 denotes German government purchases.

Equations (4) and (5) are the export functions of Germany. Equation (4) states that German exports to France are an increasing function of French income. X_{12} denotes German exports to France, and Y_2 is French income. Equation (5) states that German exports to non-union countries are an increasing function of the union exchange rate. X_{13} denotes German exports to non-union countries. And e is the exchange rate between the union and the rest of the world. For example, e is the price of the dollar as measured in euros. The message of equation (5) is that a depreciation of the euro raises German exports to non-union countries. Equation (6) is the import function of Germany. It states that German imports are an increasing function of German income. Q_1 denotes German imports from France and from non-union countries.

German output is determined by the demand for German goods $Y_1 = C_1 + I_1 + G_1 + X_{12} + X_{13} - Q_1$. Taking account of the behavioural functions (1) to (6), we arrive at the goods market equation of Germany:

$$Y_1 = C_1(Y_1) + I_1(r) + G_1 + X_{12}(Y_2) + X_{13}(e) - Q_1(Y_1) \tag{7}$$

3) The market for French goods. The behavioural functions are as follows:

$$C_2 = C_2(Y_2) \tag{8}$$

$$I_2 = I_2(r) \tag{9}$$

$$G_2 = \text{const} \tag{10}$$

$$X_{21} = X_{21}(Y_1) \tag{11}$$

$$X_{23} = X_{23}(e) \tag{12}$$

$$Q_2 = Q_2(Y_2) \tag{13}$$

Equation (8) is the consumption function of France. It states that French consumption is an increasing function of French income. Here C_2 denotes French consumption, and Y_2 is French income. Equation (9) is the investment function of France. It states that French investment is a decreasing function of the world interest rate. I_2 denotes French investment. According to equation (10), the French government fixes its purchases of goods and services. G_2 denotes French government purchases.

Equations (11) and (12) are the export functions of France. Equation (11) states that French exports to Germany are an increasing function of German income. X_{21} denotes French exports to Germany. Equation (12) states that French exports to non-union countries are an increasing function of the union exchange rate. X_{23} denotes French exports to non-union countries. The message of equation (12) is that a depreciation of the euro raises French exports to non-union countries. Equation (13) is the import function of France. It states that French imports are an increasing function of French income. Q_2 denotes French imports from Germany and from non-union countries.

French output is determined by the demand for French goods $Y_2 = C_2 + I_2 + G_2 + X_{21} + X_{23} - Q_2$. Upon substituting the behavioural functions (8) to (13), we reach the goods market equation of France:

$$Y_2 = C_2(Y_2) + I_2(r) + G_2 + X_{21}(Y_1) + X_{23}(e) - Q_2(Y_2) \tag{14}$$

4) The money market of the union. The behavioural functions are as follows:

$$L_1 = L_1(r, Y_1) \tag{15}$$

$$L_2 = L_2(r, Y_2) \tag{16}$$

$$M = \text{const} \tag{17}$$

Equation (15) is the money demand function of Germany. It states that German money demand is a decreasing function of the world interest rate and an increasing function of German income. L_1 denotes German money demand. Equation (16) is the money demand function of France. It states that French money demand is a decreasing function of the world interest rate and an increasing function of French income. L_2 denotes French money demand.

Equation (17) is the money supply function of the union. It states that the union central bank fixes the money supply of the union. M denotes union money supply. The money demand of the union is equal to the money supply of the union $L_1 + L_2 = M$. Upon inserting the behavioural functions (15) to (17), we get to the money market equation of the union:

$$L_1(r, Y_1) + L_2(r, Y_2) = M \tag{18}$$

5) The model. On this foundation, the full model can be represented by a system of three equations:

$$Y_1 = C_1(Y_1) + I_1(r) + G_1 + X_{12}(Y_2) + X_{13}(e) - Q_1(Y_1) \tag{19}$$

$$Y_2 = C_2(Y_2) + I_2(r) + G_2 + X_{21}(Y_1) + X_{23}(e) - Q_2(Y_2) \tag{20}$$

$$M = L_1(r, Y_1) + L_2(r, Y_2) \tag{21}$$

Equation (19) is the goods market equation of Germany, as measured in German goods. (20) is the goods market equation of France, as measured in French goods. And (21) is the money market equation of the union, as measured in euros. It is worth pointing out here that the goods market equations are well consistent with microfoundations, see Carlberg (2002). The exogenous variables are union money supply M, German government purchases G_1, French government purchases G_2, and the world interest rate r. The endogenous variables are German income Y_1, French income Y_2, and the union exchange rate e.

6) The total differential. It is useful to take the total differential of the model:

$$dY_1 = c_1 dY_1 + dG_1 + m_2 dY_2 + h_1 de - q_1 dY_1 \tag{22}$$

$$dY_2 = c_2 dY_2 + dG_2 + m_1 dY_1 + h_2 de - q_2 dY_2 \tag{23}$$

$$dM = k_1 dY_1 + k_2 dY_2 \tag{24}$$

Here is a list of the new symbols:

c_1 marginal consumption rate of Germany

c_2 marginal consumption rate of France

h_1 exchange rate sensitivity of German exports

h_2 exchange rate sensitivity of French exports

k_1 income sensitivity of German money demand

k_2 income sensitivity of French money demand

m_1 marginal import rate of Germany relative to France

m_2 marginal import rate of France relative to Germany

q_1 marginal import rate of Germany relative to France and non-union countries

q_2 marginal import rate of France relative to Germany and non-union countries

We assume that the union countries are the same size and have the same behavioural functions. In terms of the model this means:

$$c = c_1 = c_2 \tag{25}$$

$$h = h_1 = h_2 \tag{26}$$

$$k = k_1 = k_2 \tag{27}$$

$$m = m_1 = m_2 \tag{28}$$

$$q = q_1 = q_2 \tag{29}$$

These assumptions prove to be particularly fruitful. In addition we make some standard assumptions:

$$0 < c < 1 \tag{30}$$

$$h > 0 \tag{31}$$

$$k > 0 \tag{32}$$

$$0 < m < 1 \tag{33}$$

$$0 < q < 1 \tag{34}$$

7) Fiscal policy. Take for instance an increase in German government purchases. Then what will be the effect on German income, and what on French income? The total differential of the model is as follows:

$$dY_1 = cdY_1 + dG_1 + mdY_2 + hde - qdY_1 \tag{35}$$

$$dY_2 = cdY_2 + mdY_1 + hde - qdY_2 \tag{36}$$

$$0 = dY_1 + dY_2 \tag{37}$$

Subtract equation (36) from equation (35) to verify $(1 - c + m + q)(dY_1 - dY_2) = dG_1$. Further note equation (37) and solve for:

$$\frac{dY_1}{dG_1} = \frac{1}{2(1 - c + m + q)} \tag{38}$$

$$\frac{dY_2}{dG_1} = -\frac{1}{2(1 - c + m + q)} \tag{39}$$

As a fundamental result, these are the fiscal policy multipliers. An increase in German government purchases raises German income. On the other hand, it lowers French income. And what is more, the increase in German income is equal in amount to the decline in French income. That is to say, union income does not change. Now have a closer look at the process of adjustment. The increase in German government purchases causes an appreciation of the euro. This in turn reduces both German exports and French exports. The net effect is that German income goes up, while French income goes down.

To illustrate this, consider a numerical example with $c = 0.72$, $m = 0.16$, and $q = 0.24$. Let the sensitivity of consumption to net income be 0.9, and let the tax rate be 0.2. Then the sensitivity of consumption to gross income is $c = 0.8 * 0.9 = 0.72$. The marginal import rate of Germany is $q = 0.24$. The marginal import rate of Germany relative to France is $m = 0.16$. And the marginal import rate of Germany relative to non-union countries is $q - m = 0.08$. Likewise, the marginal import rate of France is $q = 0.24$. The marginal import rate of France relative to Germany is $m = 0.16$. And the marginal import rate of

France relative to non-union countries is $q - m = 0.08$. Hence the fiscal policy multipliers are $dY_1 / dG_1 = 0.735$ and $dY_2 / dG_1 = -0.735$. That means, an increase in German government purchases of 100 causes an increase in German income of 74 and a decline in French income of equally 74. In a sense, the internal effect of fiscal policy is very small, while the external effect of fiscal policy is very large.

8) Monetary policy. Take for instance an increase in union money supply. Then what will be the effect on German income, and what on French income? The total differential of the model is:

$$dY_1 = cdY_1 + mdY_2 + hde - qdY_1 \tag{40}$$

$$dY_2 = cdY_2 + mdY_1 + hde - qdY_2 \tag{41}$$

$$dM = kdY_1 + kdY_2 \tag{42}$$

Subtract equation (41) from equation (40) to get $dY_1 = dY_2$. Put this into equation (42) and rearrange terms:

$$\frac{dY_1}{dM} = \frac{dY_2}{dM} = \frac{1}{2k} \tag{43}$$

As a principal result, these are the monetary policy multipliers. An increase in union money supply raises both German income and French income, to the same extent respectively. Moreover have a closer look at the channels of transmission. The increase in union money supply causes a depreciation of the euro. This in turn enhances both German exports and French exports. That is why German income and French income move up. To illustrate this, consider a numerical example with $k = 0.25$. So the monetary policy multipliers are $dY_1 / dM = dY_2 / dM = 2$. In other words, an increase in union money supply of 100 causes an increase in German income of 200 and an increase in French income of equally 200.

Chapter 2
Monetary Policy in the Union

1) The model. The output model can be characterized by a system of two equations:

$$Y_1 = A_1 + \alpha M \tag{1}$$

$$Y_2 = A_2 + \alpha M \tag{2}$$

According to equation (1), German output Y_1 is determined by union money supply M and by some other factors called A_1. According to equation (2), French output Y_2 is determined by union money supply M and by some other factors called A_2. The monetary policy multiplier is positive $\alpha > 0$. The endogenous variables are German output and French output. The primary target of the union central bank is price stability in the union. The secondary target of the union central bank is high employment in Germany and France. The instrument of the union central bank is union money supply. It proves useful to consider two distinct cases:
- unemployment in Germany and France
- inflation in Germany and France.

First consider unemployment in Germany and France. More precisely, let unemployment in Germany exceed unemployment in France. Then the specific target of the union central bank is full employment in France. Aiming at full employment in Germany would imply overemployment in France and, hence, inflation in France. Here a comment is in place. Full employment is defined as the equilibrium rate of unemployment (the natural rate of unemployment or NAIRU). So unemployment means that actual unemployment is above equilibrium unemployment. And overemployment means that actual unemployment is below equilibrium unemployment.

Second consider inflation in Germany and France. Let there be overemployment in Germany and France, and let overemployment in Germany

24

exceed overemployment in France. Then the specific target of the union central bank is full employment in Germany and, thus, price stability in Germany. Aiming at full employment in France would imply overemployment in Germany and, hence, inflation in Germany.

2) Some numerical examples. Let the monetary policy multiplier be $\alpha = 2$. Then the output model can be written as follows:

$$Y_1 = A_1 + 2M \tag{3}$$

$$Y_2 = A_2 + 2M \tag{4}$$

The endogenous variables are German and French output. Obviously, an increase in union money supply of 100 causes an increase in German output of 200 and an increase in French output of equally 200. Further let full-employment output in Germany be 1000, and let full-employment output in France be the same. Again it proves useful to consider two cases:
- unemployment in Germany and France
- inflation in Germany and France.

First consider unemployment in Germany and France. More precisely, let unemployment in Germany exceed unemployment in France. Let German output be 940, and let French output be 970. That is to say, the output gap in Germany is 60, and the output gap in France is 30. In this situation, the specific target of the union central bank is to close the output gap in France. The monetary policy multiplier in France is 2. So what is needed is an increase in union money supply of 15. This policy action raises German output and French output by 30 each. As a consequence, German output goes from 940 to 970, and French output goes from 970 to 1000. In France there is now full employment. In Germany unemployment comes down, but there is still some unemployment left. Table 1.1 presents a synopsis. As a result, monetary policy in the union can achieve full employment in France. Moreover, monetary policy in the union can reduce unemployment in Germany. However, monetary policy in the union cannot achieve full employment in Germany and France.

Table 1.1
Monetary Policy in the Union
Unemployment in Germany and France

	Germany	France
Initial Output	940	970
Change in Money Supply	15
Output	970	1000

Table 1.2
Monetary Policy in the Union
Inflation in Germany and France

	Germany	France
Initial Output	1060	1030
Change in Money Supply	−30
Output	1000	970

Second consider inflation in Germany and France. Let there be overemployment in Germany and France, and let overemployment in Germany exceed overemployment in France. Let German output be 1060, and let French output be 1030. That is to say, the inflationary gap in Germany is 60, and the inflationary gap in France is 30. In this situation, the specific target of the union central bank is to close the inflationary gap in Germany. The monetary policy multiplier in Germany is 2. So what is needed is a reduction in union money supply of 30. This policy action lowers German output and French output by 60 each. As a consequence, German output goes from 1060 to 1000, and French output goes from 1030 to 970. There is now price stability in the union. In addition, there is full employment in Germany. As an adverse side effect, there is unemployment in France. Table 1.2 gives on overview. As a result, monetary policy in the union can achieve price stability in the union. On the other hand, monetary policy in the union cannot achieve full employment in Germany and France.

Chapter 3
Fiscal Competition between Germany and France

1. The Dynamic Model

1) The static model. As a point of reference, consider the static model. It can be represented by a system of two equations:

$$Y_1 = A_1 + \gamma G_1 - \delta G_2 \tag{1}$$

$$Y_2 = A_2 + \gamma G_2 - \delta G_1 \tag{2}$$

According to equation (1), German output Y_1 is determined by German government purchases G_1, French government purchases G_2, and some other factors called A_1. According to equation (2), French output Y_2 is determined by French government purchases G_2, German government purchases G_1, and some other factors called A_2. The internal effect of fiscal policy is positive $\gamma > 0$. By contrast, the external effect of fiscal policy is negative $\delta > 0$. And what is more, the internal effect and the external effect are the same size $\gamma = \delta$. The endogenous variables are German output and French output. Along these lines, the static model can be rewritten as follows:

$$Y_1 = A_1 + \gamma G_1 - \gamma G_2 \tag{3}$$

$$Y_2 = A_2 + \gamma G_2 - \gamma G_1 \tag{4}$$

Again the endogenous variables are German and French output.

2) The dynamic model. At the beginning there is unemployment in both Germany and France. More precisely, unemployment in Germany exceeds unemployment in France. The target of the German government is full employment in Germany. The instrument of the German government is German government purchases. The German government raises German government purchases so as to close the output gap in Germany:

$$G_1 - G_1^{-1} = \frac{\overline{Y_1} - Y_1}{\gamma} \tag{5}$$

Here is a list of the new symbols:

Y_1 German output this period

$\overline{Y_1}$ full-employment output in Germany

$\overline{Y_1} - Y_1$ output gap in Germany this period

G_1^{-1} German government purchases last period

G_1 German government purchases this period

$G_1 - G_1^{-1}$ increase in German government purchases.

Here the endogenous variable is German government purchases this period G_1.

The target of the French government is full employment in France. The instrument of the French government is French government purchases. The French government raises French government purchases so as to close the output gap in France:

$$G_2 - G_2^{-1} = \frac{\overline{Y_2} - Y_2}{\gamma} \tag{6}$$

Here is a list of the new symbols:

Y_2 French output this period

$\overline{Y_2}$ full-employment output in France

$\overline{Y_2} - Y_2$ output gap in France this period

G_2^{-1} French government purchases last period

G_2 French government purchases this period

$G_2 - G_2^{-1}$ increase in French government purchases.

Here the endogenous variable is French government purchases this period G_2. We assume that the German government and the French government decide simultaneously and independently.

In addition there is an output lag. German output next period is determined by German government purchases this period as well as by French government purchases this period:

$$Y_1^{+1} = A_1 + \gamma G_1 - \gamma G_2 \tag{7}$$

Here Y_1^{+1} denotes German output next period. In the same way, French output next period is determined by French government purchases this period as well as by German government purchases this period:

$$Y_2^{+1} = A_2 + \gamma G_2 - \gamma G_1 \tag{8}$$

Here Y_2^{+1} denotes French output next period.

On this basis, the dynamic model can be characterized by a system of four equations:

$$G_1 - G_1^{-1} = \frac{\overline{Y}_1 - Y_1}{\gamma} \tag{9}$$

$$G_2 - G_2^{-1} = \frac{\overline{Y}_2 - Y_2}{\gamma} \tag{10}$$

$$Y_1^{+1} = A_1 + \gamma G_1 - \gamma G_2 \tag{11}$$

$$Y_2^{+1} = A_2 + \gamma G_2 - \gamma G_1 \tag{12}$$

Equation (9) shows the policy response in Germany, (10) shows the policy response in France, (11) shows the output lag in Germany, and (12) shows the output lag in France. The endogenous variables are German government purchases this period G_1, French government purchases this period G_2, German output next period Y_1^{+1}, and French output next period Y_2^{+1}.

3) The steady state. In the steady state by definition we have:

$$G_1 = G_1^{-1} \tag{13}$$

$$G_2 = G_2^{-1} \tag{14}$$

Equation (13) has it that German government purchases do not change any more. Similarly, equation (14) has it that French government purchases do not change any more. Therefore the steady state can be captured by a system of four equations:

$$Y_1 = \overline{Y}_1 \tag{15}$$

$$Y_2 = \overline{Y}_2 \tag{16}$$

$$Y_1 = A_1 + \gamma G_1 - \gamma G_2 \tag{17}$$

$$Y_2 = A_2 + \gamma G_2 - \gamma G_1 \tag{18}$$

Here the endogenous variables are German output Y_1, French output Y_2, German government purchases G_1, and French government purchases G_2. According to equation (15) there is full employment in Germany, so German output is constant. According to equation (16) there is full employment in France, so French output is constant too. Further, equations (17) and (18) give the steady-state levels of German and French government purchases.

Now add up equations (17) and (18), taking account of equations (15) and (16), to reach:

$$\overline{Y}_1 + \overline{Y}_2 = A_1 + A_2 \tag{19}$$

However, this is in direct contradiction to the assumption that $\overline{Y}_1$, $\overline{Y}_2$, A_1 and A_2 are given independently. As a result, there is no steady state of fiscal competition. In other words, fiscal competition between Germany and France does not lead to full employment in Germany and France. The underlying reason is the large external effect of fiscal policy.

2. Some Numerical Examples

To illustrate the dynamic model, have a look at some numerical examples. For ease of exposition, without loss of generality, assume $\gamma = 1$. On this assumption, the static model can be written as follows:

$$Y_1 = A_1 + G_1 - G_2 \tag{1}$$

$$Y_2 = A_2 + G_2 - G_1 \tag{2}$$

The endogenous variables are German and French output. Obviously, an increase in German government purchases of 100 causes an increase in German output of 100 and a decline in French output of equally 100. Correspondingly, an increase in French government purchases of 100 causes an increase in French output of 100 and a decline in German output of equally 100. Further let full-employment output in Germany be 1000, and let full-employment output in France be the same.

It proves useful to study four distinct cases:
- unemployment in Germany exceeds unemployment in France
- unemployment in Germany equals unemployment in France
- unemployment in Germany exceeds overemployment in France
- unemployment in Germany equals overemployment in France.

1) Unemployment in Germany exceeds unemployment in France. At the beginning there is unemployment in both Germany and France. More precisely, unemployment in Germany exceeds unemployment in France. Let initial output in Germany be 940, and let initial output in France be 970. Step 1 refers to the policy response. The output gap in Germany is 60. The fiscal policy multiplier in Germany is 1. So what is needed in Germany is an increase in German government purchases of 60. The output gap in France is 30. The fiscal policy multiplier in France is 1. So what is needed in France is an increase in French government purchases of 30.

Step 2 refers to the output lag. The increase in German government purchases of 60 causes an increase in German output of 60. As a side effect, it causes a decline in French output of equally 60. The increase in French government purchases of 30 causes an increase in French output of 30. As a side effect, it causes a decline in German output of equally 30. The net effect is an increase in German output of 30 and a decline in French output of equally 30. As a consequence, German output goes from 940 to 970, and French output goes from 970 to 940. Put another way, the output gap in Germany narrows from 60 to 30, and the output gap in France widens from 30 to 60.

Why does the German government not succeed in closing the output gap in Germany? The underlying reason is the negative external effect of the increase in French government purchases. And why does the French government not succeed in closing the output gap in France? The underlying reason is the negative external effect of the increase in German government purchases.

Step 3 refers to the policy response. The output gap in Germany is 30. The fiscal policy multiplier in Germany is 1. So what is needed in Germany is an increase in German government purchases of 30. The output gap in France is 60. The fiscal policy multiplier in France is 1. So what is needed in France is an increase in French government purchases of 60.

Step 4 refers to the output lag. The increase in German government purchases of 30 causes an increase in German output of 30. As a side effect, it causes a decline in French output of equally 30. The increase in French government purchases of 60 causes an increase in French output of 60. As a side effect, it causes a decline in German output of equally 60. The net effect is a decline in German output of 30 and an increase in French output of equally 30. As a consequence, German output goes from 970 to 940, and French output goes from 940 to 970. With this, German output and French output are back at their initial levels. That means, the process will repeat itself step by step. Table 1.3 presents a synopsis.

Table 1.3

Fiscal Competition between Germany and France

Unemployment in Germany Exceeds Unemployment in France

	Germany	France
Initial Output	940	970
Change in Government Purchases	60	30
Output	970	940
Change in Government Purchases	30	60
Output	940	970
and so on	...	...

What are the dynamic characteristics of this process? There is a continuous increase in German government purchases, as there is in French government purchases. There are uniform oscillations in German output, as there are in French output. The German economy oscillates between high and low unemployment, as does the French economy. There is a continuous appreciation of the euro. Accordingly, there is a continuous decline in both German exports and French exports. Moreover, after a certain number of steps, German exports are down to zero. And much the same holds for French exports. Budget deficits and current account deficits rise step by step. That is why public debt and foreign debt tend to explode. As a result, fiscal competition between Germany and France does not lead to full employment in Germany and France. Instead, fiscal competition gives rise to a vicious circle.

2) Unemployment in Germany equals unemployment in France. Let initial output in Germany be 970, and let initial output in France be the same. Step 1 refers to the policy response. The output gap in Germany is 30. The fiscal policy multiplier in Germany is 1. So what is needed in Germany is an increase in German government purchases of 30. The output gap in France is 30. The fiscal policy multiplier in France is 1. So what is needed in France is an increase in French government purchases of 30.

Step 2 refers to the output lag. The increase in German government purchases of 30 causes an increase in German output of 30. As a side effect, it causes a decline in French output of 30. The increase in French government purchases of 30 causes an increase in French output of 30. As a side effect, it causes a decline in German output of 30. The net effect is that German output does not change, and neither does French output. As a consequence, German output is still 970, as is French output.

Step 3 refers to the policy response. The output gap in Germany is 30. The fiscal policy multiplier in Germany is 1. So what is needed in Germany is an increase in German government purchases of 30. The output gap in France is 30. The fiscal policy multiplier in France is 1. So what is needed in France is an increase in French government purchases of 30.

Step 4 refers to the output lag. The increase in German government purchases of 30 causes an increase in German output of 30. As a side effect, it causes a decline in French output of 30. The increase in French government purchases of 30 causes an increase in French output of 30. As a side effect, it causes a decline in German output of 30. The net effect is that German output does not change, and neither does French output. As a consequence, German output is still 970, as is French output.

That means, German output and French output stay at their initial levels. This process will repeat itself step by step. Table 1.4 gives an overview. There is a continuous increase in German government purchases, as there is in French government purchases. However, there is no change in German output, and the same is true of French output. There is unemployment in both Germany and France. As a result, the process of fiscal competition does not lead to full employment.

Table 1.4

Fiscal Competition between Germany and France

Unemployment in Germany Equals Unemployment in France

	Germany	France
Initial Output	970	970
Change in Government Purchases	30	30
Output	970	970
Change in Government Purchases	30	30
Output	970	970
and so on	...	...

3) Unemployment in Germany exceeds overemployment in France. At the start there is unemployment in Germany but overemployment in France. Thus there is inflation in France. Let initial output in Germany be 940, and let initial output in France be 1030. Step 1 refers to the policy response. The output gap in Germany is 60. The fiscal policy multiplier in Germany is 1. So what is needed in Germany is an increase in German government purchases of 60. The inflationary gap in France is 30. The fiscal policy multiplier in France is 1. So what is needed in France is a reduction in French government purchases of 30.

Step 2 refers to the output lag. The increase in German government purchases of 60 causes an increase in German output of 60. As a side effect, it causes a decline in French output of 60. The reduction in French government purchases of 30 causes a decline in French output of 30. As a side effect, it causes an increase in German output of 30. The total effect is an increase in German output of 90 and a decline in French output of equally 90. As a consequence, German output goes from 940 to 1030, and French output goes from 1030 to 940.

Step 3 refers to the policy response. The inflationary gap in Germany is 30. The fiscal policy multiplier in Germany is 1. So what is needed in Germany is a reduction in German government purchases of 30. The output gap in France is

60. The fiscal policy multiplier in France is 1. So what is needed in France is an increase in French government purchases of 60.

Step 4 refers to the output lag. The reduction in German government purchases of 30 causes a decline in German output of 30. As a side effect, it causes an increase in French output of 30. The increase in French government purchases of 60 causes an increase in French output of 60. As a side effect, it causes a decline in German output of 60. The total effect is a decline in German output of 90 and an increase in French output of equally 90. As a consequence, German output goes from 1030 to 940, and French output goes from 940 to 1030.

At this point in time, output is back at its initial level. So this process will repeat itself. For a synopsis see Table 1.5. What are the dynamic characteristics? There is an upward trend in German government purchases, as there is in French government purchases. There are uniform oscillations in German output, as there are in French output. The German economy oscillates between unemployment and overemployment, and the same holds for the French economy. As a result, fiscal competition does not lead to full employment.

Table 1.5

Fiscal Competition between Germany and France

Unemployment in Germany Exceeds Overemployment in France

	Germany	France
Initial Output	940	1030
Change in Government Purchases	60	−30
Output	1030	940
Change in Government Purchases	−30	60
Output	940	1030
and so on	...	...

4) Unemployment in Germany equals overemployment in France. Let initial output in Germany be 970, and let initial output in France be 1030. Step 1 refers to the policy response. The output gap in Germany is 30. The fiscal policy multiplier in Germany is 1. So what is needed in Germany is an increase in German government purchases of 30. The inflationary gap in France is 30. The fiscal policy multiplier in France is 1. So what is needed in France is a reduction in French government purchases of 30.

Step 2 refers to the output lag. The increase in German government purchases of 30 causes an increase in German output of 30. As a side effect, it causes a decline in French output of 30. The reduction in French government purchases of 30 causes a decline in French output of 30. As a side effect, it causes an increase in German output of 30. The total effect is an increase in German output of 60 and a decline in French output of equally 60. As a consequence, German output goes from 970 to 1030, and French output goes from 1030 to 970.

Step 3 refers to the policy response. The inflationary gap in Germany is 30. The fiscal policy multiplier in Germany is 1. So what is needed in Germany is a reduction in German government purchases of 30. The output gap in France is 30. The fiscal policy multiplier in France is 1. So what is needed in France is an increase in French government purchases of 30.

Step 4 refers to the output lag. The reduction in German government purchases of 30 causes a decline in German output of 30. As a side effect, it causes an increase in French output of 30. The increase in French government purchases of 30 causes an increase in French output of 30. As a side effect, it causes a decline in German output of 30. The total effect is a decline in German output of 60 and an increase in French output of equally 60. As a consequence, German output goes from 1030 to 970, and French output goes from 970 to 1030.

With this, output is back at its initial level, hence the process will repeat itself. For an overview see Table 1.6. There are uniform oscillations in German government purchases, and the same applies to French government purchases. There are uniform oscillations in German output, and the same is true of French output. As a result, fiscal competition does not lead to full employment.

Table 1.6

Fiscal Competition between Germany and France

Unemployment in Germany Equals Overemployment in France

	Germany	France
Initial Output	970	1030
Change in Government Purchases	30	−30
Output	1030	970
Change in Government Purchases	−30	30
Output	970	1030
and so on	...	...

5) Summary. Fiscal competition cannot achieve full employment. Fiscal competition cannot even reduce unemployment. As an adverse side effect, government purchases tend to explode. And output tends to oscillate uniformly.

Chapter 4
Fiscal Cooperation between Germany and France

1. The Model

As a starting point, take the output model. It can be represented by a system of two equations:

$$Y_1 = A_1 + \gamma G_1 - \gamma G_2 \qquad (1)$$
$$Y_2 = A_2 + \gamma G_2 - \gamma G_1 \qquad (2)$$

Here Y_1 denotes German output, Y_2 is French output, G_1 is German government purchases, and G_2 is French government purchases. The endogenous variables are German output and French output. At the beginning there is unemployment in both Germany and France. More precisely, unemployment in Germany exceeds unemployment in France. The targets of fiscal cooperation are full employment in Germany and full employment in France. The instruments of fiscal cooperation are German government purchases and French government purchases. So there are two targets and two instruments.

On this basis, the policy model can be characterized by a system of two equations:

$$\overline{Y}_1 = A_1 + \gamma G_1 - \gamma G_2 \qquad (3)$$
$$\overline{Y}_2 = A_2 + \gamma G_2 - \gamma G_1 \qquad (4)$$

Here $\overline{Y}_1$ denotes full-employment output in Germany, and $\overline{Y}_2$ denotes full-employment output in France. The endogenous variables are German government purchases and French government purchases. Now take the sum of equations (3) and (4) to find out:

$$\overline{Y}_1 + \overline{Y}_2 = A_1 + A_2 \qquad (5)$$

However, this is in direct contradiction to the assumption that $\overline{Y}_1$, $\overline{Y}_2$, A_1 and A_2 are given independently. As a result, there is no solution to fiscal cooperation. That is to say, fiscal cooperation between Germany and France cannot achieve full employment in Germany and France. The underlying reason is the large external effect of fiscal policy.

2. Some Numerical Examples

To illustrate the policy model, have a look at some numerical examples. For ease of exposition, without losing generality, assume $\gamma = 1$. On this assumption, the output model can be written as follows:

$$Y_1 = A_1 + G_1 - G_2 \tag{1}$$
$$Y_2 = A_2 + G_2 - G_1 \tag{2}$$

The endogenous variables are German and French output. Evidently, an increase in German government purchases of 100 causes an increase in German output of 100 and a decline in French output of equally 100. Further let full-employment output in Germany be 1000, and let full-employment output in France be the same.

It proves useful to consider three distinct cases:
- unemployment in Germany exceeds unemployment in France
- unemployment in Germany exceeds overemployment in France
- unemployment in Germany equals overemployment in France.

1) Unemployment in Germany exceeds unemployment in France. Let initial output in Germany be 940, and let initial output in France be 970. In this case, fiscal cooperation cannot increase union employment. Fiscal cooperation can only redistribute employment among union countries. Take for instance an

increase in German government purchases of 15. This policy measure raises German output by 15 and lowers French output by equally 15. As a consequence, German output goes from 940 to 955, and French output goes from 970 to 955. As a result, in this case, there is no solution to fiscal cooperation. Table 1.7 presents a synopsis.

Table 1.7

Fiscal Cooperation between Germany and France

Unemployment in Germany Exceeds Unemployment in France

	Germany	France
Initial Output	940	970
Change in Government Purchases	15	0
Output	955	955

2) Unemployment in Germany exceeds overemployment in France. At the start there is unemployment in Germany but overemployment in France. Thus there is inflation in France. Let initial output in Germany be 940, and let initial output in France be 1030. In this case, the specific target of fiscal cooperation is full employment in France and, hence, price stability in France. Aiming at full employment in Germany would imply unemployment in France. So what is needed is a decline in French output of 30. What is needed, for instance, is an increase in German government purchases of 15 and a reduction in French government purchases of equally 15.

The increase in German government purchases of 15 raises German output by 15 and lowers French output by equally 15. The reduction in French government purchases of 15 lowers French output by 15 and raises German output by equally 15. The total effect is an increase in German output of 30 and a decline in French output of equally 30. As a consequence, German output goes from 940 to 970, and French output goes from 1030 to 1000. In France there is full employment.

In Germany unemployment comes down, but there is still some unemployment left. As a result, in this case, there is a certain solution to fiscal cooperation. Fiscal cooperation can reduce both unemployment in Germany and overemployment in France. On the other hand, fiscal cooperation cannot achieve full employment in Germany and France. Table 1.8 gives an overview.

Table 1.8
Fiscal Cooperation between Germany and France
Unemployment in Germany Exceeds Overemployment in France

	Germany	France
Initial Output	940	1030
Change in Government Purchases	15	−15
Output	970	1000

3) Unemployment in Germany equals overemployment in France. Let initial output in Germany be 970, and let initial output in France be 1030. What is needed, then, is an increase in German government purchases of 15 and a reduction in French government purchases of equally 15. The overall effect is an increase in German output of 30 and a decline in French output of equally 30. As a consequence, German output goes from 970 to 1000, and French output goes from 1030 to 1000. In this special case, fiscal cooperation can in fact achieve full employment in Germany and France. For a synopsis see Table 1.9.

Table 1.9

Fiscal Cooperation between Germany and France

Unemployment in Germany Equals Overemployment in France

	Germany	France
Initial Output	970	1030
Change in Government Purchases	15	−15
Output	1000	1000

4) Summary. Fiscal cooperation between Germany and France generally cannot achieve full employment in Germany and France.

5) Comparing fiscal cooperation with fiscal competition. Fiscal competition cannot achieve full employment. The same applies to fiscal cooperation. Fiscal competition cannot reduce unemployment. Fiscal cooperation can reduce unemployment in some cases. Under fiscal competition there is a tendency for government purchases to explode. And there is a tendency for output to oscillate uniformly. Under fiscal cooperation there are no such tendencies. Judging from these points of view, fiscal cooperation seems to be superior to fiscal competition.

Chapter 5
Competition between the Union Central Bank, the German Government, and the French Government

1. The Dynamic Model

1) The static model. As a point of reference, consider the static model. It can be represented by a system of two equations:

$$Y_1 = A_1 + \alpha M + \gamma G_1 - \delta G_2 \tag{1}$$

$$Y_2 = A_2 + \alpha M + \gamma G_2 - \delta G_1 \tag{2}$$

According to equation (1), German output Y_1 is determined by union money supply M, German government purchases G_1, French government purchases G_2, and some other factors called A_1. According to equation (2), French output Y_2 is determined by union money supply M, French government purchases G_2, German government purchases G_1, and some other factors called A_2. The internal effect of monetary policy is positive $\alpha > 0$. The internal effect of fiscal policy is positive as well $\gamma > 0$. By contrast, the external effect of fiscal policy is negative $\delta > 0$. And what is more, the internal effect of fiscal policy and the external effect of fiscal policy are the same size $\gamma = \delta$. The endogenous variables are German output Y_1 and French output Y_2. Along these lines, the static model can be rewritten as follows:

$$Y_1 = A_1 + \alpha M + \gamma G_1 - \gamma G_2 \tag{3}$$

$$Y_2 = A_2 + \alpha M + \gamma G_2 - \gamma G_1 \tag{4}$$

Again the endogenous variables are German and French output.

2) The dynamic model. At the beginning there is unemployment in both Germany and France. More precisely, unemployment in Germany exceeds

unemployment in France. The primary target of the union central bank is price stability in the union. The secondary target of the union central bank is high employment in Germany and France. The instrument of the union central bank is union money supply. The target of the German government is full employment in Germany. The instrument of the German government is German government purchases. The target of the French government is full employment in France. The instrument of the French government is French government purchases.

We assume that the central bank and the governments decide sequentially. First the central bank decides, and then the governments decide. In step 1, the union central bank decides. In step 2, the German government and the French government decide simultaneously and independently. In step 3, the union central bank decides. In step 4, the German government and the French government decide simultaneously and independently. And so on. The reasons for this stepwise procedure are: First, the inside lag of monetary policy is short, whereas the inside lag of fiscal policy is long. And second, the internal effect of monetary policy is very large, whereas the internal effect of fiscal policy is very small.

2. Some Numerical Examples

To illustrate the dynamic model, have a look at some numerical examples. For ease of exposition, without loss of generality, assume $\alpha = 2$ and $\gamma = 1$. On this assumption, the static model can be written as follows:

$$Y_1 = A_1 + 2M + G_1 - G_2 \tag{1}$$
$$Y_2 = A_2 + 2M + G_2 - G_1 \tag{2}$$

The endogenous variables are German and French output. Obviously, an increase in union money supply of 100 causes an increase in German output of 200 and an increase in French output of equally 200. An increase in German government purchases of 100 causes an increase in German output of 100 and a decline in French output of equally 100. Correspondingly, an increase in French government purchases of 100 causes an increase in French output of 100 and a decline in German output of equally 100. Further let full-employment output in Germany be 1000, and let full-employment output in France be the same.

It proves useful to study three distinct cases:
- unemployment in Germany and France
- another interpretation
- inflation in Germany and France.

1) Unemployment in Germany and France. Let initial output in Germany be 940, and let initial output in France be 970. Step 1 refers to monetary policy. The output gap in Germany is 60, and the output gap in France is 30. In this situation, the specific target of the union central bank is to close the output gap in France. Closing the output gap in Germany would imply overemployment in France and, hence, inflation in France. The output gap in France is 30. The monetary policy multiplier in France is 2. So what is needed is an increase in union money supply of 15. Step 2 refers to the output lag. The increase in union money supply of 15 causes an increase in German output of 30 and an increase in French output of equally 30. As a consequence, German output goes from 940 to 970, and French output goes from 970 to 1000.

Step 3 refers to fiscal policy. The output gap in Germany is 30. The fiscal policy multiplier in Germany is 1. So what is needed in Germany is an increase in German government purchases of 30. The output gap in France is zero. So there is no need for a change in French government purchases. Step 4 refers to the output lag. The increase in German government purchases of 30 causes an increase in German output of 30. As a side effect, it causes a decline in French output of equally 30. As a consequence, German output goes from 970 to 1000, and French output goes from 1000 to 970.

Step 5 refers to monetary policy. The output gap in Germany is zero, and the output gap in France is 30. So there is no need for a change in union money supply. Step 6 refers to the output lag. As a consequence, German output stays at 1000, and French output stays at 970.

Step 7 refers to fiscal policy. The output gap in Germany is zero. So there is no need for a change in German government purchases. The output gap in France is 30. The fiscal policy multiplier in France is 1. So what is needed in France is an increase in French government purchases of 30. Step 8 refers to the output lag. The increase in French government purchases of 30 causes an increase in French output of 30. As a side effect, it causes a decline in German output of equally 30. As a consequence, French output goes from 970 to 1000, and German output goes from 1000 to 970. With this, German output and French output are back at the levels reached in step 2. That means, the process will repeat itself step by step. Table 1.10 presents a synopsis.

Table 1.10

Competition between the Union Central Bank, the German Government, and the French Government

Unemployment in Germany and France

	Germany	France
Initial Output	940	970
Change in Money Supply	15	
Output	970	1000
Change in Government Purchases	30	0
Output	1000	970
Change in Money Supply	0	
Output	1000	970
Change in Government Purchases	0	30
Output	970	1000
and so on	...	...

48

What are the dynamic characteristics of this process? There is a one-time increase in union money supply. There is an upward trend in German government purchases, as there is in French government purchases. There are uniform oscillations in German output, as there are in French output. The German economy oscillates between unemployment and full employment, as does the French economy. As a result, competition between the union central bank, the German government, and the French government does not lead to full employment in Germany and France. Technically speaking, there is no steady state.

2) Another interpretation. Let initial output in Germany be 940, and let initial output in France be 970. Step 1 refers to monetary policy. The output gap in Germany is 60, and the output gap in France is 30. The monetary policy multiplier in Germany is 2, as is the monetary policy multiplier in France. So what is needed is an increase in union money supply of 15.

Step 2 refers to fiscal policy. The German government and the French government anticipate the effect of the increase in union money supply. The German government expects that, due to the increase in union money supply of 15, German output will rise to 970. The French government expects that, due to the increase in union money supply of 15, French output will rise to 1000. The expected output gap in Germany is 30. The fiscal policy multiplier in Germany is 1. So what is needed in Germany is an increase in German government purchases of 30. The expected output gap in France is zero. So there is no need for a change in French government purchases.

Step 3 refers to the output lag. The increase in union money supply of 15 causes an increase in German output of 30 and an increase in French output of equally 30. The increase in German government purchases of 30 causes an increase in German output of 30. As a side effect, it causes a decline in French output of equally 30. The net effect is an increase in German output of 60 and an increase in French output of zero. As a consequence, German output goes from 940 to 1000, while French output stays at 970.

Step 4 refers to monetary policy. The output gap in Germany is zero, and the output gap in France is 30. So there is no need for a change in union money supply. Step 5 refers to fiscal policy. The German government expects that, due to the constancy of union money supply, German output will stay at 1000. The French government expects that, due to the constancy of union money supply, French output will stay at 970. The expected output gap in Germany is zero. So there is no need for a change in German government purchases. The expected output gap in France is 30. The fiscal policy multiplier in France is 1. So what is needed in France is an increase in French government purchases of 30. Step 6 refers to the output lag. The increase in French government purchases of 30 causes an increase in French output of 30. As a side effect, it causes a decline in German output of equally 30. As a consequence, French output goes from 970 to 1000, and German output goes from 1000 to 970. And so on. Table 1.11 gives an overview.

Table 1.11

Competition between the Union Central Bank, the German Government, and the French Government

Another Interpretation

	Germany	France
Initial Output	940	970
Change in Money Supply	15	
Change in Government Purchases	30	0
Output	1000	970
Change in Money Supply	0	
Change in Government Purchases	0	30
Output	970	1000
and so on	...	...

3) Inflation in Germany and France. At the start there is overemployment in both Germany and France. For that reason there is inflation in both Germany and France. Let overemployment in Germany exceed overemployment in France. Let

initial output in Germany be 1060, and let initial output in France be 1030. Step 1 refers to monetary policy. The inflationary gap in Germany is 60, and the inflationary gap in France is 30. In this situation, the specific target of the union central bank is to close the inflationary gap in Germany. Closing the inflationary gap in France would imply overemployment in Germany and, hence, inflation in Germany. The inflationary gap in Germany is 60. The monetary policy multiplier in Germany is 2. So what is needed is a reduction in union money supply of 30. Step 2 refers to the output lag. The reduction in union money supply of 30 causes a decline in German output of 60 and a decline in French output of equally 60. As a consequence, German output goes from 1060 to 1000, and French output goes from 1030 to 970.

Step 3 refers to fiscal policy. The output gap in Germany is zero. So there is no need for a change in German government purchases. The output gap in France is 30. The fiscal policy multiplier in France is 1. So what is needed in France is an increase in French government purchases of 30. Step 4 refers to the output lag. The increase in French government purchases of 30 causes an increase in French output of 30. As a side effect, it causes a decline in German output of equally 30. As a consequence, French output goes from 970 to 1000, and German output goes from 1000 to 970.

Step 5 refers to monetary policy. The output gap in Germany is 30, and the output gap in France is zero. So there is no need for a change in union money supply. Step 6 refers to the output lag. As a consequence, German output stays at 970, and French output stays at 1000.

Step 7 refers to fiscal policy. The output gap in Germany is 30. The fiscal policy multiplier in Germany is 1. So what is needed in Germany is an increase in German government purchases of 30. The output gap in France is zero. So there is no need for a change in French government purchases. Step 8 refers to the output lag. The increase in German government purchases of 30 causes an increase in German output of 30. As a side effect, it causes a decline in French output of equally 30. As a consequence, German output goes from 970 to 1000, and French output goes from 1000 to 970. With this, German output and French output are back at the levels reached in step 2. That is to say, the process will repeat itself step by step. For a synopsis see Table 1.12.

Table 1.12

Competition between the Union Central Bank, the German Government, and the French Government

Inflation in Germany and France

	Germany	France
Initial Output	1060	1030
Change in Money Supply	−30	
Output	1000	970
Change in Government Purchases	0	30
Output	970	1000
Change in Government Purchases	30	0
Output	1000	970
and so on	...	...

What are the dynamic characteristics of this process? There is a one-time reduction in union money supply. There is an upward trend in German government purchases, as there is in French government purchases. There are uniform oscillations in German output, as there are in French output. The German economy oscillates between unemployment and full employment, as does the French economy. As a result, the process of monetary and fiscal competition leads to price stability. However, the process of monetary and fiscal competition does not lead to full employment.

4) Summary. Monetary and fiscal competition can reduce unemployment. Monetary and fiscal competition can achieve price stability. But monetary and fiscal competition cannot achieve full employment.

5) Comparing monetary and fiscal competition with pure fiscal competition. Fiscal competition cannot achieve full employment. The same applies to monetary and fiscal competition. Fiscal competition cannot even reduce

unemployment. Monetary and fiscal competition can reduce unemployment to a certain extent. Judging from these points of view, monetary and fiscal competition is superior to fiscal competition.

Chapter 6
Cooperation between the Union Central Bank, the German Government, and the French Government

1. The Model

1) Introduction. As a starting point, take the output model. It can be represented by a system of two equations:

$$Y_1 = A_1 + \alpha M + \gamma G_1 - \gamma G_2 \tag{1}$$

$$Y_2 = A_2 + \alpha M + \gamma G_2 - \gamma G_1 \tag{2}$$

Here Y_1 denotes German output, Y_2 is French output, M is union money supply, G_1 is German government purchases, and G_2 is French government purchases. The endogenous variables are German output and French output.

At the beginning there is unemployment in both Germany and France. More precisely, unemployment in Germany exceeds unemployment in France. The policy makers are the union central bank, the German government, and the French government. The targets of policy cooperation are full employment in Germany and full employment in France. The instruments of policy cooperation are union money supply, German government purchases, and French government purchases. There are two targets and three instruments, so there is one degree of freedom. As a result, there is an infinite number of solutions. In other words, cooperation between the union central bank, the German government, and the French government can achieve full employment in Germany and France.

3) The policy model. On this basis, the policy model can be characterized by a system of two equations:

$$\Delta Y_1 = \alpha \Delta M + \gamma \Delta G_1 - \gamma \Delta G_2 \tag{3}$$

54

$$\Delta Y_2 = \alpha \Delta M + \gamma \Delta G_2 - \gamma \Delta G_1 \tag{4}$$

Here ΔY_1 denotes the output gap in Germany, ΔY_2 is the output gap in France, ΔM is the required increase in union money supply, ΔG_1 is the required increase in German government purchases, and ΔG_2 is the required increase in French government purchases. The endogenous variables are ΔM, ΔG_1 and ΔG_2.

We now introduce a third target. We assume that the increase in German government purchases should be equal in size to the reduction in French government purchases $\Delta G_1 + \Delta G_2 = 0$. Put another way, we assume that the sum total of union government purchases should be constant. Add up equations (3) and (4) to find out:

$$\Delta M = \frac{\Delta Y_1 + \Delta Y_2}{2\alpha} \tag{5}$$

Then subtract equation (4) from equation (3), taking account of $\Delta G_1 + \Delta G_2 = 0$, and solve for:

$$\Delta G_1 = \frac{\Delta Y_1 - \Delta Y_2}{4\gamma} \tag{6}$$

$$\Delta G_2 = - \frac{\Delta Y_1 - \Delta Y_2}{4\gamma} \tag{7}$$

Equation (5) shows the required increase in union money supply, (6) shows the required increase in German government purchases, and (7) shows the required increase in French government purchases.

2. Some Numerical Examples

To illustrate the policy model, have a look at some numerical examples. For ease of exposition, without losing generality, assume $\alpha = 2$ and $\gamma = 1$. On this assumption, the output model can be written as follows:

$$Y_1 = A_1 + 2M + G_1 - G_2 \tag{1}$$

$$Y_2 = A_2 + 2M + G_2 - G_1 \tag{2}$$

The endogenous variables are German and French output. Evidently, an increase in union money supply of 100 causes an increase in German output of 200 and an increase in French output of equally 200. An increase in German government purchases of 100 causes an increase in German output of 100 and a decline in French output of equally 100. Further let full-employment output in Germany be 1000, and let full-employment output in France be the same.

It proves useful to consider two distinct cases:
- unemployment in Germany and France
- inflation in Germany and France.

1) Unemployment in Germany and France. Let unemployment in Germany exceed unemployment in France. Let initial output in Germany be 940, and let initial output in France be 970. The solution can be found in two logical steps. Step 1 refers to monetary policy. The output gap in the union is 90. The monetary policy multiplier in the union is 4. So what is needed is an increase in union money supply of 22.5. This policy action raises German output and French output by 45 each. As a consequence, German output goes from 940 to 985, and French output goes from 970 to 1015. In Germany there is still some unemployment left, and in France there is now some overemployment. Strictly speaking, unemployment in Germany and overemployment in France are the same size.

Step 2 refers to fiscal policy. The output gap in Germany is 15, and the output gap in France is -15. So what is needed, according to equations (6) and (7) from

56

the previous section, is an increase in German government purchases of 7.5 and a reduction in French government purchases of equally 7.5. The increase in German government purchases of 7.5 raises German output by 7.5 and lowers French output by equally 7.5. The reduction in French government purchases of 7.5 lowers French output by 7.5 and raises German output by equally 7.5. The total effect is an increase in German output of 15 and a decline in French output of equally 15. As a consequence, German output goes from 985 to 1000, and French output goes from 1015 to 1000. In Germany there is now full employment, and the same holds for France.

As a result, cooperation between the union central bank, the German government, and the French government can achieve full employment in Germany and France. What is needed is an increase in union money supply, an increase in German government purchases, and a reduction in French government purchases. Here the increase in German government purchases is equal in size to the reduction in French government purchases. Table 1.13 presents a synopsis.

Tables 1.14 and 1.15 give some alternative solutions. Table 1.14 is marked by an increase in union money supply and an increase in German government purchases. Table 1.15 is marked by an increase in union money supply and a reduction in French government purchases.

2) Inflation in Germany and France. At the start there is overemployment in both Germany and France. For that reason there is inflation in both Germany and France. Let overemployment in Germany exceed overemployment in France. Let initial output in Germany be 1060, and let initial output in France be 1030. The solution can be determined in two logical steps. Step 1 refers to monetary policy. The inflationary gap in the union is 90. The monetary policy multiplier in the union is 4. So what is needed is a reduction in union money supply of 22.5. This policy action lowers German output and French output by 45 each. As a consequence, German output goes from 1060 to 1015, and French output goes from 1030 to 985. In Germany there is still some overemployment left, and in France there is now some unemployment. Strictly speaking, overemployment in Germany and unemployment in France are the same size.

Table 1.13

Cooperation between the Union Central Bank, the German Government, and the French Government

Unemployment in Germany and France

	Germany	France
Initial Output	940	970
Change in Money Supply	22.5	
Output	985	1015
Change in Government Purchases	7.5	−7.5
Output	1000	1000

Table 1.14

Cooperation between the Union Central Bank, the German Government, and the French Government

A Second Solution

	Germany	France
Initial Output	940	970
Change in Money Supply	22.5	
Output	985	1015
Change in Government Purchases	15	0
Output	1000	1000

Step 2 refers to fiscal policy. The inflationary gap in Germany is 15, and the inflationary gap in France is −15. What is needed, then, is a reduction in German government purchases of 7.5 and an increase in French government purchases of equally 7.5. The total effect is a decline in German output of 15 and an increase in French output of equally 15. As a consequence, German output goes from 1015 to 1000, and French output goes from 985 to 1000. In Germany there is now full employment and, hence, price stability. And the same applies to France.

As a result, monetary and fiscal cooperation can achieve both price stability and full employment. What is needed is a reduction in union money supply, a reduction in German government purchases, and an increase in French government purchases. For an overview see Table 1.16.

3) Comparing monetary and fiscal cooperation with monetary and fiscal competition. Monetary and fiscal competition cannot achieve full employment. By contrast, monetary and fiscal cooperation can indeed achieve full employment. Under monetary and fiscal competition there is a tendency for government purchases to explode. Besides there is a tendency for output to oscillate uniformly. Under monetary and fiscal cooperation there are no such tendencies. Judging from these points of view, monetary and fiscal cooperation seems to be superior to monetary and fiscal competition.

Table 1.15

Cooperation between the Union Central Bank, the German Government, and the French Government

A Third Solution

	Germany	France
Initial Output	940	970
Change in Money Supply	22.5	
Output	985	1015
Change in Government Purchases	0	−15
Output	1000	1000

Table 1.16

Cooperation between the Union Central Bank, the German Government, and the French Government

Inflation in Germany and France

	Germany	France
Initial Output	1060	1030
Change in Money Supply	−22.5	
Output	1015	985
Change in Government Purchases	−7.5	7.5
Output	1000	1000

Chapter 7
Competition between the German Labour Union and the French Labour Union

1. The Dynamic Model

1) The basic model. An increase in German nominal wages causes an increase in the price of German goods. Then what will be the effect on German output, and what on French output? The solution to this problem is as follows:

$$\hat{Y}_1 = -\frac{1-c+2m+2q}{2(1-c+m+q)} \hat{W}_1 \tag{1}$$

$$\hat{Y}_2 = -\frac{1-c}{2(1-c+m+q)} \hat{W}_1 \tag{2}$$

Here W_1 denotes German nominal wages, Y_1 is German output, and Y_2 is French output. The hat denotes the rate of change. $\hat{W}_1 = dW_1 / W_1$ is the rate of change of German nominal wages. $\hat{Y}_1$ is the rate of change of German output. And $\hat{Y}_2$ is the rate of change of French output. For the proof see Carlberg (2001) p. 68.

As an important result, an increase in German nominal wages lowers German output. And what is more, it lowers French output as well. To illustrate this, consider a numerical example with $c = 0.72$, $m = 0.16$, and $q = 0.24$. Then the wage policy multipliers are $\hat{Y}_1 = -0.794\hat{W}_1$ and $\hat{Y}_2 = -0.206\hat{W}_1$. That means, a 1 percent increase in German nominal wages causes a 0.79 percent decline in German output and a 0.21 percent decline in French output. The internal effect of wage policy is very large, and the external effect of wage policy is large. Next have a closer look at the process of adjustment. An increase in German nominal wages causes an increase in the price of German goods and an appreciation of the euro. The increase in the price of German goods lowers German output but raises French output. The appreciation of the euro lowers both German exports and French exports. The net effect is that German output and French output go down.

2) The static model. As a point of reference, consider the static model. It can be represented by a system of two equations:

$$Y_1 = A_1 - \varepsilon W_1 - \eta W_2 \tag{3}$$

$$Y_2 = A_2 - \varepsilon W_2 - \eta W_1 \tag{4}$$

According to equation (3), German output Y_1 is determined by German nominal wages W_1, French nominal wages W_2, and some other factors called A_1. According to equation (4), French output Y_2 is determined by French nominal wages W_2, German nominal wages W_1, and some other factors called A_2. The coefficients ε and η are positive with $\varepsilon > \eta$. An increase in German nominal wages reduces both German output and French output, where the fall in German output exceeds the fall in French output. Similarly, an increase in French nominal wages reduces both French output and German output, where the fall in French output exceeds the fall in German output. The endogenous variables are German output and French output.

3) The dynamic model. At the beginning there is unemployment in both Germany and France. More precisely, unemployment in Germany exceeds unemployment in France. The target of the German labour union is full employment in Germany. The instrument of the German labour union is German nominal wages. The German labour union lowers German nominal wages so as to close the output gap in Germany:

$$W_1 - W_1^{-1} = - \frac{\overline{Y}_1 - Y_1}{\varepsilon} \tag{5}$$

Here is a list of the new symbols:

Y_1	German output this period
$\overline{Y}_1$	full-employment output in Germany
$\overline{Y}_1 - Y_1$	output gap in Germany this period
W_1^{-1}	German nominal wages last period
W_1	German nominal wages this period
$W_1 - W_1^{-1}$	change in German nominal wages.

Here the endogenous variable is German nominal wages this period W_1.

The target of the French labour union is full employment in France. The instrument of the French labour union is French nominal wages. The French labour union lowers French nominal wages so as to close the output gap in France:

$$W_2 - W_2^{-1} = - \frac{\overline{Y}_2 - Y_2}{\varepsilon} \tag{6}$$

Here is a list of the new symbols:

Y_2	French output this period
$\overline{Y}_2$	full-employment output in France
$\overline{Y}_2 - Y_2$	output gap in France this period
W_2^{-1}	French nominal wages last period
W_2	French nominal wages this period
$W_2 - W_2^{-1}$	change in French nominal wages.

Here the endogenous variable is French nominal wages this period W_2. We assume that the German labour union and the French labour union decide simultaneously and independently.

In addition there is an output lag. German output next period is determined by German nominal wages this period as well as by French nominal wages this period:

$$Y_1^{+1} = A_1 - \varepsilon W_1 - \eta W_2 \tag{7}$$

Here Y_1^{+1} denotes German output next period. In the same way, French output next period is determined by French nominal wages this period as well as by German nominal wages this period:

$$Y_2^{+1} = A_2 - \varepsilon W_2 - \eta W_1 \tag{8}$$

Here Y_2^{+1} denotes French output next period.

On this basis, the dynamic model can be characterized by a system four equations:

$$W_1 - W_1^{-1} = - \frac{\overline{Y}_1 - Y_1}{\epsilon} \tag{9}$$

$$W_2 - W_2^{-1} = - \frac{\overline{Y}_2 - Y_2}{\epsilon} \tag{10}$$

$$Y_1^{+1} = A_1 - \epsilon W_1 - \eta W_2 \tag{11}$$
$$Y_2^{+1} = A_2 - \epsilon W_2 - \eta W_1 \tag{12}$$

Equation (9) shows the wage response by the German labour union, (10) shows the wage response by the French labour union, (11) shows the output lag in Germany, and (12) shows the output lag in France. The endogenous variables are German nominal wages this period W_1, French nominal wages this period W_2, German output next period Y_1^{+1}, and French output next period Y_2^{+1}.

4) The steady state. In the steady state by definition we have:

$$W_1 = W_1^{-1} \tag{13}$$
$$W_2 = W_2^{-1} \tag{14}$$

Equation (13) has it that German nominal wages do not move any more. Likewise, equation (14) has it that French nominal wages do not move any more. Therefore the steady state can be captured by a system of four equations:

$$Y_1 = \overline{Y}_1 \tag{15}$$
$$Y_2 = \overline{Y}_2 \tag{16}$$
$$Y_1 = A_1 - \epsilon W_1 - \eta W_2 \tag{17}$$
$$Y_2 = A_2 - \epsilon W_2 - \eta W_1 \tag{18}$$

Here the endogenous variables are German output Y_1, French output Y_2, German nominal wages W_1, and French nominal wages W_2. According to equation (15) there is full employment in Germany, so German output is constant. According to equation (16) there is full employment in France, so French output is constant too. Further, equations (17) and (18) give the steady-state levels of German and French nominal wages.

The model of the steady state can be compressed to a system of only two equations:

$$\overline{Y}_1 = A_1 - \varepsilon W_1 - \eta W_2 \tag{19}$$

$$\overline{Y}_2 = A_2 - \varepsilon W_2 - \eta W_1 \tag{20}$$

Here the endogenous variables are German nominal wages and French nominal wages. To simplify notation we introduce:

$$B_1 = A_1 - \overline{Y}_1 \tag{21}$$

$$B_2 = A_2 - \overline{Y}_2 \tag{22}$$

With this, the model of the steady state can be written as follows:

$$B_1 = \varepsilon W_1 + \eta W_2 \tag{23}$$

$$B_2 = \varepsilon W_2 + \eta W_1 \tag{24}$$

The endogenous variables are still W_1 and W_2.

Next we solve the model for the endogenous variables:

$$W_1 = \frac{\varepsilon B_1 - \eta B_2}{\varepsilon^2 - \eta^2} \tag{25}$$

$$W_2 = \frac{\varepsilon B_2 - \eta B_1}{\varepsilon^2 - \eta^2} \tag{26}$$

Equation (25) shows the steady-state level of German nominal wages, and equation (26) shows the steady-state level of French nominal wages. As a result, there is a steady state if and only if $\varepsilon \neq \eta$. Owing to the assumption $\varepsilon > \eta$, this condition is fulfilled. The steady-state levels of W_1 and W_2 are positive if $\eta / \varepsilon < B_1 / B_2 < \varepsilon / \eta$.

5) Stability. Eliminate Y_1 in equation (9) by means of equation (11) and rearrange terms $\overline{Y}_1 = A_1 - \varepsilon W_1 - \eta W_2^{-1}$. By analogy, eliminate Y_2 in equation (10) by means of equation (12) to arrive at $\overline{Y}_2 = A_2 - \varepsilon W_2 - \eta W_1^{-1}$. On this basis, the dynamic model can be described by a system of two equations:

$$\overline{Y}_1 = A_1 - \varepsilon W_1 - \eta W_2^{-1} \tag{27}$$

$$\overline{Y}_2 = A_2 - \varepsilon W_2 - \eta W_1^{-1} \tag{28}$$

Here the endogenous variables are German nominal wages this period W_1 and French nominal wages this period W_2. To simplify notation we make use of equations (21) and (22). With this, the dynamic model can be written as follows:

$$B_1 = \varepsilon W_1 + \eta W_2^{-1} \tag{29}$$

$$B_2 = \varepsilon W_2 + \eta W_1^{-1} \tag{30}$$

The endogenous variables are still W_1 and W_2.

Now substitute equation (30) into equation (29) and solve for:

$$\varepsilon W_1 = B_1 - \frac{\eta B_2}{\varepsilon} + \frac{\eta^2 W_1^{-2}}{\varepsilon} \tag{31}$$

Then differentiate equation (31) for W_1^{-2}:

$$\frac{dW_1}{dW_1^{-2}} = \frac{\eta^2}{\varepsilon^2} \tag{32}$$

Finally the stability condition is $\eta^2 / \varepsilon^2 < 1$ or:

$$\eta < \varepsilon \tag{33}$$

That means, the steady state is stable if and only if the external effect of wage policy is smaller than the internal effect of wage policy. This condition is satisfied. As a result, there is a stable steady state of wage policy competition. In other words, competition between the German labour union and the French labour union leads to full employment in Germany and France.

2. A Numerical Example

To illustrate the dynamic model, have a look at a numerical example. For ease of exposition, without loss of generality, assume $\varepsilon = 4$ and $\eta = 1$. On this assumption, the static model can be written as follows:

$$Y_1 = A_1 - 4W_1 - W_2 \tag{1}$$

$$Y_2 = A_2 - 4W_2 - W_1 \tag{2}$$

The endogenous variables are German and French output. Obviously, an increase in German nominal wages of 100 causes a decline in German output of 400 and a decline in French output of 100. Strictly speaking, what matters here is the change in German output relative to the change in French output 400/100 = 4. Compare this with the results given in the basic model, where we had 0.8/0.2 = 4. Further, an increase in French nominal wages of 100 causes a decline in French output of 400 and a decline in German output of 100. Let full-employment output in Germany be 1000, and let full-employment output in France be the same.

At the beginning there is unemployment in both Germany and France. More precisely, unemployment in Germany exceeds unemployment in France. Let initial output in Germany be 940, and let initial output in France be 970. Step 1 refers to the policy response. The output gap in Germany is 60. The wage policy multiplier in Germany is -4. So what is needed in Germany is a reduction in German nominal wages of 15. The output gap in France is 30. The wage policy multiplier in France is -4. So what is needed in France is a reduction in French nominal wages of 7.5.

Step 2 refers to the output lag. The reduction in German nominal wages of 15 causes an increase in German output of 60. As a side effect, it causes an increase in French output of 15. The reduction in French nominal wages of 7.5 causes an increase in French output of 30. As a side effect, it causes an increase in German output of 7.5. The total effect is an increase in German output of 67.5 and an increase in French output of 45. As a consequence, German output goes from 940 to 1007.5, and French output goes from 970 to 1015. That means, the output gap in Germany of 60 turns into an inflationary gap of 7.5 And the output gap in France of 30 turns into an inflationary gap of 15.

Why does the German labour union not succeed in closing the output gap in Germany (or, for that matter, the inflationary gap in Germany)? The underlying reason is the positive external effect of the reduction in French nominal wages. And why does the French labour union not succeed in closing the output gap in France (or the inflationary gap in France)? The underlying reason is the positive external effect of the reduction in Germany nominal wages.

Step 3 refers to the policy response. The inflationary gap in Germany is 7.5. The wage policy multiplier in Germany is -4. So what is needed in Germany is an increase in German nominal wages of 1.9. The inflationary gap in France is 15. The wage policy multiplier in France is -4. So what is needed in France is an increase in French nominal wages of 3.8.

Step 4 refers to the output lag. The increase in German nominal wages of 1.9 causes a decline in German output of 7.5. As a side effect, it causes a decline in French output of 1.9. The increase in French nominal wages of 3.8 causes a decline in French output of 15. As a side effect, it causes a decline in German output of 3.8. The total effect is a decline in German output of 11.3 and a decline in French output of 16.9. As a consequence, German output goes from 1007.5 to 996.2, and French output goes from 1015 to 998.1. And so on. Table 1.17 presents a synopsis.

What are the dynamic characteristics of this process? There are damped oscillations in German nominal wages, as there are in French nominal wages. Moreover, there are damped oscillations in German output, as there are in French output. The German economy oscillates between unemployment and overemployment, as does the French economy. As a result, competition between the German labour union and the French labour union leads to full employment in Germany and France.

Finally compare wage policy competition with fiscal competition. Fiscal competition cannot achieve full employment. By contrast, wage policy competition can indeed achieve full employment. Judging from this point of view, wage policy competition seems to be superior to fiscal competition.

Table 1.17
Competition between the German Labour Union and the French Labour Union
Unemployment in Germany and France

	Germany	France
Initial Output	940	970
Change in Nominal Wages	−15	−7.5
Output	1007.5	1015
Change in Nominal Wages	1.9	3.8
Output	996.2	998.1
Change in Nominal Wages	−1.0	−0.5
Output	1000.5	1001.0
and so on	...	...

Chapter 8
Cooperation between the German Labour Union and the French Labour Union

1. The Model

1) Introduction. As a starting point, take the output model. It can be represented by a system of two equations:

$$Y_1 = A_1 - \varepsilon W_1 - \eta W_2 \tag{1}$$
$$Y_2 = A_2 - \varepsilon W_2 - \eta W_1 \tag{2}$$

Here Y_1 denotes German output, Y_2 is French output, W_1 is German nominal wages, and W_2 is French nominal wages. The endogenous variables are German output and French output. At the beginning there is unemployment in both Germany and France. More precisely, unemployment in Germany exceeds unemployment in France. The targets of wage policy cooperation are full employment in Germany and full employment in France. The instruments of wage policy cooperation are German nominal wages and French nominal wages. So there are two targets and two instruments.

2) The policy model. On this basis, the policy model can be characterized by a system of two equations:

$$\overline{Y}_1 = A_1 - \varepsilon W_1 - \eta W_2 \tag{3}$$
$$\overline{Y}_2 = A_2 - \varepsilon W_2 - \eta W_1 \tag{4}$$

Here $\overline{Y}_1$ denotes full-employment output in Germany, and $\overline{Y}_2$ denotes full-employment output in France. The endogenous variables are German nominal wages and French nominal wages.

To simplify notation, we introduce $B_1 = A_1 - \overline{Y}_1$ and $B_2 = A_2 - \overline{Y}_2$. Then we solve the model for the endogenous variables:

$$W_1 = \frac{\varepsilon B_1 - \eta B_2}{\varepsilon^2 - \eta^2} \tag{5}$$

$$W_2 = \frac{\varepsilon B_2 - \eta B_1}{\varepsilon^2 - \eta^2} \tag{6}$$

Equation (5) shows the required level of German nominal wages, and equation (6) shows the required level of French nominal wages. There is a solution if and only if $\varepsilon \neq \eta$. Due to the assumption $\varepsilon > \eta$, this condition is met. The solution is positive if $\eta / \varepsilon < B_1 / B_2 < \varepsilon / \eta$. As a result, cooperation between the German labour union and the French labour union can achieve full employment in Germany and France. It is worth pointing out here that the solution to wage policy cooperation is identical to the steady state of wage policy competition.

3) Another version of the policy model. As an alternative, the policy model can be stated in terms of the output gap and the required change in nominal wages:

$$\Delta Y_1 = -\varepsilon \Delta W_1 - \eta \Delta W_2 \tag{7}$$
$$\Delta Y_2 = -\varepsilon \Delta W_2 - \eta \Delta W_1 \tag{8}$$

Here ΔY_1 denotes the output gap in Germany, ΔY_2 is the output gap in France, ΔW_1 is the required change in German nominal wages, and ΔW_2 is the required change in French nominal wages. The endogenous variables are ΔW_1 and ΔW_2. The solution to the system (7) and (8) is as follows:

$$\Delta W_1 = -\frac{\varepsilon \Delta Y_1 - \eta \Delta Y_2}{\varepsilon^2 - \eta^2} \tag{9}$$

$$\Delta W_2 = -\frac{\varepsilon \Delta Y_2 - \eta \Delta Y_1}{\varepsilon^2 - \eta^2} \tag{10}$$

2. Some Numerical Examples

To illustrate the policy model, have a look at some numerical examples. For ease of exposition, without losing generality, assume $\varepsilon = 4$ and $\eta = 1$. On this assumption, the output model can be written as follows:

$$Y_1 = A_1 - 4W_1 - W_2 \tag{1}$$

$$Y_2 = A_2 - 4W_2 - W_1 \tag{2}$$

The endogenous variables are German and French output. Evidently, an increase in German nominal wages of 100 causes a decline in German output of 400 and a decline in French output of 100. Further let full-employment output in Germany be 1000, and let full-employment output in France be the same.

It proves useful to consider four distinct cases:
- unemployment in Germany exceeds unemployment in France
- unemployment in Germany, full employment in France
- unemployment in Germany equals unemployment in France
- unemployment in Germany, overemployment in France.

1) Unemployment in Germany exceeds unemployment in France. Let initial output in Germany be 940, and let initial output in France be 970. The output gap in Germany is 60, and the output gap in France is 30. So what is needed, according to equations (9) and (10) from the previous section, is a reduction in German nominal wages of 14 and a reduction in French nominal wages of 4. The reduction in German nominal wages of 14 increases German output by 56 and French output by 14. The reduction in French nominal wages of 4 increases French output by 16 and German output by 4. The total effect is an increase in German output of 60 and an increase in French output of 30. As a consequence, German output goes from 940 to 1000, and French output goes from 970 to 1000. In Germany there is now full employment, and the same holds for France. The effective multiplier in Germany is -4.3, because of $60/14 = 4.3$. And the effective multiplier in France is -7.5, because of $30/4 = 7.5$. As a result,

72

cooperation between the German labour union and the French labour union can achieve full employment in Germany and France. Table 1.18 gives an overview.

Table 1.18
**Cooperation between the German Labour Union and
the French Labour Union**
Unemployment in Germany and France

	Germany	France
Initial Output	940	970
Change in Nominal Wages	−14	−4
Output	1000	1000

2) Unemployment in Germany, full employment in France. Let initial output in Germany be 940, and let initial output in France be 1000. The output gap in Germany is 60, and the output gap in France is zero. What is needed, then, is a reduction in German nominal wages of 16 and an increase in French nominal wages of 4. The reduction in German nominal wages of 16 increases German output by 64 and French output by 16. The increase in French nominal wages of 4 reduces French output by 16 and German output by 4. The net effect is an increase in German output of 60 and an increase in French output of zero. The effective multiplier in Germany is −3.8, and the effective multiplier in France is zero.

3) Unemployment in Germany equals unemployment in France. Let initial output in Germany be 970, and let initial output in France be the same. The output gap in Germany is 30, as is the output gap in France. What is needed, then, is a reduction in German nominal wages of 6 and a reduction in French nominal wages of equally 6. The reduction in German nominal wages of 6 increases German output by 24 and French output by 6. The reduction in French nominal wages of 6 increases French output by 24 and German output by 6. The overall effect is an increase in German output of 30 and an increase in French

output of equally 30. The effective multiplier in Germany is -5, as is the effective multiplier in France.

4) Unemployment in Germany, overemployment in France. Let initial output in Germany be 970, and let initial output in France be 1030. The output gap in Germany is 30, and the output gap in France is -30. What is needed, then, is a reduction in German nominal wages of 10 and an increase in French nominal wages of equally 10. The reduction in German nominal wages of 10 increases German output by 40 and French output by 10. The increase in French nominal wages of 10 reduces French output by 40 and German output by 10. The net effect is an increase in German output of 30 and a decline in French output of equally 30. The effective multiplier in Germany is -3, as is the effective multiplier in France.

5) Comparing wage policy cooperation with wage policy competition. Wage policy competition can achieve full employment. The same applies to wage policy cooperation. Wage policy competition is a slow process. Wage policy cooperation is a fast process. Judging from these points of view, wage policy cooperation seems to be superior to wage policy competition.

Chapter 9
Competition between the Central Bank,
the German Labour Union,
and the French Labour Union

1. The Dynamic Model

1) The static model. As a point of reference, consider the static model. It can be represented by a system of two equations:

$$Y_1 = A_1 + \alpha M - \varepsilon W_1 - \eta W_2 \tag{1}$$

$$Y_2 = A_2 + \alpha M - \varepsilon W_2 - \eta W_1 \tag{2}$$

According to equation (1), German output Y_1 is determined by union money supply M, German nominal wages W_1, French nominal wages W_2, and some other factors called A_1. According to equation (2), French output Y_2 is determined by union money supply M, French nominal wages W_2, German nominal wages W_1, and some other factors called A_2. The coefficients α, ε and η are positive with $\varepsilon > \eta$.

An increase in union money supply raises both German output and French output, to the same extent respectively. An increase in German nominal wages lowers both German output and French output, where the fall in German output exceeds the fall in French output. Likewise, an increase in French nominal wages lowers both French output and German output, where the fall in French output exceeds the fall in German output. Of course, the endogenous variables are German output and French output.

2) The dynamic model. At the beginning there is unemployment in both Germany and France. More precisely, unemployment in Germany exceeds unemployment in France. The primary target of the union central bank is price stability in the union. The secondary target of the union central bank is high

employment in Germany and France. The instrument of the union central bank is union money supply. The target of the German labour union is full employment in Germany. The instrument of the German labour union is German nominal wages. The target of the French labour union is full employment in France. The instrument of the French labour union is French nominal wages.

We assume that the central bank and the labour unions decide sequentially. First the central bank decides, and then the labour unions decide. In step 1, the central bank decides. In step 2, the German labour union and the French labour union decide simultaneously and independently. In step 3, the central bank decides. In step 4, the German labour union and the French labour union decide simultaneously and independently. And so on.

2. Some Numerical Examples

To illustrate the dynamic model, have a look at some numerical examples. For ease of exposition, without loss of generality, assume $\alpha = 2$, $\varepsilon = 4$, and $\eta = 1$. On this assumption, the static model can be written as follows:

$$Y_1 = A_1 + 2M - 4W_1 - W_2 \tag{1}$$
$$Y_2 = A_2 + 2M - 4W_2 - W_1 \tag{2}$$

The endogenous variables are German and French output. Obviously, an increase in union money supply of 100 causes an increase in German output of 200 and an increase in French output of equally 200. An increase in German nominal wages of 100 causes a decline in German output of 400 and a decline in French output of 100. Correspondingly, an increase in French nominal wages of 100 causes a decline in French output of 400 and a decline in German output of 100. Further let full-employment output in Germany be 1000, and let full-employment output in France be the same.

It proves useful to study two distinct cases:
- unemployment in Germany and France
- inflation in Germany and France.

1) Unemployment in Germany and France. Let initial output in Germany be 940, and let initial output in France be 970. Step 1 refers to monetary policy. The output gap in Germany is 60, and the output gap in France is 30. In this situation, the specific target of the union central bank is to close the output gap in France. Closing the output gap in Germany would imply overemployment in France and, hence, inflation in France. The output gap in France is 30. The monetary policy multiplier in France is 2. So what is needed is an increase in union money supply of 15. Step 2 refers to the output lag. The increase in union money supply of 15 causes an increase in German output of 30 and an increase in French output of equally 30. As a consequence, German output goes from 940 to 970, and French output goes from 970 to 1000.

Step 3 refers to wage policy. The output gap in Germany is 30. The wage policy multiplier in Germany is -4. So what is needed in Germany is a reduction in German nominal wages of 7.5. The output gap in France is zero. So there is no need for a change in French nominal wages. Step 4 refers to the output lag. The reduction in German nominal wages of 7.5 causes an increase in German output of 30. As a side effect, it causes an increase in French output of 7.5. As a consequence, German output goes from 970 to 1000, and French output goes from 1000 to 1007.5.

Step 5 refers to monetary policy. The inflationary gap in Germany is zero, and the inflationary gap in France is 7.5. In this situation, the specific target of the union central bank is to close the inflationary gap in France. The monetary policy multiplier in France is 2. So what is needed is a reduction in union money supply of 3.8. Step 6 refers to the output lag. The reduction in union money supply of 3.8 causes a decline in German output of 7.5 and a decline in French output of equally 7.5. As a consequence, German output goes from 1000 to 992.5, and French output goes from 1007.5 to 1000.

Step 7 refers to wage policy. The output gap in Germany is 7.5. The wage policy multiplier in Germany is -4. So what is needed in Germany is a reduction in German nominal wages of 1.9. The output gap in France is zero. So there is no need for a change in French nominal wages. Step 8 refers to the output lag. The reduction in German nominal wages of 1.9 causes an increase in German output of 7.5. As a side effect, it causes an increase in French output of 1.9. As a consequence, German output goes from 992.5 to 1000, and French output goes from 1000 to 1001.9. And so on. Table 1.19 presents a synopsis.

Table 1.19

Competition between the Central Bank, the German Labour Union, and the French Labour Union

Unemployment in Germany and France

	Germany	France
Initial Output	940	970
Change in Money Supply	15	
Output	970	1000
Change in Nominal Wages	−7.5	0
Output	1000	1007.5
Change in Money Supply	−3.8	
Output	992.5	1000
Change in Nominal Wages	−1.9	0
Output	1000	1001.9
Change in Money Supply	−0.9	
Output	998.1	1000
and so on	...	...

What are the dynamic characteristics of this process? There is an initial increase in union money supply, followed by a continuous reduction in union money supply. There is a continuous decline in German nominal wages, but there is no change in French nominal wages. There are damped oscillations in German output, as there are in French output. The German economy oscillates between unemployment and full employment, while the French economy oscillates between overemployment and full employment. As a result, competition between the central bank, the German labour union, and the French labour union leads to full employment in Germany and France. Technically speaking, there is a stable steady state.

2) Inflation in Germany and France. At the start there is overemployment in both Germany and France. For that reason there is inflation in both Germany and France. Let overemployment in Germany exceed overemployment in France. Let initial output in Germany be 1060, and let initial output in France be 1030. Step 1 refers to monetary policy. The inflationary gap in Germany is 60, and the inflationary gap in France is 30. In this situation, the specific target of the union central bank is to close the inflationary gap in Germany. Closing the inflationary gap in France would imply overemployment in Germany and, hence, inflation in Germany. The inflationary gap in Germany is 60. The monetary policy multiplier in Germany is 2. So what is needed is a reduction in union money supply of 30. Step 2 refers to the output lag. The reduction in union money supply of 30 causes a decline in German output of 60 and a decline in French output of equally 60. As a consequence, German output goes from 1060 to 1000, and French output goes from 1030 to 970.

Step 3 refers to wage policy. The output gap in Germany is zero. So there is no need for a change in German nominal wages. The output gap in France is 30. The wage policy multiplier in France is -4. So what is needed in France is a reduction in French nominal wages of 7.5. Step 4 refers to the output lag. The reduction in French nominal wages of 7.5 causes an increase in French output of 30. As a side effect, it causes an increase in German output of 7.5. As a consequence, French output goes from 970 to 1000, and German output goes from 1000 to 1007.5

Step 5 refers to monetary policy. The inflationary gap in Germany is 7.5, and the inflationary gap in France is zero. In this situation, the specific target of the union central bank is to close the inflationary gap in Germany. The monetary policy multiplier in Germany is 2. So what is needed is a reduction in union money supply of 3.8. Step 6 refers to the output lag. The reduction in union money supply of 3.8 causes a decline in German output of 7.5 and a decline in

French output of equally 7.5. As a consequence, German output goes from 1007.5 to 1000, and French output goes from 1000 to 992.5

Step 7 refers to wage policy. The output gap in Germany is zero. So there is no need for a change in German nominal wages. The output gap in France is 7.5. The wage policy multiplier in France is -4. So what is needed in France is a reduction in French nominal wages of 1.9. Step 8 refers to the output lag. The reduction in French nominal wages of 1.9 causes an increase in French output of 7.5. As a side effect, it causes an increase in German output of 1.9. As a consequence, French output goes from 992.5 to 1000, and German output goes from 1000 to 1001.9. And so on. Table 1.20 gives an overview.

Table 1.20

Competition between the Central Bank, the German Labour Union, and the French Labour Union

Inflation in Germany and France

	Germany	France
Initial Output	1060	1030
Change in Money Supply	-30	
Output	1000	970
Change in Nominal Wages	0	-7.5
Output	1007.5	1000
Change in Money Supply	-3.8	
Output	1000	992.5
Change in Nominal Wages	0	-1.9
Output	1001.9	1000
and so on	...	...

What are the dynamic characteristics of this process? There is a continuous reduction in union money supply. There is no change in German nominal wages, but there is a continuous decline in French nominal wages. There are damped oscillations in German output, as there are in French output. The German economy oscillates between overemployment and full employment, while the French economy oscillates between unemployment and full employment. As a result, competition between the central bank, the German labour union, and the French labour union leads to price stability and full employment.

3) Comparing monetary and wage competition with pure wage competition. Wage competition can achieve full employment. The same holds for monetary and wage competition. Wage competition is a (relatively) slow process. Monetary and wage competition is a (relatively) fast process. Wage competition leads to a large reduction in nominal wages. Monetary and wage competition leads to a small reduction in nominal wages. Judging from these points of view, monetary and wage competition is superior to wage competition.

4) Comparing monetary and wage competition with monetary and fiscal competition. Monetary and fiscal competition cannot achieve full employment. By contrast, monetary and wage competition can indeed achieve full employment. Judging from this perspective, monetary and wage competition is superior to monetary and fiscal competition.

Chapter 10
Cooperation between the Central Bank,
the German Labour Union,
and the French Labour Union

1. The Model

1) Introduction. As a starting point, take the output model. It can be represented by a system of two equations:

$$Y_1 = A_1 + \alpha M - \varepsilon W_1 - \eta W_2 \tag{1}$$

$$Y_2 = A_2 + \alpha M - \varepsilon W_2 - \eta W_1 \tag{2}$$

Here Y_1 denotes German output, Y_2 is French output, M is union money supply, W_1 is German nominal wages, and W_2 is French nominal wages. The endogenous variables are German output and French output.

At the beginning there is unemployment in both Germany and France. More precisely, unemployment in Germany exceeds unemployment in France. The policy makers are the central bank, the German labour union, and the French labour union. The targets of policy cooperation are full employment in Germany and full employment in France. The instruments of policy cooperation are union money supply, German nominal wages, and French nominal wages. There are two targets and three instruments, so there is one degree of freedom. As a result, there is an infinite number of solutions. In other words, monetary and wage cooperation can achieve full employment.

2) The policy model. On this basis, the policy model can be characterized by a system of two equations:

$$\Delta Y_1 = \alpha \Delta M - \varepsilon \Delta W_1 - \eta \Delta W_2 \tag{3}$$

$$\Delta Y_2 = \alpha \Delta M - \varepsilon \Delta W_2 - \eta \Delta W_1 \tag{4}$$

Here ΔY_1 denotes the output gap in Germany, ΔY_2 is the output gap in France, ΔM is the required change in union money supply, ΔW_1 is the required change in German nominal wages, and ΔW_2 is the required change in French nominal wages. The endogenous variables are ΔM, ΔW_1, and ΔW_2.

We now introduce a third target. We assume that the reduction in German nominal wages should be equal in size to the increase in French nominal wages $\Delta W_1 + \Delta W_2 = 0$. Put another way, we assume that the price level of union goods should be constant. Take the sum of equations (3) and (4), observe $\Delta W_1 + \Delta W_2 = 0$, and solve for:

$$\Delta M = \frac{\Delta Y_1 + \Delta Y_2}{2\alpha} \tag{5}$$

Then take the difference between equations (3) and (4), observe $\Delta W_1 + \Delta W_2 = 0$, and solve for:

$$\Delta W_1 = -\frac{\Delta Y_1 - \Delta Y_2}{2(\varepsilon - \eta)} \tag{6}$$

$$\Delta W_2 = \frac{\Delta Y_1 - \Delta Y_2}{2(\varepsilon - \eta)} \tag{7}$$

Equation (5) shows the required change in union money supply, (6) shows the required change in German nominal wages, and (7) shows the required change in French nominal wages. There is a solution to policy cooperation if and only if $\varepsilon \neq \eta$. This condition is met.

2. Some Numerical Examples

To illustrate the policy model, have a look at some numerical examples. For ease of exposition, without losing generality, assume $\alpha = 2$, $\varepsilon = 4$, and $\eta = 1$. On this assumption, the output model can be written as follows:

$$Y_1 = A_1 + 2M - 4W_1 - W_2 \tag{1}$$

$$Y_2 = A_2 + 2M - 4W_2 - W_1 \tag{2}$$

The endogenous variables are German and French output. Evidently, an increase in union money supply of 100 causes an increase in German output of 200 and an increase in French output of equally 200. An increase in German nominal wages of 100 causes a decline in German output of 400 and a decline in French output of 100. Further let full-employment output in Germany be 1000, and let full-employment output in France be the same.

It proves useful to consider two distinct cases:
- unemployment in Germany and France
- inflation in Germany and France.

1) Unemployment in Germany and France. Let unemployment in Germany exceed unemployment in France. Let initial output in Germany be 940, and let initial output in France be 970. The solution can be found in two logical steps. Step 1 refers to monetary policy. The output gap in the union is 90. The monetary policy multiplier in the union is 4. So what is needed is an increase in union money supply of 22.5. This policy action raises German output and French output by 45 each. As a consequence, German output goes from 940 to 985, and French output goes from 970 to 1015. In Germany there is still some unemployment left, and in France there is now some overemployment. Strictly speaking, unemployment in Germany and overemployment in France are the same size.

Step 2 refers to wage policy. The output gap in Germany is 15, and the output gap in France is -15. So what is needed, according to equations (6) and (7) from the previous section, is a reduction in German nominal wages of 5 and an increase in French nominal wages of equally 5. The reduction in German nominal wages of 5 increases German output by 20 and French output by 5. Conversely, the increase in French nominal wages of 5 reduces French output by 20 and German output by 5. The net effect is an increase in German output of 15 and a decline in French output of equally 15. As a consequence, German output goes from 985 to 1000, and French output goes from 1015 to 1000. In Germany there is now full employment, and the same holds for France.

As a result, cooperation between the central bank, the German labour union, and the French labour union can achieve full employment in Germany and France. What is needed is an increase in union money supply, a reduction in German nominal wages, and an increase in French nominal wages. Here the reduction in German nominal wages is equal in size to the increase in French nominal wages. On this account, the price level of union goods is constant. Table 1.21 presents a synopsis.

Tables 1.22 and 1.23 give some alternative solutions. In Table 1.22, the increase in union money supply is rather small. To compensate for this, the reduction in German nominal wages is greater than the increase in French nominal wages. Thus the price level of union goods is falling. In Table 1.23, the increase in union money supply is quite large. To balance this, the reduction in German nominal wages is less than the increase in French nominal wages. Thus the price level of union goods is rising.

2) Inflation in Germany and France. At the start there is overemployment in both Germany and France. Let overemployment in Germany exceed overemployment in France. Let initial output in Germany be 1060, and let initial output in France be 1030. The solution can be determined in two logical steps. Step 1 refers to monetary policy. The inflationary gap in the union is 90. The monetary policy multiplier in the union is 4. So what is needed is a reduction in union money supply of 22.5. This policy action lowers German output and French output by 45 each. As a consequence, German output goes from 1060 to 1015, and French output goes from 1030 to 985. In Germany there is still some overemployment left, and in France there is now some unemployment. Strictly speaking, overemployment in Germany and unemployment in France are the same size.

Table 1.21

Cooperation between the Central Bank, the German Labour Union, and the French Labour Union

Unemployment in Germany and France

	Germany	France
Initial Output	940	970
Change in Money Supply	22.5	
Output	985	1015
Change in Nominal Wages	−5	5
Output	1000	1000

Table 1.22

Cooperation between the Central Bank, the German Labour Union, and the French Labour Union

A Second Solution

	Germany	France
Initial Output	940	970
Change in Money Supply	15	
Output	970	1000
Change in Nominal Wages	−8	2
Output	1000	1000

Step 2 refers to wage policy. The output gap in Germany is -15, and the output gap in France is 15. What is needed, then, is an increase in German nominal wages of 5 and a reduction in French nominal wages of equally 5. The increase in German nominal wages of 5 reduces German output by 20 and French output by 5. Conversely, the reduction in French nominal wages of 5 increases French output by 20 and German output by 5. The net effect is a decline in German output of 15 and an increase in French output of equally 15. As a consequence, German output goes from 1015 to 1000, and French output goes from 985 to 1000. In Germany there is now full employment and, hence, price stability. The same applies to France.

As a result, monetary and wage cooperation can achieve price stability and full employment. What is needed is a reduction in union money supply, an increase in German nominal wages, and a reduction in French nominal wages. Here the increase in German nominal wages is equal in size to the reduction in French nominal wages. On this account, the price level of union goods is constant. For a synopsis see Table 1.24.

3) Comparing monetary and wage cooperation with monetary and wage competition. Monetary and wage competition can achieve full employment. The same is true of monetary and wage cooperation. Monetary and wage competition is a slow process. Monetary and wage cooperation is a fast process. Under monetary and wage competition, nominal wages and prices are declining. Under monetary and wage cooperation, nominal wages and prices are constant on aggregate. Judging from these points of view, monetary and wage cooperation seems to be superior to monetary and wage competition.

4) Comparing monetary and wage cooperation with pure wage cooperation. Wage cooperation can achieve full employment. The same holds for monetary and wage cooperation. Under wage cooperation, nominal wages and prices come down. Under monetary and wage cooperation, nominal wages and prices are constant on aggregate. Judging from this perspective, monetary and wage cooperation seems to be superior to wage cooperation.

Table 1.23
Cooperation between the Central Bank, the German Labour Union, and the French Labour Union
A Third Solution

	Germany	France
Initial Output	940	970
Change in Money Supply	30	
Output	1000	1030
Change in Nominal Wages	−2	8
Output	1000	1000

Table 1.24
Cooperation between the Central Bank, the German Labour Union, and the French Labour Union
Inflation in Germany and France

	Germany	France
Initial Output	1060	1030
Change in Money Supply	−22.5	
Output	1015	985
Change in Nominal Wages	5	−5
Output	1000	1000

Chapter 11
Inflation in Germany and France

1. Monetary Policy in the Union

1) The model. To begin with, consider a stylized model of output and inflation:

$$Y_1 = A_1 + \alpha M / P_1 \tag{1}$$

$$Y_2 = A_2 + \alpha M / P_2 \tag{2}$$

$$\hat{P}_1 = \lambda (Y_1 - \overline{Y}_1) / \overline{Y}_1 \tag{3}$$

$$\hat{P}_2 = \lambda (Y_2 - \overline{Y}_2) / \overline{Y}_2 \tag{4}$$

According to equation (1), German output Y_1 is determined by union money supply M, the price of German goods P_1, and some other factors called A_1. According to equation (2), French output Y_2 is determined by union money supply M, the price of French goods P_2, and some other factors called A_2. The coefficient α is positive. An increase in union money supply raises both German output and French output. An increase in the price of German goods lowers German output. On the other hand, it has no effect on French output. An increase in the price of French goods lowers French output. On the other hand, it has no effect on German output.

In equation (3), $\hat{P}_1$ is the rate of growth of the price of German goods. The hat denotes the rate of growth $\hat{P}_1 = \dot{P}_1 / P_1$, and the dot denotes the time derivative $\dot{P}_1 = dP_1 / dt$. In other words, $\hat{P}_1$ is producer inflation in Germany. $\overline{Y}_1$ is full-employment output in Germany. $Y_1 - \overline{Y}_1$ is the inflationary gap in Germany. $(Y_1 - \overline{Y}_1) / \overline{Y}_1$ is the inflationary gap in Germany, expressed as a percentage of full-employment output in Germany. And λ is the speed of price adjustment. According to equation (3), producer inflation in Germany is proportional to the inflationary gap in Germany.

In equation (4), $\hat{P}_2$ is the rate of growth of the price of French goods. In other words, $\hat{P}_2$ is producer inflation in France. $\overline{Y}_2$ is full-employment output in France. $Y_2 - \overline{Y}_2$ is the inflationary gap in France. And $(Y_2 - \overline{Y}_2)/\overline{Y}_2$ is the inflationary gap in France, expressed as a percentage of full-employment output in France. According to equation (4), producer inflation in France is proportional to the inflationary gap in France. In equations (1) to (4), the endogenous variables are German output, French output, producer inflation in Germany, and producer inflation in France. For the behavioural foundations of the model see Carlberg (2000, 2001).

The target of the union central bank is price stability in the union. The instrument of the union central bank is union money supply. Producer inflation in the union is composed of producer inflation in Germany and producer inflation in France $\hat{P} = 0.5\hat{P}_1 + 0.5\hat{P}_2$. Here price stability in the union is defined as zero inflation in the union $\hat{P} = 0$. This implies $\hat{P}_1 + \hat{P}_2 = 0$. On this basis, the policy model can be represented by a system of five equations:

$$Y_1 = A_1 + \alpha M / P_1 \tag{5}$$

$$Y_2 = A_2 + \alpha M / P_2 \tag{6}$$

$$\hat{P}_1 = \lambda(Y_1 - \overline{Y}_1)/\overline{Y}_1 \tag{7}$$

$$\hat{P}_2 = \lambda(Y_2 - \overline{Y}_2)/\overline{Y}_2 \tag{8}$$

$$\hat{P}_1 + \hat{P}_2 = 0 \tag{9}$$

Here the endogenous variables are union money supply, German output, French output, producer inflation in Germany, and producer inflation in France.

Initially let the union countries be the same size $P_1\overline{Y}_1 = P_2\overline{Y}_2$ To simplify notation, let initial prices be $P_1 = P_2 = 1$. Then equations (7), (8) and (9) give:

$$Y_1 + Y_2 = \overline{Y}_1 + \overline{Y}_2 \tag{10}$$

Then equations (5) and (6) yield:

$$M = \frac{\overline{Y}_1 + \overline{Y}_2 - A_1 - A_2}{2\alpha} \tag{11}$$

As a result, this is the level of union money supply required for price stability in the union.

2) A numerical example. To illustrate the policy model, take a numerical example with $\alpha = 2$ and $\lambda = 1$. Then an increase in union money supply of 100 causes an increase in German output of 200 and an increase in French output of equally 200. Further let full-employment output in Germany be 1000, and let full-employment output in France be the same. At the beginning there is overemployment in both Germany and France. For that reason there is inflation in both Germany and France. More precisely, overemployment in Germany exceeds overemployment in France. For that reason, inflation in Germany exceeds inflation in France. Let initial output in Germany by 1060, and let initial output in France be 1030. That means, the inflationary gap in Germany is 60, and the inflationary gap in France is 30. Then, according to equations (3) and (4), inflation in Germany is 6 percent, and inflation in France is 3 percent.

The target of the union central bank is price stability in the union. So what is needed is a reduction in union money supply of 22.5. This policy action lowers German output and French output by 45 each. As a consequence, German output goes from 1060 to 1015, and French output goes from 1030 to 985. Now the inflationary gap in Germany is 15, and the inflationary gap in France is −15. Therefore inflation in Germany is 1.5 percent, and inflation in France is −1.5 percent. The net effect is that inflation in the union is zero. In Germany there is some overemployment left, while in France there is now some unemployment. Strictly speaking, overemployment in Germany is equal in size to unemployment in France. Table 1.25 presents a synopsis. As a result, monetary policy in the union can achieve price stability in the union. However, monetary policy in the union cannot achieve full employment in Germany and France.

Table 1.25
Monetary Policy in the Union
Inflation in Germany and France

	Germany	France
Initial Output	1060	1030
Inflation	6	3
Change in Money Supply	-22.5	
Output	1015	985
Inflation	1.5	-1.5
Inflation	0	

2. Downwards Sticky Wages

1) The model. In this section we assume that nominal wages are downwards sticky. In terms of the model that means: In the case of unemployment, the speed of price adjustment is low. And in the case of overemployment, the speed of price adjustment is high. Accordingly, the model of output and inflation can be written as follows:

$$Y_1 = A_1 + \alpha M / P_1 \tag{1}$$
$$Y_2 = A_2 + \alpha M / P_2 \tag{2}$$
$$\hat{P}_1 = \lambda_1 (Y_1 - \overline{Y}_1) / \overline{Y}_1 \tag{3}$$
$$\hat{P}_2 = \lambda_2 (Y_2 - \overline{Y}_2) / \overline{Y}_2 \tag{4}$$

Here λ_1 denotes the speed of price adjustment in Germany, and λ_2 denotes the speed of price adjustment in France. The endogenous variables are German output, French output, producer inflation in Germany, and producer inflation in France.

The target of the union central bank is price stability in the union $\hat{P}_1 + \hat{P}_2 = 0$. Accordingly, the policy model can be characterized by a system of five equations:

$$Y_1 = A_1 + \alpha M / P_1 \tag{5}$$

$$Y_2 = A_2 + \alpha M / P_2 \tag{6}$$

$$\hat{P}_1 = \lambda_1 (Y_1 - \overline{Y}_1) / \overline{Y}_1 \tag{7}$$

$$\hat{P}_2 = \lambda_2 (Y_2 - \overline{Y}_2) / \overline{Y}_2 \tag{8}$$

$$\hat{P}_1 + \hat{P}_2 = 0 \tag{9}$$

Here the endogenous variables are union money supply, German output, French output, producer inflation in Germany, and producer inflation in France. The solution to the policy model is:

$$M = \frac{\lambda_1 \overline{Y}_1 + \lambda_2 \overline{Y}_2 - \lambda_1 A_1 - \lambda_2 A_2}{\alpha \lambda_1 + \alpha \lambda_2} \tag{10}$$

As a result, this is the level of union money supply required for price stability in the union.

2) A numerical example. To illustrate the policy model, consider a numerical example with $\alpha = 2$. In the case of unemployment, let the speed of price adjustment be $\lambda = 0.5$. And in the case of overemployment, let the speed of price adjustment be $\lambda = 1$. At the start there is inflation in both Germany and France. More precisely, inflation in Germany exceeds inflation in France. Let initial output in Germany be 1060, and let initial output in France be 1030. Thus the inflationary gap in Germany is 60, and the inflationary gap in France is 30. Then, according to equations (3) and (4), inflation in Germany is 6 percent, and inflation in France is 3 percent.

The target of the union central bank is price stability in the union. So what is needed is a reduction in union money supply of 25. This policy action lowers German output and French output by 50 each. As a consequence, German output goes from 1060 to 1010, and French output goes from 1030 to 980. Now the inflationary gap in Germany is 10, and the inflationary gap in France is -20. Hence inflation in Germany is 1 percent, and inflation in France is -1 percent. The net effect is that inflation in the union is zero. In Germany there is some overemployment left, while in France there is now some unemployment. Strictly speaking, unemployment in France exceeds overemployment in Germany. Table 1.26 gives an overview.

Table 1.26
Monetary Policy in the Union
Downwards Sticky Wages

	Germany	France
Initial Output	1060	1030
Inflation	6	3
Change in Money Supply	-25	
Output	1010	980
Inflation	1	-1
Inflation	0	

3. Cooperation between the Union Central Bank, the German Government, and the French Government

1) The model. The model of output and inflation can be captured by a system of four equations:

$$Y_1 = A_1 + \alpha M / P_1 + \gamma G_1 - \gamma G_2 \tag{1}$$

$$Y_2 = A_2 + \alpha M / P_2 + \gamma G_2 - \gamma G_1 \tag{2}$$

$$\hat{P}_1 = \lambda (Y_1 - \overline{Y}_1) / \overline{Y}_1 \tag{3}$$

$$\hat{P}_2 = \lambda (Y_2 - \overline{Y}_2) / \overline{Y}_2 \tag{4}$$

Here G_1 denotes German government purchases, and G_2 denotes French government purchases. The coefficient γ is positive. An increase in German government purchases raises German output. On the other hand, it lowers French output. An increase in French government purchases raises French output. On the other hand, it lowers German output. The endogenous variables are German output, French output, producer inflation in Germany, and producer inflation in France.

At the beginning there is inflation in both Germany and France. Let inflation in Germany exceed inflation in France. The policy makers are the union central bank, the German government, and the French government. The targets of policy cooperation are price stability in the union, full employment in Germany, and full employment in France. According to the model, full employment in Germany and full employment in France imply price stability in the union. Hence there are only two independent targets. The instruments of policy cooperation are union money supply, German government purchases, and French government purchases. There are two targets and three instruments, so there is one degree of freedom. That is to say, there is an infinite number of solutions.

A solution can be found in two logical steps. In step 1, union money supply is determined such that overemployment in Germany is equal in size to unemployment in France $Y_1 + Y_2 = \overline{Y}_1 + \overline{Y}_2$. In step 2, German government purchases and French government purchases are determined such that there is full employment in Germany and full employment in France $Y_1 = \overline{Y}_1$, $Y_2 = \overline{Y}_2$. As a result, there is price stability in Germany, price stability in France, and thus price stability in the union.

2) A numerical example. To illustrate this, consider a numerical example with $\alpha = 2$, $\gamma = 1$, and $\lambda = 1$. Then an increase in union money supply of 100 causes an increase in German output of 200 and an increase in French output of equally 200. An increase in German government purchases of 100 causes an increase in German output of 100 and a decline in French output of equally 100. Further let full-employment output in Germany be 1000, and let full-employment output in France be the same. Let initial output in Germany be 1060, and let initial output in France be 1030. That means, the inflationary gap in Germany is 60, and the inflationary gap in France is 30. Then, according to equations (3) and (4), inflation in Germany is 6 percent, and inflation in France is 3 percent.

Step 1 refers to monetary policy. What is needed is a reduction in union money supply of 22.5. This policy action lowers German output and French output by 45 each. As a consequence, German output goes from 1060 to 1015, and French output goes from 1030 to 985. Now the inflationary gap in Germany is 15, and the inflationary gap in France is −15. Therefore inflation in German is 1.5 percent, and inflation in France is −1.5 percent. The net effect is that inflation in the union is zero. In Germany there is some overemployment left, while in France there is now some unemployment. Properly speaking, overemployment in Germany is equal in size to unemployment in France.

Step 2 refers to fiscal policy. What is needed is a reduction in German government purchases of 7.5 and an increase in French government purchases of equally 7.5. These policy measures lower German output by 15 and raise French output by equally 15. As a consequence, German output goes from 1015 to 1000, and French output goes from 985 to 1000. Now the inflationary gap in Germany is zero, as is the inflationary gap in France. Therefore inflation in Germany is zero, as is inflation in France. Hence inflation in the union is zero too. In Germany there is full employment, as there is in France. For a synopsis see Table 1.27.

As a result, cooperation between the union central bank, the German government, and the French government can achieve both price stability and full employment.

Table 1.27

Cooperation between the Union Central Bank, the German Government, and the French Government

Inflation in Germany and France

	Germany	France
Initial Output	1060	1030
Inflation	6	3
Change in Money Supply	−22.5	
Output	1015	985
Inflation	1.5	−1.5
Inflation	0	
Change in Government Purchases	−7.5	7.5
Output	1000	1000
Inflation	0	0
Inflation	0	

Part Two

The World of
Two Monetary Regions

Chapter 1
The Basic Model

1. The World as a Whole

1) The model. Understanding the world as a whole is helpful in understanding the world of two monetary regions. Take for instance an increase in world government purchases of 100. Then what will be the effect on world income? Alternatively, take a 1 percent increase in world money supply. Again what will be the effect on world income?

Of course, the world as a whole is a closed economy. Therefore the model can be represented by a system of two equations:

$$Y = C(Y) + I(r) + G \tag{1}$$

$$M = L(r, Y) \tag{2}$$

$C(Y)$ is the consumption function. It states that world consumption is an increasing function of world income. $I(r)$ is the investment function. It states that world investment is a decreasing function of the world interest rate. G denotes world government purchases. Thus equation (1) is the goods market equation of the world as a whole. M denotes world money supply. $L(r, Y)$ is the money demand function. It states that world money demand is a decreasing function of the world interest rate and an increasing function of world income. Hence equation (2) is the money market equation of the world as a whole. The exogenous variables are world government purchases G and world money supply M. The endogenous variables are world income Y and the world interest rate r.

Now take the total differential of the model:

$$dY = cdY - bdr + dG \tag{3}$$

$$dM = kdY - jdr \tag{4}$$

Here c denotes the marginal consumption rate with $0 < c < 1$, b is the interest sensitivity of investment with $b > 0$, k is the income sensitivity of money demand with $k > 0$, and j is the interest sensitivity of money demand with $j > 0$.

2) Fiscal policy. To begin with, solve equations (3) and (4) for the fiscal policy multiplier:

$$\frac{dY}{dG} = \frac{j}{bk + js} \tag{5}$$

Here s is shorthand for $1 - c$. As a result, an increase in world government purchases raises world income. To illustrate this, have a look at a numerical example with $c = 0.72$ and $k = 0.25$. Empirically speaking, however, b and j are not well known.

Therefore, as a point of reference, consider the special case that the interest rate is given exogenously. Then the total differential of the goods market equation is $dY = cdY + dG$. Accordingly, the fiscal policy multiplier is:

$$\frac{dY}{dG} = \frac{1}{s} \tag{6}$$

In the numerical example with $c = 0.72$, the fiscal policy multiplier is 3.5714. That is, an increase in world government purchases of 100 causes an increase in world income of 357.

Let us return now to the general case that the interest rate is endogenous. We assume here that the damping effect of the money market on the fiscal policy multiplier is 0.5:

$$\frac{dY}{dG} = \frac{1}{2s} \tag{7}$$

In the numerical example with $c = 0.72$, the fiscal policy multiplier is 1.7857. That is, an increase in world government purchases of 100 causes an increase in world income of 179. Finally, the comparison of equation (5) with equation (7) yields:

$$bk = js \tag{8}$$

In the numerical example with c = 0.72 and k = 0.25, we have b/j = 1.12.

  3) Monetary policy. To start with, solve equations (3) and (4) for the monetary policy multiplier:

$$\frac{dY}{dM} = \frac{b}{bk + js} \tag{9}$$

Obviously, an increase in world money supply raises world income. Further, taking account of equation (8), the monetary policy multiplier simplifies as follows:

$$\frac{dY}{dM} = \frac{1}{2k} \tag{10}$$

In the numerical example with k = 0.25, the monetary policy multiplier is 2. That is, an increase in world money supply of 100 causes an increase in world income of 200.

  As a point of reference, consider the small open economy with flexible exchange rates and perfect capital mobility. There the monetary policy multiplier is:

$$\frac{dY}{dM} = \frac{1}{k} \tag{11}$$

This is well known, see for instance the small monetary union of two countries. In the numerical example with k = 0.25, the monetary policy multiplier is 4. That is, an increase in domestic money supply of 100 causes an increase in domestic income of 400. Let us return now to the world as a whole. As a finding, the damping effect on the monetary policy multiplier of closing the economy is 0.5.

Finally, what does this mean in terms of elasticities? As a starting point, take the monetary policy multiplier $dY/dM = 1/2k$ with $k = \partial L/\partial Y$. Assume that the income elasticity of money demand is unity $(\partial L/\partial Y)(Y/L) = 1$. This implies $k = L/Y$. Due to $L = M$, we have $k = M/Y$. This together with $dY/dM = 1/2k$ yields:

$$\hat{Y} = \frac{1}{2}\hat{M} \tag{12}$$

Here the hat denotes the rate of change (e.g. $\hat{Y} = dY/Y$). That is, a 1 percent increase in world money supply produces a 0.5 percent increase in world income.

4) Extensions. So far we assumed that the damping effect of the money market on the fiscal multiplier is 0.5. Now, instead, we assume that the damping effect is 0.75 or 0.25. First assume that the damping effect is 0.75. In this case, the fiscal multiplier is $dY/dG = 3/4s$ and the monetary multiplier is $dY/dM = 1/4k$. In the numerical example, an increase in world government purchases of 100 causes an increase in world income of 268. And an increase in world money supply of 100 causes an increase in world income of 100. More generally, a 1 percent increase in world money supply produces a 0.25 percent increase in world income.

Second assume that the damping effect is 0.25. In this case, the fiscal multiplier is $dY/dG = 1/4s$ and the monetary multiplier is $dY/dM = 3/4k$. In the numerical example, an increase in world government purchases of 100 causes an increase in world income of 89. And an increase in world money supply of 100 causes an increase in world income of 300. More generally, a 1 percent increase in world money supply produces a 0.75 percent increase in world income.

2. The World of Two Monetary Regions

1) Introduction. In this section we consider a world of two monetary regions, let us say Europe and America. The exchange rate between Europe and America is flexible. Take for example an increase in European government purchases. Then what will be the effect on European income, and what on American income? Correspondingly, take an increase in European money supply. Then how will European income respond, and how American income?

In dealing with these problems we make the following assumptions. European goods and American goods are imperfect substitutes for each other. European output is determined by the demand for European goods. American output is determined by the demand for American goods. European money demand is equal to European money supply. American money demand is equal to American money supply. There is perfect capital mobility between Europe and America, so the European interest rate agrees with the American interest rate. In the short run, nominal wages and prices are rigid. P_1 denotes the price of European goods, as measured in euros. And P_2 denotes the price of American goods, as measured in dollars. To simplify notation let be $P_1 = P_2 = 1$. The letter e denotes the exchange rate between Europe and America. Properly speaking, e is the price of the dollar as measured in euros. Let the initial value of the exchange rate be unity.

2) The market for European goods. The behavioural functions underlying the analysis are as follows:

$$C_1 = C_1(Y_1) \tag{1}$$
$$I_1 = I_1(r) \tag{2}$$
$$G_1 = const \tag{3}$$
$$X_1 = X_1(e, Y_2) \tag{4}$$
$$Q_1 = Q_1(Y_1) \tag{5}$$

Equation (1) is the consumption function of Europe. It states that European consumption is an increasing function of European income. Here C_1 denotes

European consumption, and Y_1 is European income. Equation (2) is the investment function of Europe. It states that European investment is a decreasing function of the world interest rate. I_1 denotes European investment, and r is the world interest rate. According to equation (3), the European government fixes its purchases of goods and services. G_1 denotes European government purchases.

Equation (4) is the export function of Europe. It states that European exports are an increasing function of the exchange rate and an increasing function of American income. X_1 denotes European exports to America, and Y_2 is American income. The message of equation (4) is that a depreciation of the euro raises European exports. Equation (5) is the import function Europe. It states that European imports are an increasing function of European income. Q_1 denotes European imports from America. European output is determined by the demand for European goods $Y_1 = C_1 + I_1 + G_1 + X_1 - Q_1$. Taking account of the behavioural functions (1) to (5), we arrive at the goods market equation of Europe:

$$Y_1 = C_1(Y_1) + I_1(r) + G_1 + X_1(e, Y_2) - Q_1(Y_1) \tag{6}$$

3) The market for American goods. The behavioural functions are as follows:

$$C_2 = C_2(Y_2) \tag{7}$$
$$I_2 = I_2(r) \tag{8}$$
$$G_2 = \text{const} \tag{9}$$
$$X_2 = X_2(e, Y_1) \tag{10}$$
$$Q_2 = Q_2(Y_2) \tag{11}$$

Equation (7) is the consumption function of America. It states that American consumption is an increasing function of American income. Here C_2 denotes American consumption. Equation (8) is the investment function of America. It states that American investment is a decreasing function of the world interest rate. I_2 denotes American investment. According to equation (9), the American government fixes its purchases of goods and services. G_2 denotes American government purchases.

Equation (10) is the export function of America. It states that American exports are a decreasing function of the exchange rate and an increasing function of European income. X_2 denotes American exports to Europe. The message of equation (10) is that a depreciation of the dollar raises American exports. Equation (11) is the import function of America. It states that American imports are an increasing function of American income. Q_2 denotes American imports from Europe. American output is determined by the demand for American goods $Y_2 = C_2 + I_2 + G_2 + X_2 - Q_2$. Paying attention to the behavioural functions (7) to (11), we reach the goods market equation of America:

$$Y_2 = C_2(Y_2) + I_2(r) + G_2 + X_2(e, Y_1) - Q_2(Y_2) \tag{12}$$

4) The European money market. The behavioural functions are:

$$L_1 = L_1(r, Y_1) \tag{13}$$
$$M_1 = \text{const} \tag{14}$$

Equation (13) is the money demand function of Europe. It states that European money demand is a decreasing function of the world interest rate and an increasing function of European income. L_1 denotes European money demand. Equation (14) is the money supply function of Europe. It states that the European central bank fixes European money supply. M_1 denotes European money supply. European money demand equals European money supply $L_1 = M_1$. Upon substituting the behavioural functions (13) and (14), we get to the money market equation of Europe $L_1(r, Y_1) = M_1$.

5) The American money market. The behavioural functions are:

$$L_2 = L_2(r, Y_2) \tag{15}$$
$$M_2 = \text{const} \tag{16}$$

Equation (15) is the money demand function of America. It states that American money demand is a decreasing function of the world interest rate and an increasing function of American income. L_2 denotes American money demand.

Equation (16) is the money supply function of America. It states that the American central bank fixes American money supply. M_2 denotes American money supply. American money demand equals American money supply $L_2 = M_2$. Upon inserting the behavioural functions (15) and (16), we get to the money market equation of America $L_2(r, Y_2) = M_2$.

6) The model. On this foundation, the full model can be characterized by a system of four equations:

$$Y_1 = C_1(Y_1) + I_1(r) + G_1 + X_1(e, Y_2) - Q_1(Y_1) \tag{17}$$

$$Y_2 = C_2(Y_2) + I_2(r) + G_2 + X_2(e, Y_1) - Q_2(Y_2) \tag{18}$$

$$M_1 = L_1(r, Y_1) \tag{19}$$

$$M_2 = L_2(r, Y_2) \tag{20}$$

Equation (17) is the goods market equation of Europe, as measured in European goods. (18) is the goods market equation of America, as measured in American goods. (19) is the money market equation of Europe, as measured in euros. And (20) is the money market equation of America, as measured in dollars. It is worth pointing out here that the goods market equations are well consistent with microfoundations, see Carlberg (2002). The exogenous variables are European money supply M_1, American money supply M_2, European government purchases G_1, and American government purchases G_2. The endogenous variables are European income Y_1, American income Y_2, the exchange rate e, and the world interest rate r.

7) The total differential. It is useful to take the total differential of the model:

$$dY_1 = c_1 dY_1 - b_1 dr + dG_1 + h_1 de + q_2 dY_2 - q_1 dY_1 \tag{21}$$

$$dY_2 = c_2 dY_2 - b_2 dr + dG_2 - h_2 de + q_1 dY_1 - q_2 dY_2 \tag{22}$$

$$dM_1 = k_1 dY_1 - j_1 dr \tag{23}$$

$$dM_2 = k_2 dY_2 - j_2 dr \tag{24}$$

Here is a list of the new symbols:

b_1 interest sensitivity of European investment
b_2 interest sensitivity of American investment
c_1 marginal consumption rate of Europe
c_2 marginal consumption rate of America
h_1 exchange rate sensitivity of European exports
h_2 exchange rate sensitivity of American exports
j_1 interest sensitivity of European money demand
j_2 interest sensitivity of American money demand
k_1 income sensitivity of European money demand
k_2 income sensitivity of American money demand
q_1 marginal import rate of Europe
q_2 marginal import rate of America.

We assume that the monetary regions are the same size and have the same behavioural functions. In terms of the model that means:

$$b = b_1 = b_2 \tag{25}$$

$$c = c_1 = c_2 \tag{26}$$

$$h = h_1 = h_2 \tag{27}$$

$$j = j_1 = j_2 \tag{28}$$

$$k = k_1 = k_2 \tag{29}$$

$$q = q_1 = q_2 \tag{30}$$

These assumptions prove to be particularly fruitful. In addition we make some standard assumptions:

$$b > 0 \tag{31}$$

$$0 < c < 1 \tag{32}$$

$$h > 0 \tag{33}$$

$$j > 0 \tag{34}$$

$$k > 0 \tag{35}$$

$$0 < q < 1 \tag{36}$$

8) Fiscal policy. Take for instance an increase in European government purchases. Then what will be the effect on European income, and what on American income? The total differential of the model is as follows:

$$dY_1 = cdY_1 - bdr + dG_1 + hde + qdY_2 - qdY_1 \tag{37}$$

$$dY_2 = cdY_2 - bdr - hde + qdY_1 - qdY_2 \tag{38}$$

$$0 = kdY_1 - jdr \tag{39}$$

$$0 = kdY_2 - jdr \tag{40}$$

Equations (39) and (40) give immediately:

$$dY_1 = dY_2 \tag{41}$$

$$jdr = kdY_1 \tag{42}$$

Now take the sum of equations (37) and (38), observing equation (41), to find out $2dY_1 = dG_1 + 2cdY_1 - 2bdr$. Then eliminate dr by means of equation (42), introduce $s = 1 - c$, and rearrange:

$$\frac{dY_1}{dG_1} = \frac{dY_2}{dG_1} = \frac{j}{2bk + 2js} \tag{43}$$

As a fundamental result, these are the fiscal policy multipliers. An increase in European government purchases raises both European income and American income, to the same extent respectively.

Next have a look at some further aspects. First consider the exchange rate. Take the difference between equations (37) and (38), observe equation (41), and solve for:

$$\frac{de}{dG_1} = -\frac{1}{2h} \tag{44}$$

Obviously, an increase in European government purchases causes an appreciation of the euro and a depreciation of the dollar. Second consider the world interest rate. Merge equations (42) and (43) to check:

$$\frac{dr}{dG_1} = \frac{k}{2bk + 2js} \tag{45}$$

That is, an increase in European government purchases raises the world interest rate.

Third consider the process of adjustment. An increase in European government purchases causes an appreciation of the euro and an increase in the world interest rate. The appreciation of the euro lowers European exports but raises American exports. The increase in the world interest rate lowers both European investment and American investment. The net effect is that European income and American income go up, to the same extent respectively.

Fourth consider an important special case. Assume that the world fiscal multiplier is 1/2s. This assumption was discussed in Section 1. According to equation (43), the effect on world income is:

$$\frac{dY}{dG_1} = \frac{j}{bk + js} \tag{46}$$

Now assume that the world fiscal multiplier is 1/2s:

$$\frac{dY}{dG_1} = \frac{1}{2s} \tag{47}$$

Then the comparison of equations (46) and (47) yields:

$$bk = js \tag{48}$$

What does this imply for regional incomes? To answer this question, substitute equation (48) into equation (43):

$$\frac{dY_1}{dG_1} = \frac{dY_2}{dG_1} = \frac{1}{4s} \tag{49}$$

As a result, these are the regional fiscal multipliers. To illustrate this, take a numerical example with $c = 0.72$. Then the multipliers are $dY_1 / dG_1 = dY_2 / dG_1 = 0.893$. That is, an increase in European government purchases of 100 causes an increase in European income of 90, an increase in American income of equally 90, and an increase in world income of 180. In a sense, the internal effect of fiscal policy is rather small, and the external effect of fiscal policy is quite large.

9) Monetary policy. Consider an increase in European money supply. Then how will European income respond, and how American income? The total differential of the model is as follows:

$$dY_1 = cdY_1 - bdr + hde + qdY_2 - qdY_1 \tag{50}$$

$$dY_2 = cdY_2 - bdr - hde + qdY_1 - qdY_2 \tag{51}$$

$$dM_1 = kdY_1 - jdr \tag{52}$$

$$0 = kdY_2 - jdr \tag{53}$$

Now take the difference between equations (52) and (53):

$$dY_2 = dY_1 - dM_1 / k \tag{54}$$

Then take the sum of equations (50) and (51), observing $s = 1 - c$:

$$s(dY_1 + dY_2) = -2bdr \tag{55}$$

Finally get rid of dY_2 and dr in equation (55) with the help of equations (54) and (52):

$$\frac{dY_1}{dM_1} = \frac{2bk + js}{2k(bk + js)} \tag{56}$$

$$\frac{dY_2}{dM_1} = -\frac{js}{2k(bk + js)} \tag{57}$$

As a principal result, these are the monetary policy multipliers. An increase in European money supply raises European income. On the other hand, it lowers American income. Here the rise in European income exceeds the fall in American income. That means, world income goes up. Besides, have a closer look at the mechanism of transmission. An increase in European money supply causes a depreciation of the euro and a decline in the world interest rate. The depreciation of the euro raises European exports but lowers American exports. The decline in the world interest rate raises both European investment and American investment. The net effect is that European income goes up. However, American income goes down. And what is more, world income goes up.

Next consider an important special case. Assume that the world fiscal multiplier is 1/2s. Accordingly, insert equation (48) into equations (56) and (57):

$$\frac{dY_1}{dM_1} = \frac{3}{4k} \tag{58}$$

$$\frac{dY_2}{dM_1} = -\frac{1}{4k} \tag{59}$$

As a finding, these are the monetary policy multipliers. To illustrate this, consider a numerical example with $k = 0.25$. Then the multipliers are $dY_1 / dM_1 = 3$ and $dY_2 / dM_1 = -1$. That is to say, an increase in European money supply of 100 causes an increase in European income of 300, a decline in American income 100, and an increase in world income of 200. The internal effect of monetary policy is very large, and the external effect of monetary policy is large.

Chapter 2
Monetary Competition between Europe and America

1. The Dynamic Model

1) The static model. As a point of reference, consider the static model. It can be represented by a system of two equations:

$$Y_1 = A_1 + \alpha M_1 - \beta M_2 \tag{1}$$

$$Y_2 = A_2 + \alpha M_2 - \beta M_1 \tag{2}$$

According to equation (1), European output Y_1 is determined by European money supply M_1, American money supply M_2, and some other factors called A_1. According to equation (2), American output Y_2 is determined by American money supply M_2, European money supply M_1, and some other factors called A_2. The internal effect of monetary policy is positive $\alpha > 0$. By contrast, the external effect of monetary policy is negative $\beta > 0$. In absolute values, the internal effect is larger than the external effect $\alpha > \beta$. The endogenous variables are European output and American output.

2) The dynamic model. At the beginning there is unemployment in both Europe and America. More precisely, unemployment in Europe exceeds unemployment in America. The target of the European central bank is full employment in Europe. The instrument of the European central bank is European money supply. The European central bank raises European money supply so as to close the output gap in Europe:

$$M_1 - M_1^{-1} = \frac{\overline{Y}_1 - Y_1}{\alpha} \tag{3}$$

Here is a list of the new symbols:
Y_1 European output this period

$\overline{Y}_1$ full-employment output in Europe

$\overline{Y}_1 - Y_1$ output gap in Europe this period

M_1^{-1} European money supply last period

M_1 European money supply this period

$M_1 - M_1^{-1}$ increase in European money supply.

Here the endogenous variable is European money supply this period M_1.

The target of the American central bank is full employment in America. The instrument of the American central bank is American money supply. The American central bank raises American money supply so as to close the output gap in America:

$$M_2 - M_2^{-1} = \frac{\overline{Y}_2 - Y_2}{\alpha} \tag{4}$$

Here is a list of the new symbols:

Y_2 American output this period

$\overline{Y}_2$ full-employment output in America

$\overline{Y}_2 - Y_2$ output gap in America this period

M_2^{-1} American money supply last period

M_2 American money supply this period

$M_2 - M_2^{-1}$ increase in American money supply.

Here the endogenous variable is American money supply this period M_2. We assume that the European central bank and the American central bank decide simultaneously and independently.

In addition there is an output lag. European output next period is determined by European money supply this period as well as by American money supply this period:

$$Y_1^{+1} = A_1 + \alpha M_1 - \beta M_2 \tag{5}$$

Here Y_1^{+1} denotes European output next period. In the same way, American output next period is determined by American money supply this period as well as by European money supply this period:

$$Y_2^{+1} = A_2 + \alpha M_2 - \beta M_1 \tag{6}$$

113

Here Y_2^{+1} denotes American output next period.

On this basis, the dynamic model can be characterized by a system of four equations:

$$M_1 - M_1^{-1} = \frac{\overline{Y}_1 - Y_1}{\alpha} \tag{7}$$

$$M_2 - M_2^{-1} = \frac{\overline{Y}_2 - Y_2}{\alpha} \tag{8}$$

$$Y_1^{+1} = A_1 + \alpha M_1 - \beta M_2 \tag{9}$$
$$Y_2^{+1} = A_2 + \alpha M_2 - \beta M_1 \tag{10}$$

Equation (7) shows the policy response in Europe, (8) shows the policy response in America, (9) shows the output lag in Europe, and (10) shows the output lag in America. The endogenous variables are European money supply this period M_1, American money supply this period M_2, European output next period Y_1^{+1}, and American output next period Y_2^{+1}.

3) The steady state. In the steady state by definition we have:

$$M_1 = M_1^{-1} \tag{11}$$
$$M_2 = M_2^{-1} \tag{12}$$

Equation (11) has it that European money supply does not change any more. Similarly, equation (12) has it that American money supply does not change any more. Therefore the steady state can be captured by a system of four equations:

$$Y_1 = \overline{Y}_1 \tag{13}$$
$$Y_2 = \overline{Y}_2 \tag{14}$$
$$Y_1 = A_1 + \alpha M_1 - \beta M_2 \tag{15}$$
$$Y_2 = A_2 + \alpha M_2 - \beta M_1 \tag{16}$$

Here the endogenous variables are European output Y_1, American output Y_2, European money supply M_1, and American money supply M_2. According to equation (13) there is full employment in Europe, so European output is constant. According to equation (14) there is full employment in America, so American output is constant too. Further, equations (15) and (16) give the steady-state levels of European and American money supply.

The model of the steady state can be compressed to a system of only two equations:

$$\overline{Y}_1 = A_1 + \alpha M_1 - \beta M_2 \tag{17}$$
$$\overline{Y}_2 = A_2 + \alpha M_2 - \beta M_1 \tag{18}$$

Here the endogenous variables are European money supply and American money supply. To simplify notation we introduce:

$$B_1 = \overline{Y}_1 - A_1 \tag{19}$$
$$B_2 = \overline{Y}_2 - A_2 \tag{20}$$

With this, the model of the steady state can be written as follows:

$$B_1 = \alpha M_1 - \beta M_2 \tag{21}$$
$$B_2 = \alpha M_2 - \beta M_1 \tag{22}$$

The endogenous variables are still M_1 and M_2.

Next we solve the model for the endogenous variables:

$$M_1 = \frac{\alpha B_1 + \beta B_2}{\alpha^2 - \beta^2} \tag{23}$$

$$M_2 = \frac{\alpha B_2 + \beta B_1}{\alpha^2 - \beta^2} \tag{24}$$

Equation (23) shows the steady-state level of European money supply, and equation (24) shows the steady-state level of American money supply. As a result, there is a steady state if and only if $\alpha \neq \beta$. Owing to the assumption $\alpha > \beta$, this condition is fulfilled.

4) Stability. Eliminate Y_1 in equation (7) by means of equation (9) and rearrange terms $\overline{Y}_1 = A_1 + \alpha M_1 - \beta M_2^{-1}$. By analogy, eliminate Y_2 in equation (8) by means of equation (10) to arrive at $\overline{Y}_2 = A_2 + \alpha M_2 - \beta M_1^{-1}$. On this basis, the dynamic model can be described by a system of two equations:

$$\overline{Y}_1 = A_1 + \alpha M_1 - \beta M_2^{-1} \tag{25}$$

$$\overline{Y}_2 = A_2 + \alpha M_2 - \beta M_1^{-1} \tag{26}$$

Here the endogenous variables are European money supply this period M_1 and American money supply this period M_2. To simplify notation we make use of equations (19) and (20). With this, the dynamic model can be written as follows:

$$B_1 = \alpha M_1 - \beta M_2^{-1} \tag{27}$$

$$B_2 = \alpha M_2 - \beta M_1^{-1} \tag{28}$$

The endogenous variables are still M_1 and M_2.

Now substitute equation (28) into equation (27) and solve for:

$$\alpha M_1 = B_1 + \frac{\beta B_2}{\alpha} + \frac{\beta^2 M_1^{-2}}{\alpha} \tag{29}$$

Then differentiate equation (29) for M_1^{-2}:

$$\frac{dM_1}{dM_1^{-2}} = \frac{\beta^2}{\alpha^2} \tag{30}$$

Finally the stability condition is $\beta^2 / \alpha^2 < 1$ or:

$$\beta < \alpha \tag{31}$$

That means, the steady state is stable if and only if the external effect of monetary policy is smaller than the internal effect of monetary policy. This condition is satisfied. As a result, there is a stable steady state of monetary competition. In other words, monetary competition between Europe and America leads to full employment in Europe and America.

2. Some Numerical Examples

To illustrate the dynamic model, have a look at some numerical examples. In line with the basic model in the previous chapter, assume $\alpha = 3$ and $\beta = 1$. On this assumption, the static model can be written as follows:

$$Y_1 = A_1 + 3M_1 - M_2 \tag{1}$$
$$Y_2 = A_2 + 3M_2 - M_1 \tag{2}$$

The endogenous variables are European output and American output. Obviously, an increase in European money supply of 100 causes an increase in European output of 300 and a decline in American output of 100. Correspondingly, an increase in American money supply of 100 causes an increase in American output of 300 and a decline in European output of 100. Further let full-employment output in Europe be 1000, and let full-employment output in America be the same.

It proves useful to study four distinct cases:
- unemployment in Europe and America
- another interpretation
- inflation in Europe and America
- unemployment in Europe, inflation in America.

1) Unemployment in Europe and America. At the beginning there is unemployment in both Europe and America. More precisely, unemployment in Europe exceeds unemployment in America. Let initial output in Europe be 940, and let initial output in America be 970. Step 1 refers to the policy response. The output gap in Europe is 60. The monetary policy multiplier in Europe is 3. So what is needed in Europe is an increase in European money supply of 20. The output gap in America is 30. The monetary policy multiplier in America is 3. So what is needed in America is an increase in American money supply of 10.

Step 2 refers to the output lag. The increase in European money supply of 20 causes an increase in European output of 60. As a side effect, it causes a decline in American output of 20. The increase in American money supply of 10 causes an increase in American output of 30. As a side effect, it causes a decline in European output of 10. The net effect is an increase in European output of 50 and an increase in American output of 10. As a consequence, European output goes from 940 to 990, and American output goes from 970 to 980. Put another way, the output gap in Europe narrows from 60 to 10, and the output gap in America narrows from 30 to 20.

Why does the European central bank not succeed in closing the output gap in Europe? The underlying reason is the negative external effect of the increase in American money supply. And why does the American central bank not succeed in closing the output gap in America? The underlying reason is the negative external effect of the increase in European money supply.

Step 3 refers to the policy response. The output gap in Europe is 10. The monetary policy multiplier in Europe is 3. So what is needed in Europe is an increase in European money supply of 3.3. The output gap in America is 20. The monetary policy multiplier in America is 3. So what is needed in America is an increase in American money supply of 6.7.

Step 4 refers to the output lag. The increase in European money supply of 3.3 causes an increase in European output of 10. As a side effect, it causes a decline in American output of 3.3. The increase in American money supply of 6.7 causes an increase in American output of 20. As a side effect, it causes a decline in European output of 6.7. The net effect is an increase in European output of 3.3

and an increase in American output of 16.7. As a consequence, European output goes from 990 to 993.3, and American output goes from 980 to 996.7. And so on. Table 2.1 presents a synopsis.

What are the dynamic characteristics of this process? There is a continuous increase in European money supply, as there is in American money supply. There is a continuous increase in European output, as there is in American output. As a result, monetary competition between Europe and America leads to full employment in Europe and America.

Table 2.1
Monetary Competition between Europe and America
Unemployment in Europe and America

	Europe	America
Initial Output	940	970
Change in Money Supply	20	10
Output	990	980
Change in Money Supply	3.3	6.7
Output	993.3	996.7
Change in Money Supply	2.2	1.1
Output	998.9	997.8
and so on	...	...

2) Another interpretation. Again, let initial output in Europe be 940, and let initial output in America be 970. Steps 1, 2 and 3 refer to a series of policy responses. Then step 4 refers to the output lag. Let us begin with step 1. The output gap in Europe is 60. The monetary policy multiplier in Europe is 3. So what is needed in Europe is an increase in European money supply of 20. The output gap in America is 30. The monetary policy multiplier in America is 3. So what is needed in America is an increase in American money supply of 10.

In step 2, the European central bank anticipates the effect of the increase in American money supply. And the American central bank anticipates the effect of the increase in European money supply. The European central bank expects that, due to the increase in American money supply of 10, European output will only rise to 990. And the American central bank expects that, due to the increase in European money supply of 20, American output will only rise to 980. The expected output gap in Europe is 10. The monetary policy multiplier in Europe is 3. So what is needed in Europe is an increase in European money supply of 3.3. The expected output gap in America is 20. The monetary policy multiplier in America is 3. So what is needed in America is an increase in American money supply of 6.7.

We now come to step 3. The European central bank expects that, due to the increase in American money supply of 6.7, European output will only rise to 993.3. And the American central bank expects that, due to the increase in European money supply of 3.3, American output will only rise to 996.7. The expected output gap in Europe is 6.7. The monetary policy multiplier in Europe is 3. So what is needed in Europe is an increase in European money supply of 2.2. The expected output gap in America is 3.3. The monetary policy multiplier in America is 3. So what is needed in America is an increase in American money supply of 1.1.

Step 4 refers to the output lag. The accumulated increase in European money supply of 25.5 causes an increase in European output of 76.5. As a side effect, it causes a decline in American output of 25.5. The accumulated increase in American money supply of 17.8 causes an increase in American output of 53.4. As a side effect, it causes a decline in European output of 17.8. The net effect is an increase in European output of 58.7 and an increase in American output of 27.9. As a consequence, European output goes from 940 to 998.7, and American output goes from 970 to 997.9. Table 2.2 gives an overview.

Table 2.2

Monetary Competition between Europe and America

Another Interpretation

	Europe	America
Initial Output	940	970
Change in Money Supply	20	10
Change in Money Supply	3.3	6.7
Change in Money Supply	2.2	1.1
Output	998.9	997.8

3) Inflation in Europe and America. At the start there is overemployment in both Europe and America. For that reason there is inflation in both Europe and America. Let overemployment in Europe exceed overemployment in America. Let initial output in Europe be 1060, and let initial output in America be 1030. Assume that monetary competition is such a fast process that prices do not change during competition. Step 1 refers to the policy response. The inflationary gap in Europe is 60. The target of the European central bank is price stability in Europe. The monetary policy multiplier in Europe is 3. So what is needed in Europe is a reduction in European money supply of 20. The inflationary gap in America is 30. The target of the American central bank is price stability in America. The monetary policy multiplier in America is 3. So what is needed in America is a reduction in American money supply of 10.

Step 2 refers to the output lag. The reduction in European money supply of 20 causes a decline in European output of 60. As a side effect, it causes an increase in American output of 20. The reduction in American money supply of 10 causes a decline in American output of 30. As a side effect, it causes an increase in European output of 10. The net effect is a decline in European output of 50 and a decline in American output of 10. As a consequence, European output goes from 1060 to 1010, and American output goes from 1030 to 1020.

Step 3 refers to the policy response. The inflationary gap in Europe is 10. The monetary policy multiplier in Europe is 3. So what is needed in Europe is a reduction in European money supply of 3.3. The inflationary gap in America is 20. The monetary policy multiplier in America is 3. So what is needed in America is a reduction in American money supply of 6.7.

Step 4 refers to the output lag. The reduction in European money supply of 3.3 causes a decline in European output of 10. As a side effect, it causes an increase in American output of 3.3. The reduction in American money supply of 6.7 causes a decline in American output of 20. As a side effect, it causes an increase in European output of 6.7. The net effect is a decline in European output of 3.3 and a decline in American output of 16.7. As a consequence, European output goes from 1010 to 1006.7, and American output goes from 1020 to 1003.3. And so on. For a synopsis see Table 2.3.

Table 2.3
Monetary Competition between Europe and America
Inflation in Europe and America

	Europe	America
Initial Output	1060	1030
Change in Money Supply	− 20	− 10
Output	1010	1020
Change in Money Supply	− 3.3	− 6.7
Output	1006.7	1003.3
Change in Money Supply	− 2.2	− 1.1
Output	1001.1	1002.2
and so on	...	...

What are the dynamic characteristics of this process? There is a continuous reduction in European money supply, as there is in American money supply.

There is a continuous decline in European output, as there is in American output. As a result, the process of monetary competition leads to both price stability and full employment.

4) Unemployment in Europe, inflation in America. At the beginning there is unemployment in Europe but overemployment in America. Thus there is inflation in America. Let initial output in Europe be 970, and let initial output in America be 1030. Step 1 refers to the policy response. The output gap in Europe is 30. The target of the European central bank is full employment in Europe. The monetary policy multiplier in Europe is 3. So what is needed in Europe is an increase in European money supply of 10. The inflationary gap in America is 30. The target of the American central bank is price stability in America. The monetary policy multiplier in America is 3. So what is needed in America is a reduction in American money supply of 10.

Step 2 refers to the output lag. The increase in European money supply of 10 causes an increase in European output of 30. As a side effect, it causes a decline in American output of 10. The reduction in American money supply of 10 causes a decline in American output of 30. As a side effect, it causes an increase in European output of 10. The total effect is an increase in European output of 40 and a decline in American output of 40. As a consequence, European output goes from 970 to 1010, and American output goes from 1030 to 990.

Step 3 refers to the policy response. The inflationary gap in Europe is 10. The monetary policy multiplier in Europe is 3. So what is needed in Europe is a reduction in European money supply of 3.3. The output gap in America is 10. The monetary policy multiplier in America is 3. So what is needed in America is an increase in American money supply of 3.3.

Step 4 refers to the output lag. The reduction in European money supply of 3.3 causes a decline in European output of 10. As a side effect, it causes an increase in American output of 3.3. The increase in American money supply of 3.3 causes an increase in American output of 10. As a side effect, it causes a decline in European output of 3.3. The total effect is a decline in European output of 13.3 and an increase in American output of 13.3. As a consequence, European output goes from 1010 to 996.7, and American output goes from 990 to 1003.3. And so on. For an overview see Table 2.4.

What are the dynamic characteristics of this process? There are damped oscillations in European money supply, as there are in American money supply. There are damped oscillations in European output, as there are in American output. The European economy oscillates between unemployment and overemployment, and the same holds for the American economy. As a result, monetary competition leads to both price stability and full employment.

Table 2.4
Monetary Competition between Europe and America
Unemployment in Europe, Inflation in America

	Europe	America
Initial Output	970	1030
Change in Money Supply	10	– 10
Output	1010	990
Change in Money Supply	– 3.3	3.3
Output	996.7	1003.3
Change in Money Supply	1.1	– 1.1
Output	1001.1	998.9
and so on	...	...

Chapter 3
Monetary Cooperation
between Europe and America

1. The Model

1) Introduction. As a starting point, take the output model. It can be represented by a system of two equations:

$$Y_1 = A_1 + \alpha M_1 - \beta M_2 \tag{1}$$
$$Y_2 = A_2 + \alpha M_2 - \beta M_1 \tag{2}$$

Here Y_1 denotes European output, Y_2 is American output, M_1 is European money supply, and M_2 is American money supply. The endogenous variables are European output and American output. At the beginning there is unemployment in both Europe and America. More precisely, unemployment in Europe exceeds unemployment in America. The targets of monetary cooperation are full employment in Europe and full employment in America. The instruments of monetary cooperation are European money supply and American money supply. So there are two targets and two instruments.

2) The policy model. On this basis, the policy model can be characterized by a system of two equations:

$$\overline{Y}_1 = A_1 + \alpha M_1 - \beta M_2 \tag{3}$$
$$\overline{Y}_2 = A_2 + \alpha M_2 - \beta M_1 \tag{4}$$

Here $\overline{Y}_1$ denotes full-employment output in Europe, and $\overline{Y}_2$ denotes full-employment output in America. The endogenous variables are European money supply and American money supply.

To simplify notation, we introduce $B_1 = \overline{Y}_1 - A_1$ and $B_2 = \overline{Y}_2 - A_2$. Then we solve the model for the endogenous variables:

$$M_1 = \frac{\alpha B_1 + \beta B_2}{\alpha^2 - \beta^2} \tag{5}$$

$$M_2 = \frac{\alpha B_2 + \beta B_1}{\alpha^2 - \beta^2} \tag{6}$$

Equation (5) shows the required level of European money supply, and equation (6) shows the required level of American money supply. There is a solution if and only if $\alpha \neq \beta$. Due to the assumption $\alpha > \beta$, this condition is met. As a result, monetary cooperation between Europe and America can achieve full employment in Europe and America. It is worth pointing out here that the solution to monetary cooperation is identical to the steady state of monetary competition.

3) Another version of the policy model. As an alternative, the policy model can be stated in terms of the output gap and the required increase in money supply:

$$\Delta Y_1 = \alpha \Delta M_1 - \beta \Delta M_2 \tag{7}$$

$$\Delta Y_2 = \alpha \Delta M_2 - \beta \Delta M_1 \tag{8}$$

Here ΔY_1 denotes the output gap in Europe, ΔY_2 is the output gap in America, ΔM_1 is the required increase in European money supply, and ΔM_2 is the required increase in American money supply. The endogenous variables are ΔM_1 and ΔM_2. The solution to the system (7) and (8) is:

$$\Delta M_1 = \frac{\alpha \Delta Y_1 + \beta \Delta Y_2}{\alpha^2 - \beta^2} \tag{9}$$

$$\Delta M_2 = \frac{\alpha \Delta Y_2 + \beta \Delta Y_1}{\alpha^2 - \beta^2} \tag{10}$$

2. Some Numerical Examples

To illustrate the policy model, have a look at some numerical examples. For ease of exposition, without losing generality, assume $\alpha = 3$ and $\beta = 1$. On this assumption, the output model can be written as follows:

$$Y_1 = A_1 + 3M_1 - M_2 \tag{1}$$

$$Y_2 = A_2 + 3M_2 - M_1 \tag{2}$$

The endogenous variables are European output and American output. Evidently, an increase in European money supply of 100 causes an increase in European output of 300 and a decline in American output of 100. Further let full-employment output in Europe be 1000, and let full-employment output in America be the same.

It proves useful to consider five distinct cases:
- unemployment in Europe exceeds unemployment in America
- unemployment in Europe, full employment in America
- unemployment in Europe equals unemployment in America
- inflation in Europe and America
- unemployment in Europe, inflation in America.

1) Unemployment in Europe exceeds unemployment in America. Let initial output in Europe be 940, and let initial output in America be 970. The output gap in Europe is 60, and the output gap in America is 30. So what is needed, according to equations (9) and (10) from the previous section, is an increase in European money supply of 26.25 and an increase in American money supply of 18.75. The increase in European money supply of 26.25 raises European output by 78.75 and lowers American output by 26.25. The increase in American money supply of 18.75 raises American output by 56.25 and lowers European output by 18.75. The net effect is an increase in European output of 60 and an increase in American output of 30. As a consequence, European output goes from 940 to 1000, and American output goes from 970 to 1000. In Europe there is now full employment, and the same holds for America. The effective multiplier in Europe

is 2.3, because of 60/26.25 = 2.3. And the effective multiplier in America is 1.6, because of 30/18.75 = 1.6. As a result, monetary cooperation can achieve full employment. Table 2.5 presents a synopsis.

Table 2.5

Monetary Cooperation between Europe and America

Unemployment in Europe Exceeds Unemployment in America

	Europe	America
Initial Output	940	970
Change in Money Supply	26.25	18.75
Output	1000	1000

2) Unemployment in Europe, full employment in America. Let initial output in Europe be 940, and let initial output in America be 1000. The output gap in Europe is 60, and the output gap in America is zero. What is needed, then, is an increase in European money supply of 22.5 and an increase in American money supply of 7.5. The increase in European money supply of 22.5 raises European output by 67.5 and lowers American output by 22.5. The increase in American money supply of 7.5 raises American output by 22.5 and lowers European output by 7.5. The net effect is an increase in European output of 60 and an increase in American output of zero. The effective multiplier in Europe is 2.7, and the effective multiplier in America is zero. Table 2.6 gives an overview.

Table 2.6

Monetary Cooperation between Europe and America

Unemployment in Europe, Full Employment in America

	Europe	America
Initial Output	940	1000
Change in Money Supply	22.5	7.5
Output	1000	1000

3) Unemployment in Europe equals unemployment in America. Let initial output in Europe be 970, and let initial output in America be the same. The output gap in Europe is 30, as is the output gap in America. What is needed, then, is an increase in European money supply of 15 and an increase in American money supply of equally 15. The increase in European money supply of 15 raises European output by 45 and lowers American output by 15. The increase in American money supply of 15 raises American output by 45 and lowers European output by 15. The net effect is an increase in European output of 30 and an increase in American output of equally 30. The effective multiplier in Europe is 2, as is the effective multiplier in America. For a synopsis see Table 2.7.

Table 2.7

Monetary Cooperation between Europe and America

Unemployment in Europe Equals Unemployment in America

	Europe	America
Initial Output	970	970
Change in Money Supply	15	15
Output	1000	1000

4) Inflation in Europe and America. At the start there is overemployment in both Europe and America. For that reason there is inflation in both Europe and America. Let overemployment in Europe exceed overemployment in America. Let initial output in Europe be 1060, and let initial output in America be 1030. The inflationary gap in Europe is 60, and the inflationary gap in America is 30. The targets of monetary cooperation are price stability in Europe and price stability in America. What is needed, then, is a reduction in European money supply of 26.25 and a reduction in American money supply of 18.75. The reduction in European money supply of 26.25 lowers European output by 78.75 and raises American output by 26.25. The reduction in American money supply of 18.75 lowers American output by 56.25 and raises European output by 18.75. The net effect is a decline in European output of 60 and a decline in American output of 30. As a consequence, European output goes from 1060 to 1000, and American output goes from 1030 to 1000. There is now full employment in both Europe and America. For that reason there is now price stability in both Europe and America. As a result, monetary cooperation can achieve full employment and price stability. For an overview see Table 2.8.

Table 2.8
Monetary Cooperation between Europe and America
Inflation in Europe and America

	Europe	America
Initial Output	1060	1030
Change in Money Supply	− 26.25	− 18.75
Output	1000	1000

5) Unemployment in Europe, inflation in America. At the beginning there is unemployment in Europe but overemployment in America. Thus there is inflation in America. Let initial output in Europe be 970, and let initial output in America be 1030. The output gap in Europe is 30, and the output gap in America is −30. What is needed, then, is an increase in European money supply of 7.5 and

a reduction in American money supply of equally 7.5. The increase in European money supply of 7.5 raises European output by 22.5 and lowers American output by 7.5. The reduction in American money supply of 7.5 lowers American output by 22.5 and raises European output by 7.5. The total effect is an increase in European output of 30 and a decline in American output of equally 30. The effective multiplier in Europe is 4, as is the effective multiplier in America. Table 2.9 presents a synopsis.

Table 2.9
Monetary Cooperation between Europe and America
Unemployment in Europe, Inflation in America

	Europe	America
Initial Output	970	1030
Change in Money Supply	7.5	− 7.5
Output	1000	1000

6) Comparing monetary cooperation with monetary competition. Monetary competition can achieve full employment. The same applies to monetary cooperation. Monetary competition is a fast process. The same is true of monetary cooperation. Judging from these points of view, there seems to be no need for monetary cooperation.

Chapter 4
Fiscal Competition
between Europe and America

1. The Dynamic Model

1) The static model. As a point of reference, consider the static model. It can be represented by a system of two equations:

$$Y_1 = A_1 + \gamma G_1 + \delta G_2 \tag{1}$$

$$Y_2 = A_2 + \gamma G_2 + \delta G_1 \tag{2}$$

According to equation (1), European output Y_1 is determined by European government purchases G_1, American government purchases G_2, and some other factors called A_1. According to equation (2), American output Y_2 is determined by American government purchases G_2, European government purchases G_1, and some other factors called A_2. The internal effect of fiscal policy is positive $\gamma > 0$. The external effect of fiscal policy is positive too $\delta > 0$. And what is more, the internal effect and the external effect are the same size $\gamma = \delta$. The endogenous variables are European output and American output. Along these lines, the static model can be rewritten as follows:

$$Y_1 = A_1 + \gamma G_1 + \gamma G_2 \tag{3}$$

$$Y_2 = A_2 + \gamma G_2 + \gamma G_1 \tag{4}$$

2) The dynamic model. At the beginning there is unemployment in both Europe and America. More precisely, unemployment in Europe exceeds unemployment in America. The target of the European government is full employment in Europe. The instrument of the European government is European government purchases. The European government raises European government purchases so as to close the output gap in Europe:

$$G_1 - G_1^{-1} = \frac{\overline{Y}_1 - Y_1}{\gamma} \tag{5}$$

Here is a list of the new symbols:

Y_1 European output this period

$\overline{Y}_1$ full-employment output in Europe

$\overline{Y}_1 - Y_1$ output gap in Europe this period

G_1^{-1} European government purchases last period

G_1 European government purchases this period

$G_1 - G_1^{-1}$ increase in European government purchases.

Here the endogenous variable is European government purchases this period G_1.

The target of the American government is full employment in America. The instrument of the American government is American government purchases. The American government raises American government purchases so as to close the output gap in America:

$$G_2 - G_2^{-1} = \frac{\overline{Y}_2 - Y_2}{\gamma} \tag{6}$$

Here is a list of the new symbols:

Y_2 American output this period

$\overline{Y}_2$ full-employment output in America

$\overline{Y}_2 - Y_2$ output gap in America this period

G_2^{-1} American government purchases last period

G_2 American government purchases this period

$G_2 - G_2^{-1}$ increase in American government purchases.

Here the endogenous variable is American government purchases this period G_2. We assume that the European government and the American government decide simultaneously and independently.

In addition there is an output lag. European output next period is determined by European government purchases this period as well as by American government purchases this period:

$$Y_1^{+1} = A_1 + \gamma G_1 + \gamma G_2 \tag{7}$$

Here Y_1^{+1} denotes European output next period. In the same way, American output next period is determined by American government purchases this period as well as by European government purchases this period:

$$Y_2^{+1} = A_2 + \gamma G_2 + \gamma G_1 \tag{8}$$

Here Y_2^{+1} denotes American output next period.

On this basis, the dynamic model can be characterized by a system of four equations:

$$G_1 - G_1^{-1} = \frac{\overline{Y}_1 - Y_1}{\gamma} \tag{9}$$

$$G_2 - G_2^{-1} = \frac{\overline{Y}_2 - Y_2}{\gamma} \tag{10}$$

$$Y_1^{+1} = A_1 + \gamma G_1 + \gamma G_2 \tag{11}$$

$$Y_2^{+1} = A_2 + \gamma G_2 + \gamma G_1 \tag{12}$$

Equation (9) shows the policy response in Europe, (10) shows the policy response in America, (11) shows the output lag in Europe, and (12) shows the output lag in America. The endogenous variables are European government purchases this period G_1, American government purchases this period G_2, European output next period Y_1^{+1}, and American output next period Y_2^{+1}.

3) The steady state. In the steady state by definition we have:

$$G_1 = G_1^{-1} \tag{13}$$

$$G_2 = G_2^{-1} \tag{14}$$

Equation (13) has it that European government purchases do not change any more. Similarly, equation (14) has it that American government purchases do not change any more. Therefore the steady state can be captured by a system of four equations:

$$Y_1 = \overline{Y}_1 \tag{15}$$

$$Y_2 = \overline{Y}_2 \tag{16}$$

$$Y_1 = A_1 + \gamma G_1 + \gamma G_2 \tag{17}$$

$$Y_2 = A_2 + \gamma G_2 + \gamma G_1 \tag{18}$$

Here the endogenous variables are European output Y_1, American output Y_2, European government purchases G_1, and American government purchases G_2. According to equation (15) there is full employment in Europe, so European output is constant. According to equation (16) there is full employment in America, so American output is constant too. Further, equations (17) and (18) give the steady state levels of European and American government purchases.

Now subtract equation (18) from equation (17), taking account of equations (15) and (16), to reach:

$$\overline{Y}_1 - \overline{Y}_2 = A_1 - A_2 \tag{19}$$

However, this is in direct contradiction to the assumption that $\overline{Y}_1$, $\overline{Y}_2$, A_1 and A_2 are given independently. As a result, there is no steady state of fiscal competition. In other words, fiscal competition between Europe and America does not lead to full employment in Europe and America. The underlying reason is the large external effect of fiscal policy.

2. Some Numerical Examples

To illustrate the dynamic model, have a look at some numerical examples. For ease of exposition, without loss of generality, assume $\gamma = 1$. On this assumption, the static model can be written as follows:

$$Y_1 = A_1 + G_1 + G_2 \tag{1}$$
$$Y_2 = A_2 + G_2 + G_1 \tag{2}$$

The endogenous variables are European output and American output. Obviously, an increase in European government purchases of 100 causes an increase in European output of 100 and an increase in American output of equally 100. Correspondingly, an increase in American government purchases of 100 causes an increase in American output of 100 and an increase in European output of equally 100. Further let full-employment output in Europe be 1000, and let full-employment output in America be the same.

It proves useful to study four distinct cases:
- unemployment in Europe exceeds unemployment in America
- unemployment in Europe equals unemployment in America
- unemployment in Europe exceeds overemployment in America
- unemployment in Europe equals overemployment in America.

1) Unemployment in Europe exceeds unemployment in America. At the beginning there is unemployment in both Europe and America. More precisely, unemployment in Europe exceeds unemployment in America. Let initial output in Europe be 940, and let initial output in America be 970. Step 1 refers to the policy response. The output gap in Europe is 60. The fiscal policy multiplier in Europe is 1. So what is needed in Europe is an increase in European government purchases of 60. The output gap in America is 30. The fiscal policy multiplier in America is 1. So what is needed in America is an increase in American government purchases of 30.

Step 2 refers to the output lag. The increase in European government purchases of 60 causes an increase in European output of 60. As a side effect, it causes an increase in American output of equally 60. The increase in American government purchases of 30 causes an increase in American output of 30. As a side effect, it causes an increase in European output of equally 30. The total effect is an increase in European output of 90 and an increase in American output of equally 90. As a consequence, European output goes from 940 to 1030, and American output goes from 970 to 1060. Put another way, the output gap in Europe of 60 turns into an inflationary gap of 30. And the output gap in America of 30 turns into an inflationary gap of 60.

Why does the European government not succeed in closing the output gap in Europe (or, for that matter, the inflationary gap in Europe)? The underlying reason is the positive external effect of the increase in American government purchases. And why does the American government not succeed in closing the output gap in America (or the inflationary gap in America)? The underlying reason is the positive external effect of the increase in European government purchases.

Step 3 refers to the policy response. The inflationary gap in Europe is 30. The fiscal policy multiplier in Europe is 1. So what is needed in Europe is a reduction in European government purchases of 30. The inflationary gap in America is 60. The fiscal policy multiplier in America is 1. So what is needed in America is a reduction in American government purchases of 60.

Step 4 refers to the output lag. The reduction in European government purchases of 30 causes a decline in European output of 30. As a side effect, it causes a decline in American output of equally 30. The reduction in American government purchases of 60 causes a decline in American output of 60. As a side effect, it causes a decline in European output of equally 60. The total effect is a decline in European output of 90 and a decline in American output of equally 90. As a consequence, European output goes from 1030 to 940, and American output goes from 1060 to 970. With this, European output and American output are back at their initial levels. That means, the process will repeat itself step by step. Table 2.10 presents a synopsis.

What are the dynamic characteristics of this process? There is an upward trend in European government purchases. By contrast, there is a downward trend in American government purchases. There are uniform oscillations in European output, as there are in American output. The European economy oscillates between unemployment and overemployment, as does the American economy. There is a continuous appreciation of the euro and a continuous depreciation of the dollar. Accordingly, there is a continuous decline in European exports and a continuous increase in American exports. Moreover, after a certain number of steps, American government purchases are down to zero. As a result, fiscal competition between Europe and America does not lead to full employment in Europe and America.

Table 2.10

Fiscal Competition between Europe and America

Unemployment in Europe Exceeds Unemployment in America

	Europe	America
Initial Output	940	970
Change in Government Purchases	60	30
Output	1030	1060
Change in Government Purchases	− 30	− 60
Output	940	970
and so on	...	...

2) Unemployment in Europe equals unemployment in America. Let initial output in Europe be 970, and let initial output in America be the same. Step 1 refers to the policy response. The output gap in Europe is 30. The fiscal policy multiplier in Europe is 1. So what is needed in Europe is an increase in European government purchases of 30. The output gap in America is 30. The fiscal policy multiplier in America is 1. So what is needed in America is an increase in American government purchases of 30.

138

Step 2 refers to the output lag. The increase in European government purchases of 30 causes an increase in European output of 30. As a side effect, it causes an increase in American output of equally 30. The increase in American government purchases of 30 causes an increase in American output of 30. As a side effect, it causes an increase in European output of equally 30. The total effect is an increase in European output of 60 and an increase in American output of equally 60. As a consequence, European output goes from 970 to 1030, as does American output.

Step 3 refers to the policy response. The inflationary gap in Europe is 30. The fiscal policy multiplier in Europe is 1. So what is needed in Europe is a reduction in European government purchases of 30. The inflationary gap in America is 30. The fiscal policy multiplier in America is 1. So what is needed in America is a reduction in American government purchases of 30.

Step 4 refers to the output lag. The reduction in European government purchases of 30 causes a decline in European output of 30. As a side effect, it causes a decline in American output of equally 30. The reduction in American government purchases of 30 causes a decline in American output of 30. As a side effect, it causes a decline in European output of equally 30. The total effect is a decline in European output of 60 and a decline in American output of equally 60. As a consequence, European output goes from 1030 to 970, as does American output.

With this, output is back at its initial level, hence the process will repeat itself. Table 2.11 gives an overview. There are uniform oscillations in European government purchases, and the same holds for American government purchases. There are uniform oscillations in European output, and the same holds for American output. As a result, the process of fiscal competition does not lead to full employment.

Table 2.11

Fiscal Competition between Europe and America

Unemployment in Europe Equals Unemployment in America

	Europe	America
Initial Output	970	970
Change in Government Purchases		30
Output	1030	1030
Change in Government Purchases	– 30	– 30
Output	970	970
and so on	...	...

3) Unemployment in Europe exceeds overemployment in America. At the start there is unemployment in Europe but overemployment in America. Thus there is inflation in America. Let initial output in Europe be 940, and let initial output in America be 1030. Step 1 refers to the policy response. The output gap in Europe is 60. The fiscal policy multiplier in Europe is 1. So what is needed in Europe is an increase in European government purchases of 60. The inflationary gap in America is 30. The fiscal policy multiplier in America is 1. So what is needed in America is a reduction in American government purchases of 30.

Step 2 refers to the output lag. The increase in European government purchases of 60 causes an increase in European output of 60. As a side effect, it causes an increase in American output of equally 60. The reduction in American government purchases of 30 causes a decline in American output of 30. As a side effect, it causes a decline in European output of equally 30. The net effect is an increase in European output of 30 and an increase in American output of equally 30. As a consequence, European output goes from 940 to 970, and American output goes from 1030 to 1060.

Step 3 refers to the policy response. The output gap in Europe is 30. The fiscal policy multiplier in Europe is 1. So what is needed in Europe is an increase in European government purchases of 30. The inflationary gap in America is 60. The fiscal policy multiplier in America is 1. So what is needed in America is a reduction in American government purchases of 60.

Step 4 refers to the output lag. The increase in European government purchases of 30 causes an increase in European output of 30. As a side effect, it causes an increase in American output of equally 30. The reduction in American government purchases of 60 causes a decline in American output of 60. As a side effect, it causes a decline in European output of equally 60. The net effect is a decline in European output of 30 and a decline in American output of equally 30. As a consequence, European output goes from 970 to 940, and American output goes from 1060 to 1030.

At this point in time, output is back at its initial level. So this process will repeat itself. For a synopsis see Table 2.12. What are the dynamic characteristics? There is a continuous increase in European government purchases. On the other hand, there is a continuous decline in American government purchases. There are uniform oscillations in European output, as there are in American output. In Europe there is unemployment, and in America there is overemployment. As a result, fiscal competition does not lead to full employment.

Table 2.12
Fiscal Competition between Europe and America
Unemployment in Europe Exceeds Overemployment in America

	Europe	America
Initial Output	940	1030
Change in Government Purchases	60	− 30
Output	970	1060
Change in Government Purchases	30	− 60
Output	940	1030
and so on	...	...

4) Unemployment in Europe equals overemployment in America. Let initial output in Europe be 970, and let initial output in America be 1030. Step 1 refers to the policy response. The output gap in Europe is 30. The fiscal policy multiplier in Europe is 1. So what is needed in Europe is an increase in European government purchases of 30. The inflationary gap in America is 30. The fiscal policy multiplier in America is 1. So what is needed in America is a reduction in American government purchases of 30.

Step 2 refers to the output lag. The increase in European government purchases of 30 causes an increase in European output of 30. As a side effect, it causes an increase in American output of equally 30. The reduction in American government purchases of 30 causes a decline in American output of 30. As a side effect, it causes a decline in European output of equally 30. The net effect is that European output does not change, and neither does American output. As a consequence, European output is still 970, and American output is still 1030.

Step 3 refers to the policy response. The output gap in Europe is 30. The fiscal policy multiplier in Europe is 1. So what is needed in Europe is an increase in European government purchases of 30. The inflationary gap in America is 30. The fiscal policy multiplier in America is 1. So what is needed in America is a reduction in American government purchases of 30.

Step 4 refers to the output lag. The increase in European government purchases of 30 causes an increase in European output of 30. As a side effect, it causes an increase in American output of equally 30. The reduction in American government purchases of 30 causes a decline in American output of 30. As a side effect, it causes a decline in European output of equally 30. The net effect is that European output does not change, and neither does American output. As a consequence, European output is still 970, and American output is still 1030.

That means, European output and American output stay at their initial levels. This process will repeat itself step by step. For an overview see Table 2.13. There is a continuous increase in European government purchases. By contrast, there is a continuous decline in American government purchases. However, there is no change in European output, and the same applies to American output. In Europe there is unemployment, and in America there is overemployment. As a result, fiscal competition does not lead to full employment.

Table 2.13

Fiscal Competition between Europe and America

Unemployment in Europe Equals Overemployment in America

	Europe	America
Initial Output	970	1030
Change in Government Purchases	30	− 30
Output	970	1030
Change in Government Purchases	30	− 30
Output	970	1030
and so on	...	...

5) Summary. There is an upward trend in European government purchases. On the other hand, there is a downward trend in American government purchases. There are uniform oscillations in European output, and there are uniform oscillations in American output. As a finding, fiscal competition between Europe and America does not lead to full employment.

6) Comparing fiscal competition with monetary competition. Monetary competition can achieve full employment, but fiscal competition cannot do so. Judging from this point of view, monetary competition is superior to fiscal competition.

Chapter 5
Fiscal Cooperation
between Europe and America

1. The Model

As a starting point, take the output model. It can be represented by a system of two equations:

$$Y_1 = A_1 + \gamma G_1 + \gamma G_2 \tag{1}$$

$$Y_2 = A_2 + \gamma G_2 + \gamma G_1 \tag{2}$$

Here Y_1 denotes European output, Y_2 is American output, G_1 is European government purchases, and G_2 is American government purchases. The endogenous variables are European output and American output. At the beginning there is unemployment in both Europe and America. More precisely, unemployment in Europe exceeds unemployment in America. The targets of fiscal cooperation are full employment in Europe and full employment in America. The instruments of fiscal cooperation are European government purchases and American government purchases. So there are two targets and two instruments.

On this basis, the policy model can be characterized by a system of two equations:

$$\overline{Y}_1 = A_1 + \gamma G_1 + \gamma G_2 \tag{3}$$

$$\overline{Y}_2 = A_2 + \gamma G_2 + \gamma G_1 \tag{4}$$

Here $\overline{Y}_1$ denotes full-employment output in Europe, and $\overline{Y}_2$ denotes full-employment output in America. The endogenous variables are European government purchases and American government purchases. Now take the difference between equations (3) and (4) to find out:

$$\overline{Y}_1 - \overline{Y}_2 = A_1 - A_2 \tag{5}$$

However, this is in direct contradiction to the assumption that $\overline{Y}_1$, $\overline{Y}_2$, A_1 and A_2 are given independently. As a result, there is no solution to fiscal cooperation. That is to say, fiscal cooperation between Europe and America cannot achieve full employment in Europe and America. The underlying reason is the large external effect of fiscal policy.

2. Some Numerical Examples

To illustrate the policy model, have a look at some numerical examples. For ease of exposition, without losing generality, assume $\gamma = 1$. On this assumption, the output model can be written as follows:

$$Y_1 = A_1 + G_1 + G_2 \tag{1}$$
$$Y_2 = A_2 + G_2 + G_1 \tag{2}$$

The endogenous variables are European output and American output. Evidently, an increase in European government purchases of 100 causes an increase in European output of 100 and an increase in American output of equally 100. Further let full-employment output in Europe be 1000, and let full-employment output in America be the same.

It proves useful to consider three distinct cases:
- unemployment in Europe exceeds unemployment in America
- unemployment in Europe equals unemployment in America
- unemployment in Europe, overemployment in America.

1) Unemployment in Europe exceeds unemployment in America. Let initial output in Europe be 940, and let initial output in America be 970. In this case, the

specific target of fiscal cooperation is full employment in America. Aiming at full employment in Europe would imply overemployment in America and, hence, inflation in America. So what is needed is an increase in American output of 30. What is needed, for instance, is an increase in European government purchases of 15 and an increase in American government purchases of equally 15.

The increase in European government purchases of 15 raises European output and American output by 15 each. Similarly, the increase in American government purchases of 15 raises American output and European output by 15 each. The total effect is an increase in European output of 30 and an increase in American output of equally 30. As a consequence, European output goes from 940 to 970, and American output goes from 970 to 1000. In Europe unemployment comes down, but there is still some unemployment left. In America there is now full employment. As a result, in this case, fiscal cooperation can reduce unemployment in Europe and America to a certain extent. On the other hand, fiscal cooperation cannot achieve full employment in both Europe and America. Table 2.14 presents a synopsis.

Table 2.14
Fiscal Cooperation between Europe and America
Unemployment in Europe Exceeds Unemployment in America

	Europe	America
Initial Output	940	970
Change in Government Purchases	15	15
Output	970	1000

2) Unemployment in Europe equals unemployment in America. Let initial output in Europe be 970, and let initial output in America be the same. What is needed, then, is an increase in European government purchases of 15 and an increase in American government purchases of equally 15. The overall effect is to raise European output and American output by 30 each. As a consequence,

European output goes from 970 to 1000, as does American output. In this special case, fiscal cooperation can in fact achieve full employment in both Europe and America. Table 2.15 gives an overview.

Table 2.15
Fiscal Cooperation between Europe and America
Unemployment in Europe Equals Unemployment in America

	Europe	America
Initial Output	970	970
Change in Government Purchases	15	15
Output	1000	1000

3) Unemployment in Europe, overemployment in America. At the start there is unemployment in Europe but overemployment in America. Thus there is inflation in America. Let initial output in Europe be 970, and let initial output in America be 1030. First consider an increase in European government purchases of 30. This policy action raises European output and American output by 30 each. As a consequence, European output goes from 970 to 1000, and American output goes from 1030 to 1060. In Europe, unemployment comes down. In America, however, inflation goes up. So this cannot be a solution to fiscal cooperation.

Second consider a reduction in American government purchases of 30. This policy action lowers American output and European output by 30 each. As a consequence, American output goes from 1030 to 1000, and European output goes from 970 to 940. In America, inflation comes down. In Europe, however, unemployment goes up. So this cannot be a solution to fiscal cooperation either. For a synopsis see Table 2.16. The general point is that fiscal cooperation cannot raise European output and lower American output at the same time. As a result, in this case, there is no solution to fiscal cooperation.

Table 2.16

Fiscal Cooperation between Europe and America

Unemployment in Europe, Overemployment in America

	Europe	America
Initial Output	970	1030
Change in Government Purchases	0	− 30
Output	940	1000

4) Summary. Fiscal cooperation between Europe and America generally cannot achieve full employment in Europe and America. On the other hand, it can reduce unemployment in Europe and America to a certain extent.

5) Comparing fiscal cooperation with fiscal competition. Fiscal competition cannot achieve full employment. The same is true of fiscal cooperation. Fiscal competition cannot reduce unemployment. Fiscal cooperation can reduce unemployment to a certain extent. Under fiscal competition there is a tendency for government purchases to explode. And there is a tendency for output to oscillate uniformly. Under fiscal cooperation there are no such tendencies. Judging from these points of view, fiscal cooperation seems to be superior to fiscal competition.

6) Comparing fiscal cooperation with monetary cooperation. Monetary cooperation can achieve full employment. By contrast, fiscal cooperation cannot achieve full employment. From this perspective, monetary cooperation is superior to fiscal cooperation.

Part Three

The Large Monetary Union
of Two Countries

Chapter 1
The Basic Model

1) Introduction. The world consists of two monetary regions, let us say Europe and America. The exchange rate between Europe and America is flexible. Europe in turn consists of two countries, let us say Germany and France. So Germany and France form a monetary union. Take for example an increase in German government purchases. Then what will be the effect on German income, and what on French income?

In doing the analysis, we make the following assumptions. German goods, French goods and American goods are imperfect substitutes for each other. German output is determined by the demand for German goods. French output is determined by the demand for French goods. And American output is determined by the demand for American goods. European money demand equals European money supply. And American money demand equals American money supply. There is perfect capital mobility between Germany, France and America. Thus the German interest rate, the French interest rate, and the American interest rate are equalized.

In the short run, nominal wages and prices are rigid. P_1 denotes the price of German goods, as measured in euros. P_2 is the price of French goods, as measured in euros. And P_3 is the price of American goods, as measured in dollars. To simplify notation let be $P_1 = P_2 = P_3 = 1$. The letter e denotes the exchange rate between Europe and America. Properly speaking, e is the price of the dollar, as measured in euros. Let the initial value of the exchange rate be unity.

2) The market for German goods. The behavioural functions underlying the analysis are as follows:

$$C_1 = C_1(Y_1) \tag{1}$$

$$I_1 = I_1(r) \tag{2}$$

$$G_1 = \text{const} \tag{3}$$

$$X_{12} = X_{12}(Y_2) \tag{4}$$

$$X_{13} = X_{13}(e, Y_3) \tag{5}$$

$$Q_1 = Q_1(Y_1) \tag{6}$$

Equation (1) is the consumption function of Germany. It states that German consumption is an increasing function of German income. Here C_1 denotes German consumption, and Y_1 is German income. Equation (2) is the investment function of Germany. It states that German investment is a decreasing function of the world interest rate. I_1 denotes German investment, and r is the world interest rate. According to equation (3), the German government fixes its purchases of goods and services. G_1 denotes German government purchases.

Equations (4) and (5) are the export functions of Germany. Equation (4) states that German exports to France are an increasing function of French income. X_{12} denotes German exports to France, and Y_2 is French income. Equation (5) states that German exports to America are an increasing function of the exchange rate and an increasing function of American income. X_{13} denotes German exports to America, and Y_3 is American income. The message of equation (5) is that a depreciation of the euro raises German exports to America. Equation (6) is the import function of Germany. It states that German imports are an increasing function of German income. Q_1 denotes German imports from France and America.

German output is determined by the demand for German goods $Y_1 = C_1 + I_1 + G_1 + X_{12} + X_{13} - Q_1$. Taking account of the behavioural functions (1) to (6), we arrive at the goods market equation of Germany:

$$Y_1 = C_1(Y_1) + I_1(r) + G_1 + X_{12}(Y_2) + X_{13}(e, Y_3) - Q_1(Y_1) \tag{7}$$

3) The market for French goods. The behavioural functions are as follows:

$$C_2 = C_2(Y_2) \tag{8}$$

$$I_2 = I_2(r) \tag{9}$$

$$G_2 = \text{const} \tag{10}$$

$$X_{21} = X_{21}(Y_1) \tag{11}$$

$$X_{23} = X_{23}(e, Y_3) \tag{12}$$

$$Q_2 = Q_2(Y_2) \tag{13}$$

Equation (8) is the consumption function of France. It states that French consumption is an increasing function of French income. Here C_2 denotes French consumption. Equation (9) is the investment function of France. It states that French investment is a decreasing function of the world interest rate. I_2 denotes French investment. According to equation (10), the French government fixes its purchases of goods and services. G_2 denotes French government purchases.

Equations (11) and (12) are the export functions of France. Equation (11) states that French exports to Germany are an increasing function of German income. X_{21} denotes French exports to Germany. Equation (12) states that French exports to America are an increasing function of the exchange rate and an increasing function of American income. X_{23} denotes French exports to America. The message of equation (12) is that a depreciation of the euro raises French exports to America. Equation (13) is the import function of France. It states that French imports are an increasing function of French income. Q_2 denotes French imports from Germany and America.

French output is determined by the demand for French goods $Y_2 = C_2 + I_2 + G_2 + X_{21} + X_{23} - Q_2$. Upon substituting the behavioural functions (8) to (13), we reach the goods market equation of France:

$$Y_2 = C_2(Y_2) + I_2(r) + G_2 + X_{21}(Y_1) + X_{23}(e, Y_3) - Q_2(Y_2) \tag{14}$$

4) The market for American goods. The behavioural functions are as follows:

$$C_3 = C_3(Y_3) \tag{15}$$

$$I_3 = I_3(r) \tag{16}$$

$$G_3 = \text{const} \tag{17}$$

$$X_{31} = X_{31}(e, Y_1) \tag{18}$$

$$X_{32} = X_{32}(e, Y_2) \tag{19}$$

$$Q_3 = Q_3(Y_3) \tag{20}$$

Equation (15) is the consumption function of America. It states that American consumption is an increasing function of American income. Here C_3 denotes American consumption. Equation (16) is the investment function of America. It states that American investment is a decreasing function of the world interest rate. I_3 denotes American investment. According to equation (17), the American government fixes its purchases of goods and services. G_3 denotes American government purchases.

Equations (18) and (19) are the export functions of America. Equation (18) states that American exports to Germany are a decreasing function of the exchange rate and an increasing function of German income. X_{31} denotes American exports to Germany. The message of equation (18) is that a depreciation of the dollar raises American exports to Germany. Equation (19) states that American exports to France are a decreasing function of the exchange rate and an increasing function of French income. X_{32} denotes American exports to France. The message of equation (19) is that a depreciation of the dollar raises American exports to France. Equation (20) is the import function of America. It states that American imports are an increasing function of American income. Q_3 denotes American imports from Germany and France.

American output is determined by the demand for American goods $Y_3 = C_3 + I_3 + G_3 + X_{31} + X_{32} - Q_3$. Upon inserting the behavioural functions (15) to (20) we get to the goods market equation of America:

$$Y_3 = C_3(Y_3) + I_3(r) + G_3 + X_{31}(e, Y_1) + X_{32}(e, Y_2) - Q_3(Y_3) \tag{21}$$

5) The European money market. The behavioural functions are:

$$L_1 = L_1(r, Y_1) \tag{22}$$

$$L_2 = L_2(r, Y_2) \tag{23}$$

$$M_{12} = \text{const} \tag{24}$$

Equation (22) is the money demand function of Germany. It states that German money demand is a decreasing function of the world interest rate and an increasing function of German income. L_1 denotes German money demand. Equation (23) is the money demand function of France. It states that French money demand is a decreasing function of the world interest rate and an increasing function of French income. L_2 denotes French money demand. Equation (24) is the money supply function of Europe. It states that the European central bank fixes European money supply. M_{12} denotes European money supply. European money demand is equal to European money supply $L_1 + L_2 = M_{12}$. Taking account of the behavioural functions (22) to (24), we arrive at the money market equation of Europe $L_1(r, Y_1) + L_2(r, Y_2) = M_{12}$.

6) The American money market. The behavioural functions are:

$$L_3 = L_3(r, Y_3) \tag{25}$$

$$M_3 = \text{const} \tag{26}$$

Equation (25) is the money demand function of America. It states that American money demand is a decreasing function of the world interest rate and an increasing function of American income. L_3 denotes American money demand. Equation (26) is the money supply function of America. It states that the American central bank fixes American money supply. M_3 denotes American money supply. American money demand is equal to American money supply $L_3 = M_3$. Upon substituting the behavioural functions (25) and (26), we reach the money market equation of America $L_3(r, Y_3) = M_3$.

7) The model. On this foundation, the full model can be characterized by a system of five equations:

$$Y_1 = C_1(Y_1) + I_1(r) + G_1 + X_{12}(Y_2) + X_{13}(e, Y_3) - Q_1(Y_1) \tag{27}$$

$$Y_2 = C_2(Y_2) + I_2(r) + G_2 + X_{21}(Y_1) + X_{23}(e, Y_3) - Q_2(Y_2) \tag{28}$$

$$Y_3 = C_3(Y_3) + I_3(r) + G_3 + X_{31}(e, Y_1) + X_{32}(e, Y_2) - Q_3(Y_3) \tag{29}$$

$$M_{12} = L_1(r, Y_1) + L_2(r, Y_2) \tag{30}$$

$$M_3 = L_3(r, Y_3) \tag{31}$$

Equation (27) is the goods market equation of Germany, as measured in German goods. (28) is the goods market equation of France, as measured in French goods. (29) is the goods market equation of America, as measured in American goods. (30) is the money market equation of Europe, as measured in euros. And (31) is the money market equation of America, as measured in dollars. It is worth pointing out here that the goods market equations are well consistent with microfoundations, see Carlberg (2002). The exogenous variables are European money supply M_{12}, American money supply M_3, German government purchases G_1, French government purchases G_2, and American government purchases G_3. The endogenous variables are German income Y_1, French income Y_2, American income Y_3, the exchange rate between Europe and America e, and the world interest rate r.

8) The total differential. It is useful to take the total differential of the model. In doing this, we assume that the monetary regions are the same size and have the same behavioural functions. Moreover, we assume that the union countries are the same size and have the same behavioural functions. These assumptions prove to be particularly fruitful:

$$dY_1 = cdY_1 - 0.5bdr + dG_1 + 0.5hde + mdY_2 + 0.5qdY_3 - (m+q)dY_1 \tag{32}$$

$$dY_2 = cdY_2 - 0.5bdr + dG_2 + 0.5hde + mdY_1 + 0.5qdY_3 - (m+q)dY_2 \tag{33}$$

$$dY_3 = cdY_3 - bdr + dG_3 - hde + qdY_1 + qdY_2 - qdY_3 \tag{34}$$

$$dM_{12} = kdY_1 - 0.5jdr + kdY_2 - 0.5jdr \tag{35}$$

$$dM_3 = kdY_3 - jdr \tag{36}$$

Here is a list of the new symbols:

b   interest sensitivity of European investment,
         interest sensitivity of American investment
0.5b   interest sensitivity of German investment,
         interest sensitivity of French investment
c   marginal consumption rate
h   exchange rate sensitivity of European exports,
         exchange rate sensitivity of American exports
0.5h   exchange rate sensitivity of German exports,
         exchange rate sensitivity of French exports
j   interest sensitivity of European money demand,
         interest sensitivity of American money demand
0.5j   interest sensitivity of German money demand,
         interest sensitivity of French money demand
k   income sensitivity of money demand
m   marginal import rate of Germany relative to France,
         marginal import rate of France relative to Germany
q   marginal import rate of Europe relative to America,
         marginal import rate of America relative to Europe
0.5q   marginal import rate of America relative to Germany,
         marginal import rate of America relative to France.

Now take the sum of equations (32) and (33). Then define $dY_{12} = dY_1 + dY_2$ as well as $dG_{12} = dG_1 + dG_2$, where Y_{12} denotes European income and G_{12} denotes European government purchases. Hence the total differential of the model can be rewritten as follows:

$$dY_{12} = cdY_{12} - bdr + dG_{12} + hde + qdY_3 - qdY_{12} \qquad (37)$$

$$dY_3 = cdY_3 - bdr + dG_3 - hde + qdY_{12} - qdY_3 \qquad (38)$$

$$dM_{12} = kdY_{12} - jdr \qquad (39)$$

$$dM_3 = kdY_3 - jdr \qquad (40)$$

Equation (37) is the goods market equation of Europe, (38) is the goods market equation of America, (39) is the money market equation of Europe, and (40) is the money market equation of America. The exogenous variables are (the change in) European money supply dM_{12}, American money supply dM_3,

European government purchases dG_{12}, and American government purchases dG_3. The endogenous variables are European income dY_{12}, American income dY_3, the exchange rate de, and the world interest rate dr. As a result, this model is equivalent to that derived for the world of two monetary regions, cf. Chapter 1 in Part Two. Thus we can make use of the multipliers obtained there.

9) Fiscal policy. Consider for example an increase in German government purchases. Then what will be the effect on German income, French income, and American income? To solve this problem, we start with equation (32) and eliminate de, dr, dY_2 as well as dY_3. This can be done in several steps. We assume that the world fiscal multiplier is 1/2s. Then the fiscal multipliers for the world of two monetary regions are as follows:

$$\frac{dY_{12}}{dG_{12}} = \frac{dY_3}{dG_{12}} = \frac{1}{4s} \tag{41}$$

$$\frac{de}{dG_{12}} = -\frac{1}{2h} \tag{42}$$

$$\frac{dr}{dG_{12}} = \frac{1}{4b} \tag{43}$$

In equation (43) we have used the important finding $bk = js$.

Next observe $dG_{12} = dG_1$ and $dY_{12} = dY_1 + dY_2$ to get to:

$$de = -(1/2h)dG_1 \tag{44}$$

$$dr = (1/4b)dG_1 \tag{45}$$

$$dY_3 = (1/4s)dG_1 \tag{46}$$

$$dY_2 = (1/4s)dG_1 - dY_1 \tag{47}$$

Then, in equation (32), eliminate de, dr, dY_2 and dY_3 by means of equations (44) to (47), noting $s = 1 - c$:

$$\frac{dY_1}{dG_1} = \frac{2m + q + 5s}{8s(2m + q + s)} \tag{48}$$

158

As a fundamental result, this is the fiscal multiplier in Germany. An increase in German government purchases raises German income. To illustrate this, take a numerical example with c = 0.72, m = 0.08, and q = 0.08. So the multipliers are $dY_1 / dG_1 = 1.408$, $dY_2 / dG_1 = -0.515$, and $dY_3 / dG_1 = 0.893$. That is, an increase in German government purchases of 100 causes an increase in German income of 141. On the other hand, it causes a decline in French income of 52. And what is more, it causes an increase in European income of 89 and an increase in American income of equally 89.

Finally consider the process of adjustment. An increase in German government purchases causes an appreciation of the euro and an increase in the world interest rate. The appreciation of the euro lowers German exports and French exports but raises American exports. The increase in the world interest rate lowers German investment, French investment, and American investment. The net effect is that German income moves up. However, French income moves down. And American income moves up.

Chapter 2
Fiscal Competition between Germany and France

1. The Dynamic Model

1) The static model. As a point of reference, consider the static model. It can be represented by a system of two equations:

$$Y_1 = A_1 + \gamma G_1 - \delta G_2 \tag{1}$$
$$Y_2 = A_2 + \gamma G_2 - \delta G_1 \tag{2}$$

According to equation (1), German output Y_1 is determined by German government purchases G_1, French government purchases G_2, and some other factors called A_1. According to equation (2), French output Y_2 is determined by French government purchases G_2, German government purchases G_1, and some other factors called A_2. The internal effect of fiscal policy is positive $\gamma > 0$. By contrast, the external effect of fiscal policy is negative $\delta > 0$. In absolute values, the internal effect is larger than the external effect $\gamma > \delta$. The endogenous variables are German output and French output.

2) The dynamic model. At the beginning there is unemployment in both Germany and France. More precisely, unemployment in Germany exceeds unemployment in France. The target of the German government is full employment in Germany. The instrument of the German government is German government purchases. The German government raises German government purchases so as to close the output gap in Germany:

$$G_1 - G_1^{-1} = \frac{\overline{Y}_1 - Y_1}{\gamma} \tag{3}$$

Here is a list of the new symbols:

Y_1 German output this period
$\overline{Y}_1$ full-employment output in Germany
$\overline{Y}_1 - Y_1$ output gap in Germany this period

G_1^{-1} German government purchases last period
G_1 German government purchases this period
$G_1 - G_1^{-1}$ increase in German government purchases.
Here the endogenous variable is German government purchases this period G_1.

The target of the French government is full employment in France. The instrument of the French government is French government purchases. The French government raises French government purchases so as to close the output gap in France:

$$G_2 - G_2^{-1} = \frac{\overline{Y}_2 - Y_2}{\gamma}$$

(4)

Here is a list of the new symbols:
Y_2 French output this period
$\overline{Y}_2$ full-employment output in France
$\overline{Y}_2 - Y_2$ output gap in France this period
G_2^{-1} French government purchases last period
G_2 French government purchases this period
$G_2 - G_2^{-1}$ increase in French government purchases.
Here the endogenous variable is French government purchases this period G_2. We assume that the German government and the French government decide simultaneously and independently.

In addition there is an output lag. German output next period is determined by German government purchases this period as well as by French government purchases this period:

$$Y_1^{+1} = A_1 + \gamma G_1 - \delta G_2$$

(5)

Here Y_1^{+1} denotes German output next period. In the same way, French output next period is determined by French government purchases this period as well as by German government purchases this period:

$$Y_2^{+1} = A_2 + \gamma G_2 - \delta G_1$$

(6)

Here Y_2^{+1} denotes French output next period.

On this basis, the dynamic model can be characterized by a system of four equations:

$$G_1 - G_1^{-1} = \frac{\overline{Y}_1 - Y_1}{\gamma} \tag{7}$$

$$G_2 - G_2^{-1} = \frac{\overline{Y}_2 - Y_2}{\gamma} \tag{8}$$

$$Y_1^{+1} = A_1 + \gamma G_1 - \delta G_2 \tag{9}$$

$$Y_2^{+1} = A_2 + \gamma G_2 - \delta G_1 \tag{10}$$

Equation (7) shows the policy response in Germany, (8) shows the policy response in France, (9) shows the output lag in Germany, and (10) shows the output lag in France. The endogenous variables are German government purchases this period G_1, French government purchases this period G_2, German output next period Y_1^{+1}, and French output next period Y_2^{+1}.

3) The steady state. In the steady state by definition we have:

$$G_1 = G_1^{-1} \tag{11}$$

$$G_2 = G_2^{-1} \tag{12}$$

Equation (11) has it that German government purchases do not change any more. Similarly, equation (12) has it that French government purchases do not change any more. Therefore the steady state can be captured by a system of four equations:

$$Y_1 = \overline{Y}_1 \tag{13}$$

$$Y_2 = \overline{Y}_2 \tag{14}$$

$$Y_1 = A_1 + \gamma G_1 - \delta G_2 \tag{15}$$

$$Y_2 = A_2 + \gamma G_2 - \delta G_1 \tag{16}$$

Here the endogenous variables are German output Y_1, French output Y_2, German government purchases G_1, and French government purchases G_2. According to equation (13) there is full employment in Germany, so German output is constant. According to equation (14) there is full employment in France, so French output is constant too. Further, equations (15) and (16) give the steady-state levels of German and French government purchases.

The model of the steady state can be compressed to system of only two equations:

$$\overline{Y}_1 = A_1 + \gamma G_1 - \delta G_2 \tag{17}$$

$$\overline{Y}_2 = A_2 + \gamma G_2 - \delta G_1 \tag{18}$$

Here the endogenous variables are German government purchases and French government purchases. To simplify notation we introduce:

$$B_1 = \overline{Y}_1 - A_1 \tag{19}$$

$$B_2 = \overline{Y}_2 - A_2 \tag{20}$$

With this, the model of the steady state can be written as follows:

$$B_1 = \gamma G_1 - \delta G_2 \tag{21}$$

$$B_2 = \gamma G_2 - \delta G_1 \tag{22}$$

The endogenous variables are still G_1 and G_2.

Next we solve the model for the endogenous variables:

$$G_1 = \frac{\gamma B_1 + \delta B_2}{\gamma^2 - \delta^2} \tag{23}$$

$$G_2 = \frac{\gamma B_2 + \delta B_1}{\gamma^2 - \delta^2} \tag{24}$$

Equation (23) shows the steady-state level of German government purchases, and equation (24) shows the steady-state level of French government purchases. As a result, there is a steady state if and only if $\gamma \neq \delta$. Owing to the assumption $\gamma > \delta$, this condition is fulfilled.

4) Stability. Eliminate Y_1 in equation (7) by means of equation (9) and rearrange terms $\overline{Y}_1 = A_1 + \gamma G_1 - \delta G_2^{-1}$. By analogy, eliminate Y_2 in equation (8) by means of equation (10) to arrive at $\overline{Y}_2 = A_2 + \gamma G_2 - \delta G_1^{-1}$. On this basis, the dynamic model can be described by a system of two equations:

$$\overline{Y}_1 = A_1 + \gamma G_1 - \delta G_2^{-1} \tag{25}$$

$$\overline{Y}_2 = A_2 + \gamma G_2 - \delta G_1^{-1} \tag{26}$$

Here the endogenous variables are German government purchases this period G_1 and French government purchases this period G_2. To simplify notation we make use of equations (19) and (20). With this, the dynamic model can be written as follows:

$$B_1 = \gamma G_1 - \delta G_2^{-1} \tag{27}$$

$$B_2 = \gamma G_2 - \delta G_1^{-1} \tag{28}$$

The endogenous variables are still G_1 and G_2.

Now substitute equation (28) into equation (27) and solve for:

$$\gamma G_1 = B_1 + \frac{\delta B_2}{\gamma} + \frac{\delta^2 G_1^{-2}}{\gamma} \tag{29}$$

Then differentiate equation (29) for G_1^{-2}:

$$\frac{dG_1}{dG_1^{-2}} = \frac{\delta^2}{\gamma^2} \tag{30}$$

Finally the stability condition is $\delta^2 / \gamma^2 < 1$ or:

$$\delta < \gamma \tag{31}$$

That means, the steady state is stable if and only if the external effect of fiscal policy is smaller than the internal effect of fiscal policy. This condition is satisfied. As a result, there is a stable steady state of fiscal competition. In other words, fiscal competition between Germany and France leads to full employment in Germany and France.

2. Some Numerical Examples

To illustrate the dynamic model, have a look at some numerical examples. For ease of exposition, without loss of generality, assume $\gamma = 1.5$ and $\delta = 0.5$. On this assumption, the static model can be written as follows:

$$Y_1 = A_1 + 1.5G_1 - 0.5G_2 \tag{1}$$

$$Y_2 = A_2 + 1.5G_2 - 0.5G_1 \tag{2}$$

The endogenous variables are German and French output. Obviously, an increase in German government purchases of 100 causes an increase in German output of 150 and a decline in French output of 50. Correspondingly, an increase in French government purchases of 100 causes an increase in French output of 150 and a decline in German output of 50. Further let full-employment output in Germany be 1000, and let full-employment output in France be the same.

It proves useful to study two distinct cases:
- unemployment in Germany exceeds unemployment in France
- unemployment in Germany, overemployment in France.

1) Unemployment in Germany exceeds unemployment in France. At the beginning there is unemployment in both Germany and France. More precisely, unemployment in Germany exceeds unemployment in France. Let initial output

in Germany be 940, and let initial output in France be 970. Step 1 refers to the policy response. The output gap in Germany is 60. The fiscal policy multiplier in Germany is 1.5. So what is needed in Germany is an increase in German government purchases of 40. The output gap in France is 30. The fiscal policy multiplier in France is 1.5. So what is needed in France is an increase in French government purchases of 20.

Step 2 refers to the output lag. The increase in German government purchases of 40 causes an increase in German output of 60. As a side effect, it causes a decline in French output of 20. The increase in French government purchases of 20 causes an increase in French output of 30. As a side effect, it causes a decline in German output of 10. The net effect is an increase in German output of 50 and an increase in French output of 10. As a consequence, German output goes from 940 to 990, and French output goes from 970 to 980. Put another way, the output gap in Germany narrows from 60 to 10, and the output gap in France narrows from 30 to 20.

Why does the German government not succeed in closing the output gap in Germany? The underlying reason is the negative external effect of the increase in French government purchases. And why does the French government not succeed in closing the output gap in France? The underlying reason is the negative external effect of the increase in German government purchases.

Step 3 refers to the policy response. The output gap in Germany is 10. The fiscal policy multiplier in Germany is 1.5. So what is needed in Germany is an increase in German government purchases of 6.7. The output gap in France is 20. The fiscal policy multiplier in France is 1.5. So what is needed in France is an increase in French government purchases of 13.3.

Step 4 refers to the output lag. The increase in German government purchases of 6.7 causes an increase in German output of 10. As a side effect, it causes a decline in French output of 3.3. The increase in French government purchases of 13.3 causes an increase in French output of 20. As a side effect, it causes a decline in German output of 6.7. The net effect is an increase in German output of 3.3 and an increase in French output of 16.7. As a consequence, German output goes from 990 to 993.3, and French output goes from 980 to 996.7. And so on. Table 3.1 presents a synopsis.

What are the dynamic characteristics of this process? There is a continuous increase in German government purchases, as there is in French government purchases. There is a continuous increase in German output, as there is in French output. As a result, fiscal competition between Germany and France leads to full employment in Germany and France.

Taking the sum over all periods, the increase in German government purchases is 52.5, and the increase in French government purchases is 37.5. That means, the increase in German government purchases is very large, as compared to the output gap in Germany. And the increase in French government purchases is even larger, as compared to the output gap in France. The effective multiplier in Germany is only 1.1, and the effective multiplier in France is only 0.8.

Table 3.1

Fiscal Competition between Germany and France

Unemployment in Germany and France

	Germany	France
Initial Output	940	970
Change in Government Purchases	40	20
Output	990	980
Change in Government Purchases	6.7	13.3
Output	993.3	996.7
Change in Government Purchases	4.4	2.2
Output	998.9	997.8
and so on	...	...

2) Unemployment in Germany, overemployment in France. At the start there is unemployment in Germany but overemployment in France. Thus there is inflation in France. Let initial output in Germany be 970, and let initial output in

France be 1030. Step 1 refers to the policy response. The output gap in Germany is 30. The fiscal policy multiplier in Germany is 1.5. So what is needed in Germany is an increase in German government purchases of 20. The inflationary gap in France is 30. The fiscal policy multiplier in France is 1.5. So what is needed in France is a reduction in French government purchases of 20.

Step 2 refers to the output lag. The increase in German government purchases of 20 causes an increase in German output of 30. As a side effect, it causes a decline in French output of 10. The reduction in French government purchases of 20 causes a decline in French output of 30. As a side effect, it causes an increase in German output of 10. The total effect is an increase in German output of 40 and a decline in French output of equally 40. As a consequence, German output goes from 970 to 1010, and French output goes from 1030 to 990.

Step 3 refers to the policy response. The inflationary gap in Germany is 10. The fiscal policy multiplier in Germany is 1.5. So what is needed in Germany is a reduction in German government purchases of 6.7. The output gap in France is 10. The fiscal policy multiplier in France is 1.5. So what is needed in France is an increase in French government purchases of 6.7.

Step 4 refers to the output lag. The reduction in German government purchases of 6.7 causes a decline in German output of 10. As a side effect, it causes an increase in French output of 3.3. The increase in French government purchases of 6.7 causes an increase in French output of 10. As a side effect, it causes a decline in German output of 3.3. The total effect is a decline in German output of 13.3 and an increase in French output of equally 13.3. As a consequence, German output goes from 1010 to 996.7, and French output goes from 990 to 1003.3. And so on. Table 3.2 gives an overview.

What are the dynamic characteristics of this process? There are damped oscillations in German government purchases, as there are in French government purchases. There are damped oscillations in German output, as there are in French output. The German economy oscillates between unemployment and overemployment, and the same holds for the French economy. As a result, the process of fiscal competition leads to full employment.

168

Table 3.2
Fiscal Competition between Germany and France
Unemployment in Germany, Overemployment in France

	Germany	France
Initial Output	970	1030
Change in Government Purchases	20	− 20
Output	1010	990
Change in Government Purchases	− 6.7	6.7
Output	996.7	1003.3
Change in Government Purchases	2.2	− 2.2
Output	1001.1	998.9
and so on	...	...

Chapter 3
Fiscal Cooperation between Germany and France

1. The Model

1) Introduction. As a starting point, take the output model. It can be represented by a system of two equations:

$$Y_1 = A_1 + \gamma G_1 - \delta G_2 \tag{1}$$

$$Y_2 = A_2 + \gamma G_2 - \delta G_1 \tag{2}$$

Here Y_1 denotes German output, Y_2 is French output, G_1 is German government purchases, and G_2 is French government purchases. The endogenous variables are German output and French output. At the beginning there is unemployment in both Germany and France. More precisely, unemployment in Germany exceeds unemployment in France. The targets of fiscal cooperation are full employment in Germany and full employment in France. The instruments of fiscal cooperation are German government purchases and French government purchases. So there are two targets and two instruments.

2) The policy model. On this basis, the policy model can be characterized by a system of two equations:

$$\overline{Y}_1 = A_1 + \gamma G_1 - \delta G_2 \tag{3}$$

$$\overline{Y}_2 = A_2 + \gamma G_2 - \delta G_1 \tag{4}$$

Here $\overline{Y}_1$ denotes full-employment output in Germany, and $\overline{Y}_2$ denotes full-employment output in France. The endogenous variables are German government purchases and French government purchases.

To simplify notation, we introduce $B_1 = \overline{Y}_1 - A_1$ and $B_2 = \overline{Y}_2 - A_2$. Then we solve the model for the endogenous variables:

$$G_1 = \frac{\gamma B_1 + \delta B_2}{\gamma^2 - \delta^2} \tag{5}$$

$$G_2 = \frac{\gamma B_2 + \delta B_1}{\gamma^2 - \delta^2} \tag{6}$$

Equation (5) shows the required level of German government purchases, and equation (6) shows the required level of French government purchases. There is a solution if and only if $\gamma \neq \delta$. Due to the assumption $\gamma > \delta$, this condition is met. As a result, fiscal cooperation between Germany and France can achieve full employment in Germany and France. It is worth pointing out here that the solution to fiscal cooperation is identical to the steady state of fiscal competition.

3) Another version of the policy model. As an alternative, the policy model can be stated in terms of the output gap and the required increase in government purchases:

$$\Delta Y_1 = \gamma \Delta G_1 - \delta \Delta G_2 \tag{7}$$

$$\Delta Y_2 = \gamma \Delta G_2 - \delta \Delta G_1 \tag{8}$$

Here ΔY_1 denotes the output gap in Germany, ΔY_2 is the output gap in France, ΔG_1 is the required increase in German government purchases, and ΔG_2 is the required increase in French government purchases. The endogenous variables are ΔG_1 and ΔG_2. The solution to the system (7) and (8) is:

$$\Delta G_1 = \frac{\gamma \Delta Y_1 + \delta \Delta Y_2}{\gamma^2 - \delta^2} \tag{9}$$

$$\Delta G_2 = \frac{\gamma \Delta Y_2 + \delta \Delta Y_1}{\gamma^2 - \delta^2} \tag{10}$$

2. Some Numerical Examples

To illustrate the policy model, have a look at some numerical examples. For ease of exposition, without losing generality, assume $\gamma = 1.5$ and $\delta = 0.5$. On this assumption, the output model can be written as follows:

$$Y_1 = A_1 + 1.5G_1 - 0.5G_2 \tag{1}$$

$$Y_2 = A_2 + 1.5G_2 - 0.5G_1 \tag{2}$$

The endogenous variables are German output and French output. Evidently, an increase in German government purchases of 100 causes an increase in German output of 150 and a decline in French output of 50. Further let full-employment output in Germany be 1000, and let full-employment output in France be the same.

It proves useful to consider four distinct cases:
- unemployment in Germany exceeds unemployment in France
- unemployment in Germany, full employment in France
- unemployment in Germany equals unemployment in France
- unemployment in Germany, overemployment in France.

1) Unemployment in Germany exceeds unemployment in France. Let initial output in Germany be 940, and let initial output in France be 970. The output gap in Germany is 60, and the output gap in France is 30. So what is needed, according to equations (9) and (10) from the previous section, is an increase in German government purchases of 52.5 and an increase in French government purchases of 37.5. The increase in German government purchases of 52.5 raises German output by 78.75 and lowers French output by 26.25. The increase in French government purchases of 37.5 raises French output by 56.25 and lowers German output by 18.75.

The net effect is an increase in German output of 60 and an increase in French output of 30. As a consequence, German output goes from 940 to 1000, and French output goes from 970 to 1000. In Germany there is now full employment, and the same holds for France. As a result, fiscal cooperation can achieve full employment. The required increase in German government purchases is very large, as compared to the output gap in Germany. And the required increase in French government purchases is even larger, as compared to the output gap in France. The effective multiplier in Germany is only 1.1, and the effective multiplier in France is only 0.8. Table 3.3 presents a synopsis.

2) Unemployment in Germany, full employment in France. Let initial output in Germany be 940, and let initial output in France be 1000. The output gap in Germany is 60, and the output gap in France is zero. What is needed, then, is an increase in German government purchases of 45 and an increase in French government purchases of 15. The increase in German government purchases of 45 raises German output by 67.5 and lowers French output by 22.5. The increase in French government purchases of 15 raises French output by 22.5 and lowers German output by 7.5. The net effect is an increase in German output of 60 and an increase in French output of zero. The effective multiplier in Germany is 1.3, and the effective multiplier in France is zero. Table 3.4 gives an overview.

3) Unemployment in Germany equals unemployment in France. Let initial output in Germany be 970, and let initial output in France be the same. The output gap in Germany is 30, as is the output gap in France. What is needed, then, is an increase in German government purchases of 30 and an increase in French government purchases of equally 30. The increase in German government purchases of 30 raises German output by 45 and lowers French output by 15. The increase in French government purchases of 30 raises French output by 45 and lowers German output by 15. The net effect is an increase in German output of 30 and an increase in French output of equally 30. The effective multiplier in Germany is 1, as is the effective multiplier in France. For a synopsis see Table 3.5.

Table 3.3
Fiscal Cooperation between Germany and France
Unemployment in Germany Exceeds Unemployment in France

	Germany	France
Initial Output	940	970
Change in Government Purchases	52.5	37.5
Output	1000	1000

Table 3.4
Fiscal Cooperation between Germany and France
Unemployment in Germany, Full Employment in France

	Germany	France
Initial Output	940	1000
Change in Government Purchases	45	15
Output	1000	1000

Table 3.5
Fiscal Cooperation between Germany and France
Unemployment in Germany Equals Unemployment in France

	Germany	France
Initial Output	970	970
Change in Government Purchases	30	30
Output	1000	1000

4) Unemployment in Germany, overemployment in France. At the start there is unemployment in Germany but overemployment in France. Thus there is inflation in France. Let initial output in Germany be 970, and let initial output in France be 1030. The output gap in Germany is 30, and the output gap in France is −30. What is needed, then, is an increase in German government purchases of 15 and a reduction in French government purchases of equally 15. The increase in German government purchases of 15 raises German output by 22.5 and lowers French output by 7.5. The reduction in French government purchases of 15 lowers French output by 22.5 and raises German output by 7.5. The total effect is an increase in German output of 30 and a decline in French output of equally 30. The effective multiplier in Germany is 2, as is the effective multiplier in France. For an overview see Table 3.6.

5) Comparing fiscal cooperation with fiscal competition. Fiscal competition can achieve full employment. The same applies to fiscal cooperation. Fiscal competition is a slow process. By contrast, fiscal cooperation is a fast process. Judging from these points of view, fiscal cooperation seems to be superior to fiscal competition.

Table 3.6
Fiscal Cooperation between Germany and France
Unemployment in Germany, Overemployment in France

	Germany	France
Initial Output	970	1030
Change in Government Purchases	15	− 15
Output	1000	1000

Chapter 4
Competition between
the European Central Bank,
the German Government,
and the French Government

1. The Dynamic Model

1) The static model. As a point of reference, consider the static model. It can be represented by a system of two equations:

$$Y_1 = A_1 + \alpha M_{12} + \gamma G_1 - \delta G_2 \tag{1}$$

$$Y_2 = A_2 + \alpha M_{12} + \gamma G_2 - \delta G_1 \tag{2}$$

According to equation (1), German output Y_1 is determined by European money supply M_{12}, German government purchases G_1, French government purchases G_2, and some other factors called A_1. According to equation (2), French output Y_2 is determined by European money supply M_{12}, French government purchases G_2, German government purchases G_1, and some other factors called A_2. The internal effect of monetary policy is positive $\alpha > 0$. The internal effect of fiscal policy is positive as well $\gamma > 0$. By contrast, the external effect of fiscal policy is negative $\delta > 0$. In absolute values, the internal effect of fiscal policy is larger than the external effect of fiscal policy $\gamma > \delta$. The endogenous variables are German output and French output.

2) The dynamic model. At the beginning there is unemployment in both Germany and France. More precisely, unemployment in Germany exceeds unemployment in France. The primary target of the European central bank is price stability in Europe. The secondary target of the European central bank is high employment in Germany and France. The instrument of the European central bank is European money supply. The target of the German government is full employment in Germany. The instrument of the German government is

176

German government purchases. The target of the French government is full employment in France. The instrument of the French government is French government purchases.

We assume that the central bank and the governments decide sequentially. First the central bank decides, and then the governments decide. In step 1, the European central bank decides. In step 2, the German government and the French government decide simultaneously and independently. In step 3, the European central bank decides. In step 4, the German government and the French government decide simultaneously and independently. And so on. The reasons for this stepwise procedure are: First, the inside lag of monetary policy is short, whereas the inside lag of fiscal policy is long. And second, the internal effect of monetary policy is large, whereas the internal effect of fiscal policy is small.

2. Some Numerical Examples

To illustrate the dynamic model, have a look at some numerical examples. For ease of exposition, without loss of generality, assume $\alpha = 1.5$, $\gamma = 1.5$, and $\delta = 0.5$. On this assumption, the static model can be written as follows:

$$Y_1 = A_1 + 1.5M_{12} + 1.5G_1 - 0.5G_2 \tag{1}$$
$$Y_2 = A_2 + 1.5M_{12} + 1.5G_2 - 0.5G_1 \tag{2}$$

The endogenous variables are German and French output. Obviously, an increase in European money supply of 100 causes an increase in German output of 150 and an increase in French output of equally 150. An increase in German government purchases of 100 causes an increase in German output of 150 and a decline in French output of 50. Correspondingly, an increase in French government purchases of 100 causes an increase in French output of 150 and a decline in German output of 50. Further let full-employment output in Germany be 1000, and let full-employment output in France be the same.

It proves useful to study three distinct cases:
- unemployment in Germany and France
- another interpretation
- inflation in Germany and France.

1) Unemployment in Germany and France. Let initial output in Germany be 940, and let initial output in France be 970. Step 1 refers to monetary policy. The output gap in Germany is 60, and the output gap in France is 30. In this situation, the specific target of the European central bank is to close the output gap in France. Closing the output gap in Germany would imply overemployment in France and, hence, inflation in France. The output gap in France is 30. The monetary policy multiplier in France is 1.5. So what is needed is an increase in European money supply of 20. Step 2 refers to the output lag. The increase in European money supply of 20 causes an increase in German output of 30 and an increase in French output of equally 30. As a consequence, German output goes from 940 to 970, and French output goes from 970 to 1000.

Step 3 refers to fiscal policy. The output gap in Germany is 30. The fiscal policy multiplier in Germany is 1.5. So what is needed in Germany is an increase in German government purchases of 20. The output gap in France is zero. So there is no need for a change in French government purchases. Step 4 refers to the output lag. The increase in German government purchases of 20 causes an increase in German output of 30. As a side effect, it causes a decline in French output of 10. As a consequence, German output goes from 970 to 1000, and French output goes from 1000 to 990.

Step 5 refers to monetary policy. The output gap in Germany is zero, and the output gap in France is 10. So there is no need for a change in European money supply. Step 6 refers to the output lag. As a consequence, German output stays at 1000, and French output stays at 990.

Step 7 refers to fiscal policy. The output gap in Germany is zero. So there is no need for a change in German government purchases. The output gap in France is 10. The fiscal policy multiplier in France is 1.5. So what is needed in France is an increase in French government purchases of 6.7. Step 8 refers to the output lag. The increase in French government purchases of 6.7 causes an increase in

French output of 10. As a side effect, it causes a decline in German output of 3.3. As a consequence, French output goes from 990 to 1000, and German output goes from 1000 to 996.7.

Step 9 refers to monetary policy. The output gap in Germany is 3.3, and the output gap in France is zero. So there is no need for a change in European money supply. Step 10 refers to the output lag. As a consequence, German output stays at 996.7, and French output stays at 1000.

Step 11 refers to fiscal policy. The output gap in Germany is 3.3. The fiscal policy multiplier in Germany is 1.5. So what is needed in Germany is an increase in German government purchases of 2.2. The output gap in France is zero. So there is no need for a change in French government purchases. Step 12 refers to the output lag. The increase in German government purchases of 2.2 causes an increase in German output of 3.3. As a side effect, it causes a decline in French output of 1.1. As a consequence, German output goes from 996.7 to 1000, and French output goes from 1000 to 998.9. And so on. Table 3.7 presents a synopsis.

What are the dynamic characteristics of this process? There is a one-time increase in European money supply. There is an upward trend in German government purchases, as there is in French government purchases. There are damped oscillations in German output, as there are in French output. The German economy oscillates between unemployment and full employment, as does the French economy. Taking the sum over all periods, the increase in German government purchases is 22.5, and the increase in French government purchases is 7.5. As a result, competition between the European central bank, the German government, and the French government leads to full employment in Germany and France. Technically speaking, there is a stable steady state.

2) Another interpretation. Let initial output in Germany be 940, and let initial output in France be 970. Step 1 refers to monetary policy. The output gap in Germany is 60, and the output gap in France is 30. The monetary policy multiplier in Germany is 1.5, as is the monetary policy multiplier in France. So what is needed is an increase in European money supply of 20.

Table 3.7
Competition between the European Central Bank,
the German Government, and the French Government
Unemployment in Germany and France

	Germany	France
Initial Output	940	970
Change in Money Supply	20	
Output	970	1000
Change in Government Purchases	20	0
Output	1000	990
Change in Government Purchases	0	6.7
Output	996.7	1000
and so on	...	...

Step 2 refers to fiscal policy. The German government and the French government anticipate the effect of the increase in European money supply. The German government expects that, due to the increase in European money supply of 20, German output will rise to 970. The French government expects that, due to the increase in European money supply of 20, French output will rise to 1000. The expected output gap in Germany is 30. The fiscal policy multiplier in Germany is 1.5. So what is needed in Germany is an increase in German government purchases of 20. The expected output gap in France is zero. So there is no need for a change in French government purchases.

Step 3 refers to the output lag. The increase in European money supply of 20 causes an increase in German output of 30 and an increase in French output of equally 30. The increase in German government purchases of 20 causes an increase in German output of 30. As a side effect, it causes a decline in French output of 10. The net effect is an increase in German output of 60 and an increase in French output of 20. As a consequence, German output goes from 940 to 1000, and French output goes from 970 to 990.

Step 4 refers to monetary policy. The output gap in Germany is zero, and the output gap in France is 10. So there is no need for a change in European money supply. Step 5 refers to fiscal policy. The German government expects that, due to the constancy of European money supply, German output will stay at 1000. The French government expects that, due to the constancy of European money supply, French output will stay at 990. The expected output gap in Germany is zero. So there is no need for a change in German government purchases. The expected output gap in France is 10. The fiscal policy multiplier in France is 1.5. So what is needed in France is an increase in French government purchases of 6.7. Step 6 refers to the output lag. The increase in French government purchases of 6.7 causes an increase in French output of 10. As a side effect, it causes a decline in German output of 3.3. As a consequence, French output goes from 990 to 1000, and German output goes from 1000 to 996.7. And so on. Table 3.8 gives an overview.

Table 3.8
Competition between the European Central Bank,
the German Government, and the French Government
Another Interpretation

	Germany	France
Initial Output	940	970
Change in Money Supply	20	
Change in Government Purchases	20	0
Output	1000	990
Change in Government Purchases	0	6.7
Output	996.7	1000
and so on	...	...

3) Inflation in Germany and France. At the start there is overemployment in both Germany and France. For that reason there is inflation in both Germany and France. Let overemployment in Germany exceed overemployment in France. Let initial output in Germany be 1060, and let initial output in France be 1030. Step 1 refers to monetary policy. The inflationary gap in Germany is 60, and the inflationary gap in France is 30. In this situation, the specific target of the European central bank is to close the inflationary gap in Germany. Closing the inflationary gap in France would imply overemployment in Germany and, hence, inflation in Germany. The inflationary gap in Germany is 60. The monetary policy multiplier in Germany is 1.5. So what is needed is a reduction in European money supply of 40. Step 2 refers to the output lag. The reduction in European money supply of 40 causes a decline in German output of 60 and a decline in French output of equally 60. As a consequence, German output goes from 1060 to 1000, and French output goes from 1030 to 970.

Step 3 refers to fiscal policy. The output gap in Germany is zero. So there is no need for a change in German government purchases. The output gap in France is 30. The fiscal policy multiplier in France is 1.5. So what is needed in France is an increase in French government purchases of 20. Step 4 refers to the output lag. The increase in French government purchases of 20 causes an increase in French output of 30. As a side effect, it causes a decline in German output of 10. As a consequence, French output goes from 970 to 1000, and German output goes from 1000 to 990.

Step 5 refers to monetary policy. The output gap in Germany is 10, and the output gap in France is zero. So there is no need for a change in European money supply. Step 6 refers to the output lag. As a consequence, German output stays at 990, and French output stays at 1000.

Step 7 refers to fiscal policy. The output gap in Germany is 10. The fiscal policy multiplier in Germany is 1.5. So what is needed in Germany is an increase in German government purchases of 6.7. The output gap in France is zero. So there is no need for a change in French government purchases. Step 8 refers to the output lag. The increase in German government purchases of 6.7 causes an increase in German output of 10. As a side effect, it causes a decline in French output of 3.3. As a consequence, German output goes from 990 to 1000, and French output goes from 1000 to 996.7. And so on. For a synopsis see Table 3.9.

182

What are the dynamic characteristics of this process? There is a one-time reduction in European money supply. There is an upward trend in German government purchases, as there is in French government purchases. There are damped oscillations in German output, as there are in French output. The German economy oscillates between unemployment and full employment, as does the French economy. As a result, the process of monetary and fiscal competition leads to price stability and full employment.

Table 3.9
Competition between the European Central Bank,
the German Government, and the French Government
Inflation in Germany and France

	Germany	France
Initial Output	1060	1030
Change in Money Supply	− 40	
Output	1000	970
Change in Government Purchases	0	20
Output	990	1000
Change in Government Purchases	6.7	0
Output	1000	996.7
Change in Government Purchases	0	2.2
Output	998.9	1000
and so on	...	...

4) Comparing monetary and fiscal competition with pure fiscal competition. Fiscal competition can achieve full employment. The same holds for monetary and fiscal competition. Fiscal competition is a (relatively) slow process. Monetary and fiscal competition is a (relatively) fast process. Fiscal competition leads to a large increase in government purchases. Monetary and fiscal competition leads to a small increase in government purchases. Judging from these points of view, monetary and fiscal competition seems to be superior to fiscal competition.

Chapter 5
Cooperation between
the European Central Bank,
the German Government,
and the French Government

1. The Model

1) Introduction. As a starting point, take the output model. It can be represented by a system of two equations:

$$Y_1 = A_1 + \alpha M_{12} + \gamma G_1 - \delta G_2 \tag{1}$$

$$Y_2 = A_2 + \alpha M_{12} + \gamma G_2 - \delta G_1 \tag{2}$$

Here Y_1 denotes German output, Y_2 is French output, M_{12} is European money supply, G_1 is German government purchases, and G_2 is French government purchases. The endogenous variables are German output and French output.

At the beginning there is unemployment in both Germany and France. More precisely, unemployment in Germany exceeds unemployment in France. The policy makers are the European central bank, the German government, and the French government. The targets of policy cooperation are full employment in Germany and full employment in France. The instruments of policy cooperation are European money supply, German government purchases, and French government purchases. There are two targets and three instruments, so there is one degree of freedom. As a result, there is an infinite number of solutions. In other words, cooperation between the European central bank, the German government, and the French government can achieve full employment in Germany and France.

2) The policy model. On this basis, the policy model can be characterized by a system of two equations:

$$\Delta Y_1 = \alpha \Delta M_{12} + \gamma \Delta G_1 - \delta \Delta G_2 \qquad (3)$$

$$\Delta Y_2 = \alpha \Delta M_{12} + \gamma \Delta G_2 - \delta \Delta G_1 \qquad (4)$$

Here ΔY_1 denotes the output gap in Germany, ΔY_2 is the output gap in France, ΔM_{12} is the required increase in European money supply, ΔG_1 is the required increase in German government purchases, and ΔG_2 is the required increase in French government purchases. The endogenous variables are ΔM_{12}, ΔG_1 and ΔG_2.

We now introduce a third target. We assume that the increase in German government purchases should be equal in size to the reduction in French government purchases $\Delta G_1 + \Delta G_2 = 0$. Put another way, we assume that the sum total of union government purchases should be constant. Add up equations (3) and (4), taking account of $\Delta G_1 + \Delta G_2 = 0$, to find out:

$$\Delta M_{12} = \frac{\Delta Y_1 + \Delta Y_2}{2\alpha} \qquad (5)$$

Then subtract equation (4) from equation (3), taking account of $\Delta G_1 + \Delta G_2 = 0$, and solve for:

$$\Delta G_1 = \frac{\Delta Y_1 - \Delta Y_2}{2(\gamma + \delta)} \qquad (6)$$

$$\Delta G_2 = -\frac{\Delta Y_1 - \Delta Y_2}{2(\gamma + \delta)} \qquad (7)$$

Equation (5) shows the required increase in European money supply, (6) shows the required increase in German government purchases, and (7) shows the required increase in French government purchases.

2. Some Numerical Examples

To illustrate the policy model, have a look at some numerical examples. For ease of exposition, without losing generality, assume $\alpha = 1.5$, $\gamma = 1.5$, and $\delta = 0.5$. On this assumption, the output model can be written as follows:

$$Y_1 = A_1 + 1.5M_{12} + 1.5G_1 - 0.5G_2 \tag{1}$$

$$Y_2 = A_2 + 1.5M_{12} + 1.5G_2 - 0.5G_1 \tag{2}$$

The endogenous variables are German and French output. Evidently, an increase in European money supply of 100 causes an increase in German output of 150 and an increase in French output of equally 150. An increase in German government purchases of 100 causes an increase in German output of 150 and a decline in French output of 50. Further let full-employment output in Germany be 1000, and let full-employment output in France be the same.

It proves useful to consider two distinct cases:
- unemployment in Germany and France
- inflation in Germany and France.

1) Unemployment in Germany and France. Let unemployment in Germany exceed unemployment in France. Let initial output in Germany be 940, and let initial output in France be 970. The solution can be found in two logical steps. Step 1 refers to monetary policy. The output gap in Europe is 90. The monetary policy multiplier in Europe is 3. So what is needed is an increase in European money supply of 30. This policy action raises German output and French output by 45 each. As a consequence, German output goes from 940 to 985, and French output goes from 970 to 1015. In Germany there is still some unemployment left, and in France there is now some overemployment. Strictly speaking, unemployment in Germany and overemployment in France are the same size.

Step 2 refers to fiscal policy. The output gap in Germany is 15, and the output gap in France is −15. So what is needed, according to equations (6) and (7) from the previous section, is an increase in German government purchases of 7.5 and a reduction in French government purchases of equally 7.5. The increase in German government purchases of 7.5 raises German output by 11.25 and lowers French output by 3.75. The reduction in French government purchases of 7.5 lowers French output by 11.25 and raises German output by 3.75. The total effect is an increase in German output of 15 and a decline in French output of equally 15. As a consequence, German output goes from 985 to 1000, and French output goes from 1015 to 1000. In Germany there is now full employment, and the same holds for France.

As a result, cooperation between the European central bank, the German government, and the French government can achieve full employment in Germany and France. What is needed is an increase in European money supply, an increase in German government purchases, and a reduction in French government purchases. The required change in government purchases is 15. Table 3.10 presents a synopsis.

Table 3.10
Cooperation between the European Central Bank,
the German Government, and the French Government
Unemployment in Germany and France

	Germany	France
Initial Output	940	970
Change in Money Supply	30	
Output	985	1015
Change in Government Purchases	7.5	– 7.5
Output	1000	1000

Tables 3.11 and 3.12 give some alternative solutions. Table 3.11 is marked by an increase in European money supply, an increase in German government purchases, and an increase in French government purchases. The required change

in government purchases is 30. Table 3.12 is marked by an increase in European money supply, a reduction in German government purchases, and a reduction in French government purchases. The required change in government purchases is 30. The first of the three solutions minimizes the required change in government purchases.

Table 3.11
Cooperation between the European Central Bank,
the German Government, and the French Government
A Second Solution

	Germany	France
Initial Output	940	970
Change in Money Supply	20	
Output	970	1000
Change in Government Purchases	22.5	7.5
Output	1000	1000

Table 3.12
Cooperation between the European Central Bank,
the German Government, and the French Government
A Third Solution

	Germany	France
Initial Output	940	970
Change in Money Supply	40	
Output	1000	1030
Change in Government Purchases	− 7.5	− 22.5
Output	1000	1000

2) Inflation in Germany and France. At the start there is overemployment in both Germany and France. For that reason there is inflation in both Germany and France. Let overemployment in Germany exceed overemployment in France. Let initial output in Germany be 1060, and let initial output in France be 1030. The solution can be determined in two logical steps. Step 1 refers to monetary policy. The inflationary gap in Europe is 90. The monetary policy multiplier in Europe is 3. So what is needed is a reduction in European money supply of 30. This policy action lowers German output and French output by 45 each. As a consequence, German output goes from 1060 to 1015, and French output goes from 1030 to 985. In Germany there is still some overemployment left, and in France there is now some unemployment. Strictly speaking, overemployment in Germany and unemployment in France are the same size.

Step 2 refers to fiscal policy. The inflationary gap in Germany is 15, and the inflationary gap in France is −15. What is needed, then, is a reduction in German government purchases of 7.5 and an increase in French government purchases of equally 7.5. The total effect is a decline in German output of 15 and an increase in French output of equally 15. As a consequence, German output goes from 1015 to 1000, and French output goes from 985 to 1000. In Germany there is now full employment and, hence, price stability. And the same applies to France.

Table 3.13
Cooperation between the European Central Bank,
the German Government, and the French Government
Inflation in Germany and France

	Germany	France
Initial Output	1060	1030
Change in Money Supply	− 30	
Output	1015	985
Change in Government Purchases	− 7.5	7.5
Output	1000	1000

As a result, monetary and fiscal cooperation can achieve both price stability and full employment. What is needed is a reduction in European money supply, a reduction in German government purchases, and an increase in French government purchases. For an overview see Table 3.13.

3) Comparing monetary and fiscal cooperation with monetary and fiscal competition. Monetary and fiscal competition can achieve full employment. The same is true of monetary and fiscal cooperation. Monetary and fiscal competition is a (relatively) slow process. Monetary and fiscal cooperation is a (relatively) fast process. Monetary and fiscal competition leads to a large change in government purchases. Monetary and fiscal cooperation leads to a small change in government purchases. Judging from these points of view, monetary and fiscal cooperation seems to be superior to monetary and fiscal competition.

4) Comparing monetary and fiscal cooperation with pure fiscal cooperation. Fiscal cooperation can achieve full employment. The same applies to monetary and fiscal cooperation. Fiscal cooperation requires a large change in government purchases. Monetary and fiscal cooperation requires a small change in government purchases. Judging from this perspective, monetary and fiscal cooperation seems to be superior to fiscal cooperation.

Part Four

Rational
Policy Expectations

Chapter 1
The Small Monetary Union of Two Countries

1. Fiscal Competition between Germany and France

1) The output model. As a point of reference, consider the output model. It can be represented by a system of two equations:

$$Y_1 = A_1 + \gamma G_1 - \gamma G_2 \tag{1}$$

$$Y_2 = A_2 + \gamma G_2 - \gamma G_1 \tag{2}$$

According to equation (1), German output Y_1 is determined by German government purchases G_1, French government purchases G_2, and some other factors called A_1. According to equation (2), French output Y_2 is determined by French government purchases G_2, German government purchases G_1, and some other factors called A_2. The letter γ is a positive coefficient. The endogenous variables are German output and French output.

2) The policy model. At the beginning there is unemployment in both Germany and France. More precisely, unemployment in Germany exceeds unemployment in France. The target of the German government is full employment in Germany. The instrument of the German government is German government purchases. The target of the French government is full employment in France. The instrument of the French government is French government purchases. We assume that the German government and the French government decide simultaneously and independently. The German government sets German government purchases, forming rational expectations of French government purchases. And the French government sets French government purchases, forming rational expectations of German government purchases.

On this basis, the policy model can be characterized by a system of four equations:

$$\overline{Y}_1 = A_1 + \gamma G_1 - \gamma G_2^e \tag{3}$$

$$\overline{Y}_2 = A_2 + \gamma G_2 - \gamma G_1^e \tag{4}$$

$$G_1^e = G_1 \tag{5}$$

$$G_2^e = G_2 \tag{6}$$

Here is a list of the new symbols:

$\overline{Y}_1$ full-employment output in Germany

$\overline{Y}_2$ full-employment output in France

G_1^e expected government purchases in Germany, as expected by the French government

G_2^e expected government purchases in France, as expected by the German government

G_1 actual government purchases in Germany, as set by the German government

G_2 actual government purchases in France, as set by the French government.

According to equation (3), the German government sets German government purchases, forming expectations of French government purchases. According to equation (4), the French government sets French government purchases, forming expectations of German government purchases. According to equation (5), expected government purchases in Germany are equal to the forecast made by means of the model. According to equation (6), expected government purchases in France are equal to the forecast made by means of the model. That is to say, the German government sets German government purchases, predicting French government purchases with the help of the model. And the French government sets French government purchases, predicting German government purchases with the help of the model. The endogenous variables are expected government purchases in Germany G_1^e, expected government purchases in France G_2^e, actual government purchases in Germany G_1, and actual government purchases in France G_2.

The policy model can be condensed to a system of two equations:

$$\overline{Y}_1 = A_1 + \gamma G_1 - \gamma G_2 \tag{7}$$

$$\overline{Y}_2 = A_2 + \gamma G_2 - \gamma G_1 \tag{8}$$

Here the endogenous variables are actual government purchases in Germany G_1 and actual government purchases in France G_2. Now take the sum of equations (7) and (8) to reach:

$$\overline{Y}_1 + \overline{Y}_2 = A_1 + A_2 \tag{9}$$

However, this is in contradiction to the assumption that $\overline{Y}_1$, $\overline{Y}_2$, A_1 and A_2 are given independently. As a result, under rational expectations, there is no equilibrium of fiscal competition. In other words, under rational expectations, fiscal competition between Germany and France does not lead to full employment in Germany and France. The underlying reason is the large spillover effect of fiscal policy.

2. Competition between the Union Central Bank, the German Government, and the French Government

1) The output model. As a point of departure, consider the output model. It can be represented by a system of two equations:

$$Y_1 = A_1 + \alpha M + \gamma G_1 - \gamma G_2 \tag{1}$$
$$Y_2 = A_2 + \alpha M + \gamma G_2 - \gamma G_1 \tag{2}$$

According to equation (1), German output Y_1 is determined by union money supply M, German government purchases G_1, French government purchases G_2, and some other factors called A_1. According to equation (2), French output Y_2 is determined by union money supply M, French government purchases G_2, German government purchases G_1, and some other factors called A_2. The letters α and γ are positive coefficients. The endogenous variables are German output and French output.

2) The policy model. At the start there is unemployment in both Germany and France. Let unemployment in Germany exceed unemployment in France. The primary target of the union central bank is price stability in the union. The secondary target of the union central bank is high employment in Germany and France. The instrument of the union central bank is union money supply. The target of the German government is full employment in Germany. The instrument of the German government is German government purchases. The target of the French government is full employment in France. The instrument of the French government is French government purchases.

We assume that the union central bank, the German government, and the French government decide simultaneously and independently. The union central bank sets union money supply, forming rational expectations of German government purchases and French government purchases. The German government sets German government purchases, forming rational expectations of union money supply and French government purchases. The French government sets French government purchases, forming rational expectations of union money supply and German government purchases.

On this basis, the policy model can be characterized by a system of two equations:

$$\overline{Y}_1 = A_1 + \alpha M + \gamma G_1 - \gamma G_2 \tag{3}$$

$$\overline{Y}_2 = A_2 + \alpha M + \gamma G_2 - \gamma G_1 \tag{4}$$

$\overline{Y}_1$ denotes full-employment output in Germany, and $\overline{Y}_2$ denotes full-employment output in France. Here the endogenous variables are union money supply, German government purchases, and French government purchases. There are two targets and three instruments, so there is one degree of freedom. As a result, under rational expectations, there is no unique equilibrium of monetary and fiscal competition. Put another way, under rational expectations, monetary and fiscal competition does not lead to full employment in Germany and France.

Chapter 2
The World of Two Monetary Regions

1. Monetary Competition between Europe and America

1) The output model. As a point of reference, consider the output model. It can be represented by a system of two equations:

$$Y_1 = A_1 + \alpha M_1 - \beta M_2 \tag{1}$$

$$Y_2 = A_2 + \alpha M_2 - \beta M_1 \tag{2}$$

According to equation (1), European output Y_1 is determined by European money supply M_1, American money supply M_2, and some other factors called A_1. According to equation (2), American output Y_2 is determined by American money supply M_2, European money supply M_1, and some other factors called A_2. The letters α and β are positive coefficients with $\alpha > \beta$. The endogenous variables are European output and American output.

2) The policy model. At the beginning there is unemployment in both Europe and America. More precisely, unemployment in Europe exceeds unemployment in America. The target of the European central bank is full employment in Europe. The instrument of the European central bank is European money supply. The target of the American central bank is full employment in America. The instrument of the American central bank is American money supply. We assume that the European central bank and the American central bank decide simultaneously and independently. The European central bank sets European money supply, forming rational expectations of American money supply. And the American central bank sets American money supply, forming rational expectations of European money supply.

On this basis, the policy model can be characterized by a system of four equations:

$$\overline{Y}_1 = A_1 + \alpha M_1 - \beta M_2^e \tag{3}$$

$$\overline{Y}_2 = A_2 + \alpha M_2 - \beta M_1^e \tag{4}$$

$$M_1^e = M_1 \tag{5}$$

$$M_2^e = M_2 \tag{6}$$

Here is a list of the new symbols:

$\overline{Y}_1$ full-employment output in Europe

$\overline{Y}_2$ full-employment output in America

M_1^e expected money supply in Europe,
        as expected by the American central bank

M_2^e expected money supply in America,
        as expected by the European central bank

M_1 actual money supply in Europe,
        as set by the European central bank

M_2 actual money supply in America,
        as set by the American central bank.

According to equation (3), the European central bank sets European money supply, forming expectations of American money supply. According to equation (4), the American central bank sets American money supply, forming expectations of European money supply. According to equation (5), expected money supply in Europe is equal to the forecast made by means of the model. According to equation (6), expected money supply in America is equal to the forecast made by means of the model. That is to say, the European central bank sets European money supply, predicting American money supply with the help of the model. And the American central bank sets American money supply, predicting European money supply with the help of the model. The endogenous variables are expected money supply in Europe M_1^e, expected money supply in America M_2^e, actual money supply in Europe M_1, and actual money supply in America M_2.

The policy model can be compressed to a system of two equations:

$$\overline{Y}_1 = A_1 + \alpha M_1 - \beta M_2 \tag{7}$$

$$\overline{Y}_2 = A_2 + \alpha M_2 - \beta M_1 \tag{8}$$

Here the endogenous variables are actual money supply in Europe M_1 and actual money supply in America M_2. To simplify notation we introduce $B_1 = \overline{Y}_1 - A_1$ and $B_2 = \overline{Y}_2 - A_2$. Then we solve the model for the endogenous variables:

$$M_1 = \frac{\alpha B_1 + \beta B_2}{\alpha^2 - \beta^2} \tag{9}$$

$$M_2 = \frac{\alpha B_2 + \beta B_1}{\alpha^2 - \beta^2} \tag{10}$$

Equation (9) shows the equilibrium level of European money supply, and equation (10) shows the equilibrium level of American money supply. There is a solution if and only if $\alpha \neq \beta$. This condition is fulfilled. As a result, under rational expectations, monetary competition between Europe and America leads to full employment immediately. It is worth pointing out here that the equilibrium under rational expectations is identical to the steady state under adaptive expectations, see Chapter 2 of Part Two.

3) Another version of the policy model. As an alternative, the policy model can be stated in terms of the output gap and the required increase in money supply:

$$\Delta Y_1 = \alpha \Delta M_1 - \beta \Delta M_2 \tag{11}$$
$$\Delta Y_2 = \alpha \Delta M_2 - \beta \Delta M_1 \tag{12}$$

Here ΔY_1 denotes the output gap in Europe, ΔY_2 is the output gap in America, ΔM_1 is the required increase in European money supply, and ΔM_2 is the required increase in American money supply. The endogenous variables are ΔM_1 and ΔM_2. The equilibrium of the system (11) and (12) is:

$$\Delta M_1 = \frac{\alpha \Delta Y_1 + \beta \Delta Y_2}{\alpha^2 - \beta^2} \tag{13}$$

$$\Delta M_2 = \frac{\alpha \Delta Y_2 + \beta \Delta Y_1}{\alpha^2 - \beta^2} \tag{14}$$

4) A numerical example. To illustrate the policy model, have a look at a numerical example. For ease of exposition, without loss of generality, assume $\alpha = 3$ and $\beta = 1$. Obviously, an increase in European money supply of 100 causes an increase in European output of 300 and a decline in American output of 100. Let full-employment output in Europe be 1000, and let full-employment output in America be the same. Let initial output in Europe be 940, and let initial output in America be 970. The output gap in Europe is 60, and the output gap in America is 30.

So what is needed in Europe, according to equation (13), is an increase in European money supply of 26.25. And what is needed in America, according to equation (14), is an increase in American money supply of 18.75. The increase in European money supply of 26.25 raises European output by 78.75 and lowers American output by 26.25. The increase in American money supply of 18.75 raises American output by 56.25 and lowers European output by 18.75. The net effect is an increase in European output of 60 and an increase in American output of 30. As a consequence, European output goes from 940 to 1000, and American output goes from 970 to 1000. In Europe there is now full employment, and the same holds for America. As a result, under rational expectations, monetary competition leads to full employment immediately. Table 4.1 presents a synopsis.

Table 4.1
Monetary Competition between Europe and America
Rational Policy Expectations

	Europe	America
Initial Output	940	970
Change in Money Supply	26.25	18.75
Output	1000	1000

5) A comment. The European central bank closely observes the measures taken by the American central bank. And what is more, the European central bank can respond immediately to the measures taken by the American central bank. Therefore policy expectations do not seem to be very important.

2. Fiscal Competition between Europe and America

1) The output model. As a point of departure, consider the output model. It can be represented by a system of two equations:

$$Y_1 = A_1 + \gamma G_1 + \gamma G_2 \tag{1}$$

$$Y_2 = A_2 + \gamma G_2 + \gamma G_1 \tag{2}$$

According to equation (1), European output Y_1 is determined by European government purchases G_1, American government purchases G_2, and some other factors called A_1. According to equation (2), American output Y_2 is determined by American government purchases G_2, European government purchases G_1, and some other factors called A_2. The letter γ is a positive coefficient. The endogenous variables are European output and American output.

2) The policy model. At the beginning there is unemployment in both Europe and America. More precisely, unemployment in Europe exceeds unemployment in America. The target of the European government is full employment in Europe. The instrument of the European government is European government purchases. The target of the American government is full employment in America. The instrument of the American government is American government purchases. We assume that the European government and the American government decide simultaneously and independently. The European government sets European government purchases, forming rational expectations of American government purchases. And the American government sets

American government purchases, forming rational expectations of European government purchases.

On this basis, the policy model can be characterized by a system of four equations:

$$\overline{Y}_1 = A_1 + \gamma G_1 + \gamma G_2^e \tag{3}$$

$$\overline{Y}_2 = A_2 + \gamma G_2 + \gamma G_1^e \tag{4}$$

$$G_1^e = G_1 \tag{5}$$

$$G_2^e = G_2 \tag{6}$$

Here is a list of the new symbols:

$\overline{Y}_1$ full-employment output in Europe
$\overline{Y}_2$ full-employment output in America
G_1^e expected government purchases in Europe,
       as expected by the American government
G_2^e expected government purchases in America,
       as expected by the European government
G_1 actual government purchases in Europe,
       as set by the European government
G_2 actual government purchases in America,
       as set by the American government.

According to equation (3), the European government sets European government purchases, forming expectations of American government purchases. According to equation (4), the American government sets American government purchases, forming expectations of European government purchases. According to equation (5), expected government purchases in Europe are equal to the forecast made by means of the model. According to equation (6), expected government purchases in America are equal to the forecast made by means of the model. That is to say, the European government sets European government purchases, predicting American government purchases with the help of the model. And the American government sets American government purchases, predicting European government purchases with the help of the model. The endogenous variables are expected government purchases in Europe G_1^e, expected government purchases in America G_2^e, actual government purchases in Europe G_1, and actual government purchases in America G_2.

The policy model can be condensed to a system of two equations:

$$\overline{Y}_1 = A_1 + \gamma G_1 + \gamma G_2 \tag{7}$$
$$\overline{Y}_2 = A_2 + \gamma G_2 + \gamma G_1 \tag{8}$$

Here the endogenous variables are actual government purchases in Europe G_1 and actual government purchases in America G_2. Now take the difference between equations (7) and (8) to reach:

$$\overline{Y}_1 - \overline{Y}_2 = A_1 - A_2 \tag{9}$$

However, this is in contradiction to the assumption that $\overline{Y}_1$, $\overline{Y}_2$, A_1 and A_2 are given independently. As a result, under rational expectations, there is no equilibrium of fiscal competition. In other words, under rational expectations, fiscal competition between Europe and America does not lead to full employment in Europe and America. The underlying reason is the large spillover effect of fiscal policy.

Chapter 3
The Large Monetary Union of Two Countries

1. Fiscal Competition between Germany and France

1) The output model. As a point of reference, consider the output model. It can be represented by a system of two equations:

$$Y_1 = A_1 + \gamma G_1 - \delta G_2 \tag{1}$$

$$Y_2 = A_2 + \gamma G_2 - \delta G_1 \tag{2}$$

According to equation (1), German output Y_1 is determined by German government purchases G_1, French government purchases G_2, and some other factors called A_1. According to equation (2), French output Y_2 is determined by French government purchases G_2, German government purchases G_1, and some other factors called A_2. The letters γ and δ are positive coefficients with $\gamma > \delta$. The endogenous variables are German output and French output.

2) The policy model. At the beginning there is unemployment in both Germany and France. More precisely, unemployment in Germany exceeds unemployment in France. The target of the German government is full employment in Germany. The instrument of the German government is German government purchases. The target of the French government is full employment in France. The instrument of the French government is French government purchases. We assume that the German government and the French government decide simultaneously and independently. The German government sets German government purchases, forming rational expectations of French government purchases. And the French government sets French government purchases, forming rational expectations of German government purchases.

On this basis, the policy model can be characterized by a system of four equations:

$$\overline{Y}_1 = A_1 + \gamma G_1 - \delta G_2^e \tag{3}$$

$$\overline{Y}_2 = A_2 + \gamma G_2 - \delta G_1^e \tag{4}$$

$$G_1^e = G_1 \tag{5}$$

$$G_2^e = G_2 \tag{6}$$

Here is a list of the new symbols:

$\overline{Y}_1$ full-employment output in Germany

$\overline{Y}_2$ full-employment output in France

G_1^e expected government purchases in Germany,
       as expected by the French government

G_2^e expected government purchases in France,
       as expected by the German government

G_1 actual government purchases in Germany,
       as set by the German government

G_2 actual government purchases in France,
       as set by the French government.

According to equation (3), the German government sets German government purchases, forming expectations of French government purchases. According to equation (4), the French government sets French government purchases, forming expectations of German government purchases. According to equation (5), expected government purchases in Germany are equal to the forecast made by means of the model. According to equation (6), expected government purchases in France are equal to the forecast made by means of the model. That is to say, the German government sets German government purchases, predicting French government purchases with the help of the model. And the French government sets French government purchases, predicting German government purchases with the help of the model. The endogenous variables are expected government purchases in Germany G_1^e, expected government purchases in France G_2^e, actual government purchases in Germany G_1, and actual government purchases in France G_2.

The policy model can be compressed to a system of two equations:

$$\overline{Y}_1 = A_1 + \gamma G_1 - \delta G_2 \tag{7}$$

$$\overline{Y}_2 = A_2 + \gamma G_2 - \delta G_1 \qquad (8)$$

Here the endogenous variables are actual government purchases in Germany G_1 and actual government purchases in France G_2. To simplify notation we introduce $B_1 = \overline{Y}_1 - A_1$ and $B_2 = \overline{Y}_2 - A_2$. Then we solve the model for the endogenous variables:

$$G_1 = \frac{\gamma B_1 + \delta B_2}{\gamma^2 - \delta^2} \qquad (9)$$

$$G_2 = \frac{\gamma B_2 + \delta B_1}{\gamma^2 - \delta^2} \qquad (10)$$

Equation (9) shows the equilibrium level of German government purchases, and equation (10) shows the equilibrium level of French government purchases. There is a solution if and only if $\gamma \neq \delta$. This condition is fulfilled. As a result, under rational expectations, fiscal competition between Germany and France leads to full employment immediately. It is worth pointing out here that the equilibrium under rational expectations is identical to the steady state under adaptive expectations, see Chapter 2 of Part Three.

3) Another version of the policy model. As an alternative, the policy model can be stated in terms of the output gap and the required increase in government purchases:

$$\Delta Y_1 = \gamma \Delta G_1 - \delta \Delta G_2 \qquad (11)$$
$$\Delta Y_2 = \gamma \Delta G_2 - \delta \Delta G_1 \qquad (12)$$

Here ΔY_1 denotes the output gap in Germany, ΔY_2 is the output gap in France, ΔG_1 is the required increase in German government purchases, and ΔG_2 is the required increase in French government purchases. The endogenous variables are ΔG_1 and ΔG_2. The equilibrium of the system (11) and (12) is:

$$\Delta G_1 = \frac{\gamma \Delta Y_1 + \delta \Delta Y_2}{\gamma^2 - \delta^2} \qquad (13)$$

$$\Delta G_2 = \frac{\gamma \Delta Y_2 + \delta \Delta Y_1}{\gamma^2 - \delta^2} \tag{14}$$

4) A numerical example. To illustrate the policy model, have a look at a numerical example. For ease of exposition, without losing generality, assume $\gamma = 1.5$ and $\delta = 0.5$. Evidently, an increase in German government purchases of 100 causes an increase in German output of 150 and a decline in French output of 50. Let full-employment output in Germany be 1000, and let full-employment output in France be the same. Let initial output in Germany be 940, and let initial output in France be 970. The output gap in Germany is 60, and the output gap in France is 30.

So what is needed in Germany, according to equation (13), is an increase in German government purchases of 52.5. And what is needed in France, according to equation (14), is an increase in French government purchases of 37.5. The increase in German government purchases of 52.5 raises German output by 78.75 and lowers French output by 26.25. The increase in French government purchases of 37.5 raises French output by 56.25 and lowers German output by 18.75. The net effect is an increase in German output of 60 and an increase in French output of 30. As a consequence, German output goes from 940 to 1000, and French output goes from 970 to 1000. In Germany there is now full employment, and the same holds for France. As a result, under rational expectations, fiscal competition leads to full employment immediately. Table 4.2 gives an overview.

Table 4.2
Fiscal Competition between Germany and France
Rational Policy Expections

	Germany	France
Initial Output	940	970
Change in Government Purchases	52.5	37.5
Output	1000	1000

2. Competition between the European Central Bank, the German Government, and the French Government

1) The output model. As a point of departure, consider the output model. It can be represented by a system of two equations:

$$Y_1 = A_1 + \alpha M_{12} + \gamma G_1 - \delta G_2 \tag{1}$$

$$Y_2 = A_2 + \alpha M_{12} + \gamma G_2 - \delta G_1 \tag{2}$$

According to equation (1), German output Y_1 is determined by European money supply M_{12}, German government purchases G_1, French government purchases G_2, and some other factors called A_1. According to equation (2), French output Y_2 is determined by European money supply M_{12}, French government purchases G_2, German government purchases G_1, and some other factors called A_2. The letters α, γ and δ are positive coefficients with $\gamma > \delta$. The endogenous variables are German output and French output.

2) The policy model. At the start there is unemployment in both Germany and France. Let unemployment in Germany exceed unemployment in France. The primary target of the European central bank is price stability in Europe. The secondary target of the European central bank is high employment in Germany and France. The instrument of the European central bank is European money supply. The target of the German government is full employment in Germany. The instrument of the German government is German government purchases. The target of the French government is full employment in France. The instrument of the French government is French government purchases.

We assume that the European central bank, the German government and the French government decide simultaneously and independently. The European central bank sets European money supply, forming rational expectations of German government purchases and French government purchases. The German government sets German government purchases, forming rational expectations of European money supply and French government purchases. The French government sets French government purchases, forming rational expectations of European money supply and German government purchases.

On this basis, the policy model can be characterized by a system of two equations:

$$\overline{Y}_1 = A_1 + \alpha M_{12} + \gamma G_1 - \delta G_2 \tag{3}$$

$$\overline{Y}_2 = A_2 + \alpha M_{12} + \gamma G_2 - \delta G_1 \tag{4}$$

$\overline{Y}_1$ denotes full-employment output in Germany, and $\overline{Y}_2$ denotes full-employment output in France. Here the endogenous variables are European money supply, German government purchases, and French government purchases. There are two targets and three instruments, so there is one degree of freedom. As a result, under rational expectations, there is no unique equilibrium of monetary and fiscal competition. Put another way, under rational expectations, monetary and fiscal competition does not lead to full employment in Germany and France.

Synopsis

Table 5.1

The Small Monetary Union of Two Countries

Fiscal Competition between Germany and France	Unstable
Competition between the Union Central Bank, the German Government, and the French Government	Unstable
Competition between the German Labour Union and the French Labour Union	Stable
Competition between the Central Bank, the German Labour Union, and the French Labour Union	Stable
Fiscal Cooperation between Germany and France	No Solution
Cooperation between the Union Central Bank, the German Government, and the French Government	Solution
Cooperation between the German Labour Union and the French Labour Union	Solution
Cooperation between the Central Bank, the German Labour Union, and the French Labour Union	Solution

210

Table 5.2
The World of Two Monetary Regions

Monetary Competition between Europe and America	Stable
Fiscal Competition between Europe and America	Unstable
Monetary Cooperation between Europe and America	Solution
Fiscal Cooperation between Europe and America	No Solution

Table 5.3
The Large Monetary Union of Two Countries

Fiscal Competition between Germany and France	Stable
Competition between the European Central Bank, the German Government, and the French Government	Stable
Fiscal Cooperation between Germany and France	Solution
Cooperation between the European Central Bank, the German Government, and the French Government	Solution

Table 5.4
Rational Policy Expectations

The Small Monetary Union of Two Countries

Fiscal Competition between Germany and France	No Equilibrium
Competition between the Union Central Bank, the German Government, and the French Government	No Unique Equilibrium

---

The World of Two Monetary Regions

Monetary Competition between Europe and America	Unique Equilibrium
Fiscal Competition between Europe and America	No Equilibrium

The Large Monetary Union of Two Countries

Fiscal Competition between Germany and France	Unique Equilibrium
Competition between the European Central Bank, the German Government, and the French Government	No Unique Equilibrium

Conclusion

1. The Small Monetary Union of Two Countries

1.1. The Basic Model

The monetary union consists of two countries, say Germany and France. The exchange rate between the monetary union and the rest of the world is flexible. German goods and French goods are imperfect substitutes for each other. German output is determined by the demand for German goods. French output is determined by the demand for French goods. And union money demand equals union money supply. The monetary union is a small open economy with perfect capital mobility. For the small union, the world interest rate is given exogenously. Under perfect capital mobility, the union interest rate is determined by the world interest rate. Therefore the union interest rate is constant too. The union countries are the same size and have the same behavioural functions. In the short run, nominal wages and prices are rigid.

1.2. Monetary Policy in the Union

1) The model. An increase in union money supply raises both German output and French output, to the same extent respectively. In the numerical example, a 1 percent increase in union money supply causes a 1 percent increase in German output and a 1 percent increase in French output. The primary target of the union central bank is price stability in the union, and the secondary target is high employment in Germany and France. The instrument of the union central bank is union money supply. It proves useful to study two distinct cases:

- unemployment in Germany and France
- inflation in Germany and France.

First consider unemployment in Germany and France. More precisely, let unemployment in Germany exceed unemployment in France. Then the specific target of the union central bank is full employment in France. Aiming at full employment in Germany would imply overemployment in France and, hence, inflation in France. Second consider inflation in Germany and France. Let there be overemployment in Germany and France, and let overemployment in Germany exceed overemployment in France. Then the specific target of the union central bank is full employment in Germany and, thus, price stability in Germany. Aiming at full employment in France would imply overemployment in Germany and, hence, inflation in Germany.

2) Some stylized numerical examples. An increase in union money supply of 100 causes an increase in German output of 200 and an increase in French output of equally 200. Further let full-employment output in Germany be 1000, and let full-employment output in France be the same.

First consider unemployment in Germany and France. More precisely, let unemployment in Germany exceed unemployment in France. Let German output be 940, and let French output be 970. That is to say, the output gap in Germany is 60, and the output gap in France is 30. In this situation, the specific target of the union central bank is to close the output gap in France. The monetary policy multiplier in France is 2. So what is needed is an increase in union money supply of 15. This policy action raises German output and French output by 30 each. As a consequence, German output goes from 940 to 970, and French output goes from 970 to 1000. In France there is now full employment. In Germany unemployment comes down, but there is still some unemployment left. As a result, monetary policy in the union can achieve full employment in France. Moreover, monetary policy in the union can reduce unemployment in Germany. However, monetary policy in the union cannot achieve full employment in Germany and France.

Second consider inflation in Germany and France. Let there be overemployment in Germany and France, and let overemployment in Germany exceed overemployment in France. Let German output be 1060, and let French output be 1030. That is to say, the inflationary gap in Germany is 60, and the inflationary gap in France is 30. In this situation, the specific target of the union central bank is to close the inflationary gap in Germany. The monetary policy multiplier in Germany is 2. So what is needed is a reduction in union money supply of 30. This policy action lowers German output and French output by 60 each. As a consequence, German output goes from 1060 to 1000, and French output goes from 1030 to 970. There is now price stability in the union. In addition, there is full employment in Germany. As an adverse side effect, there is unemployment in France. As a result, monetary policy in the union can achieve price stability in the union. On the other hand, monetary policy in the union cannot achieve full employment in Germany and France.

1.3. Fiscal Competition between Germany and France

1) The static model. An increase in German government purchases raises German output. On the other hand, it lowers French output. And what is more, the rise in German output is equal to the fall in French output. That is to say, union output does not change. Similarly, an increase in French government purchases raises French output. On the other hand, it lowers German output. And what is more, the rise in French output is equal to the fall in German output. Once again, union output does not change. In the numerical example, an increase in German government purchases of 100 causes an increase in German output of 74 and a decline in French output of equally 74. Likewise, an increase in French government purchases of 100 causes an increase in French output of 74 and a decline in German output of equally 74. In a sense, the internal effect of fiscal policy is very small, while the external effect of fiscal policy is very large.

2) The dynamic model. At the beginning there is unemployment in both Germany and France. More precisely, unemployment in Germany exceeds unemployment in France. The target of the German government is full employment in Germany, and the instrument is German government purchases. The German government raises German government purchases so as to close the output gap in Germany. The target of the French government is full employment in France, and the instrument is French government purchases. The French government raises French government purchases so as to close the output gap in

France. We assume that the German government and the French government decide simultaneously and independently. In addition there is an output lag. As a result, there is no steady state of fiscal competition. In other words, fiscal competition between Germany and France does not lead to full employment in Germany and France. The underlying reason is the large external effect of fiscal policy.

3) A stylized numerical example. An increase in German government purchases of 100 causes an increase in German output of 100 and a decline in French output of equally 100. Correspondingly, an increase in French government purchases of 100 causes an increase in French output of 100 and a decline in German output of equally 100. Further let full-employment output in Germany be 1000, and let full-employment output in France be the same.

Let initial output in Germany be 940, and let initial output in France be 970. Step 1 refers to the policy response. The output gap in Germany is 60. The fiscal policy multiplier in Germany is 1. So what is needed in Germany is an increase in German government purchases of 60. The output gap in France is 30. The fiscal policy multiplier in France is 1. So what is needed in France is an increase in French government purchases of 30. Step 2 refers to the output lag. The increase in German government purchases of 60 causes an increase in German output of 60. As a side effect, it causes a decline in French output of equally 60. The increase in French government purchases of 30 causes an increase in French output of 30. As a side effect, it causes a decline in German output of equally 30. The net effect is an increase in German output of 30 and a decline in French output of equally 30. As a consequence, German output goes from 940 to 970, and French output goes from 970 to 940. Put another way, the output gap in Germany narrows from 60 to 30, and the output gap in France widens from 30 to 60.

Why does the German government not succeed in closing the output gap in Germany? The underlying reason is the negative external effect of the increase in French government purchases. And why does the French government not succeed in closing the output gap in France? The underlying reason is the negative external effect of the increase in German government purchases.

Step 3 refers to the policy response. The output gap in Germany is 30. The fiscal policy multiplier in Germany is 1. So what is needed in Germany is an increase in German government purchases of 30. The output gap in France is 60. The fiscal policy multiplier in France is 1. So what is needed in France is an increase in French government purchases of 60. Step 4 refers to the output lag. The increase in German government purchases of 30 causes an increase in German output of 30. As a side effect, it causes a decline in French output of equally 30. The increase in French government purchases of 60 causes an increase in French output of 60. As a side effect, it causes a decline in German output of equally 60. The net effect is a decline in German output of 30 and an increase in French output of equally 30. As a consequence, German output goes from 970 to 940, and French output goes from 940 to 970. With this, German output and French output are back at their initial levels. That means, the process will repeat itself step by step.

What are the dynamic characteristics of this process? There is a continuous increase in German government purchases, as there is in French government purchases. There are uniform oscillations in German output, as there are in French output. The German economy oscillates between high and low unemployment, as does the French economy. There is a continuous appreciation of the euro. Accordingly, there is a continuous decline in both German exports and French exports. Moreover, after a certain number of steps, German exports are down to zero. And much the same holds for French exports. Budget deficits and current account deficits rise step by step. That is why public debt and foreign debt tend to explode. As a result, fiscal competition does not lead to full employment. Instead, fiscal competition gives rise to a vicious circle.

1.4. Fiscal Cooperation between Germany and France

1) The model. At the beginning there is unemployment in both Germany and France. More precisely, unemployment in Germany exceeds unemployment in France. The targets of fiscal cooperation are full employment in Germany and

full employment in France. The instruments of fiscal cooperation are German government purchases and French government purchases. So there are two targets and two instruments. As a result, there is no solution to fiscal cooperation. That is to say, fiscal cooperation between Germany and France cannot achieve full employment in Germany and France. The underlying reason is the large external effect of fiscal policy.

2) A stylized numerical example. Let initial output in Germany be 940, and let initial output in France be 970. In this case, fiscal cooperation cannot increase union employment. Fiscal cooperation can only redistribute employment among union countries. Take for instance an increase in German government purchases of 15. This policy measure raises German output by 15 and lowers French output by equally 15. As a consequence, German output goes from 940 to 955, and French output goes from 970 to 955. As a result, in this case, there is no solution to fiscal cooperation.

3) Comparing fiscal cooperation with fiscal competition. Fiscal competition cannot achieve full employment. The same applies to fiscal cooperation. Fiscal competition cannot reduce unemployment. Fiscal cooperation can reduce unemployment in some cases. Under fiscal competition there is a tendency for government purchases to explode. And there is a tendency for output to oscillate uniformly. Under fiscal cooperation there are no such tendencies. Judging from these points of view, fiscal cooperation seems to be superior to fiscal competition.

1.5. Competition between the Union Central Bank, the German Government, and the French Government

1) The dynamic model. At the start there is unemployment in both Germany and France. Let unemployment in Germany exceed unemployment in France. The primary target of the union central bank is price stability in the union, and

the secondary target is high employment in Germany and France. The instrument of the union central bank is union money supply. The target of the German government is full employment in Germany, and the instrument is German government purchases. The target of the French government is full employment in France, and the instrument is French government purchases. We assume that the central bank and the governments decide sequentially. First the central bank decides, and then the governments decide. In step 1, the union central bank decides. In step 2, the German government and the French government decide simultaneously and independently. In step 3, the union central bank decides. In step 4, the German government and the French government decide simultaneously and independently. And so on. The reasons for this stepwise procedure are: First, the inside lag of monetary policy is short, whereas the inside lag of fiscal policy is long. And second, the internal effect of monetary policy is very large, whereas the internal effect of fiscal policy is very small.

2) Some numerical examples. An increase in union money supply of 100 causes an increase in German output of 200 and an increase in French output of equally 200. An increase in German government purchases of 100 causes an increase in German output of 100 and a decline in French output of equally 100. Correspondingly, an increase in French government purchases of 100 causes an increase in French output of 100 and a decline in German output of equally 100. Further let full-employment output in Germany be 1000, and let full-employment output in France be the same. It proves useful to study two distinct cases:

- unemployment in Germany and France
- inflation in Germany and France.

First consider unemployment in Germany and France. Let initial output in Germany be 940, and let initial output in France be 970. Step 1 refers to monetary policy. The output gap in Germany is 60, and the output gap in France is 30. In this situation, the specific target of the union central bank is to close the output gap in France. Closing the output gap in Germany would imply overemployment in France and, hence, inflation in France. The output gap in France is 30. The monetary policy multiplier in France is 2. So what is needed is an increase in union money supply of 15. Step 2 refers to the output lag. The increase in union money supply of 15 causes an increase in German output of 30 and an increase in French output of equally 30. As a consequence, German output goes from 940 to 970, and French output goes from 970 to 1000.

Step 3 refers to fiscal policy. The output gap in Germany is 30. The fiscal policy multiplier in Germany is 1. So what is needed in Germany is an increase in German government purchases of 30. The output gap in France is zero. So there is no need for a change in French government purchases. Step 4 refers to the output lag. The increase in German government purchases of 30 causes an increase in German output of 30. As a side effect, it causes a decline in French output of equally 30. As a consequence, German output goes from 970 to 1000, and French output goes from 1000 to 970.

Step 5 refers to monetary policy. The output gap in Germany is zero, and the output gap in France is 30. So there is no need for a change in union money supply. Step 6 refers to the output lag. As a consequence, German output stays at 1000, and French output stays at 970. Step 7 refers to fiscal policy. The output gap in Germany is zero. So there is no need for a change in German government purchases. The output gap in France is 30. The fiscal policy multiplier in France is 1. So what is needed in France is an increase in French government purchases of 30. Step 8 refers to the output lag. The increase in French government purchases of 30 causes an increase in French output of 30. As a side effect, it causes a decline in German output of equally 30. As a consequence, French output goes from 970 to 1000, and German output goes from 1000 to 970. With this, German output and French output are back at the levels reached in step 2. That means, the process will repeat itself step by step. Table 6.1 presents a synopsis.

What are the dynamic characteristics of this process? There is a one-time increase in union money supply. There is an upward trend in German government purchases, as there is in French government purchases. There are uniform oscillations in German output, as there are in French output. The German economy oscillates between unemployment and full employment, as does the French economy. As a result, competition between the union central bank, the German government, and the French government does not lead to full employment in Germany and France. Technically speaking, there is no steady state.

Table 6.1

Competition between the Union Central Bank, the German Government, and the French Government

Unemployment in Germany and France

	Germany	France
Initial Output	940	970
Change in Money Supply	15	
Output	970	1000
Change in Government Purchases	30	0
Output	1000	970
Change in Government Purchases	0	30
Output	970	1000
and so on	...	...

Second consider inflation in Germany and France. At the start there is overemployment in both Germany and France. For that reason there is inflation in both Germany and France. Let overemployment in Germany exceed overemployment in France. Let initial output in Germany be 1060, and let initial output in France be 1030. Step 1 refers to monetary policy. The inflationary gap in Germany is 60, and the inflationary gap in France is 30. In this situation, the specific target of the union central bank is to close the inflationary gap in Germany. Closing the inflationary gap in France would imply overemployment in Germany and, hence, inflation in Germany. The inflationary gap in Germany is 60. The monetary policy multiplier in Germany is 2. So what is needed is a reduction in union money supply of 30. Step 2 refers to the output lag. The reduction in union money supply of 30 causes a decline in German output of 60 and a decline in French output of equally 60. As a consequence, German output goes from 1060 to 1000, and French output goes from 1030 to 970.

Step 3 refers to fiscal policy. The output gap in Germany is zero. So there is no need for a change in German government purchases. The output gap in France is 30. The fiscal policy multiplier in France is 1. So what is needed in France is an increase in French government purchases of 30. Step 4 refers to the output lag. The increase in French government purchases of 30 causes an increase in French output of 30. As a side effect, it causes a decline in German output of equally 30. As a consequence, French output goes from 970 to 1000, and German output goes from 1000 to 970.

Step 5 refers to monetary policy. The output gap in Germany is 30, and the output gap in France is zero. So there is no need for a change in union money supply. Step 6 refers to the output lag. As a consequence, German output stays at 970, and French output stays at 1000. Step 7 refers to fiscal policy. The output gap in Germany is 30. The fiscal policy multiplier in Germany is 1. So what is needed in Germany is an increase in German government purchases of 30. The output gap in France is zero. So there is no need for a change in French government purchases. Step 8 refers to the output lag. The increase in German government purchases of 30 causes an increase in German output of 30. As a side effect, it causes a decline in French output of equally 30. As a consequence, German output goes from 970 to 1000, and French output goes from 1000 to 970. With this, German output and French output are back at the levels reached in step 2. That is to say, the process will repeat itself step by step.

What are the dynamic characteristics of this process? There is a one-time reduction in union money supply. There is an upward trend in German government purchases, as there is in French government purchases. There are uniform oscillations in German output, as there are in French output. The German economy oscillates between unemployment and full employment, as does the French economy. As a result, the process of monetary and fiscal competition leads to price stability. However, the process of monetary and fiscal competition does not lead to full employment.

3) Summary. Monetary and fiscal competition can reduce unemployment. Monetary and fiscal competition can achieve price stability. But monetary and fiscal competition cannot achieve full employment.

4) Comparing monetary and fiscal competition with pure fiscal competition. Fiscal competition cannot achieve full employment. The same applies to monetary and fiscal competition. Fiscal competition cannot even reduce unemployment. Monetary and fiscal competition can reduce unemployment to a certain extent. Judging from these points of view, monetary and fiscal competition is superior to fiscal competition.

1.6. Cooperation between the Union Central Bank, the German Government, and the French Government

1) The model. At the beginning there is unemployment in both Germany and France. More precisely, unemployment in Germany exceeds unemployment in France. The targets of policy cooperation are full employment in Germany and full employment in France. The instruments of policy cooperation are union money supply, German government purchases, and French government purchases. There are two targets and three instruments, so there is one degree of freedom. As a result, there is an infinite number of solutions. In other words, cooperation between the union central bank, the German government, and the French government can achieve full employment in Germany and France.

2) Some numerical examples. It proves useful to study two distinct cases:
- unemployment in Germany and France
- inflation in Germany and France.

First consider unemployment in Germany and France. Let unemployment in Germany exceed unemployment in France. Let initial output in Germany be 940, and let initial output in France be 970. The solution can be found in two logical steps. Step 1 refers to monetary policy. The output gap in the union is 90. The monetary policy multiplier in the union is 4. So what is needed is an increase in union money supply of 22.5. This policy action raises German output and French output by 45 each. As a consequence, German output goes from 940 to 985, and French output goes from 970 to 1015. In Germany there is still some unemployment left, and in France there is now some overemployment. Strictly speaking, unemployment in Germany and overemployment in France are the same size.

Step 2 refers to fiscal policy. The output gap in Germany is 15, and the output gap in France is −15. What is needed, then, is an increase in German government purchases of 7.5 and a reduction in French government purchases of equally 7.5. The increase in German government purchases of 7.5 raises German output by 7.5 and lowers French output by equally 7.5. The reduction in French government purchases of 7.5 lowers French output by 7.5 and raises German output by equally 7.5. The total effect is an increase in German output of 15 and a decline in French output of equally 15. As a consequence, German output goes from 985 to 1000, and French output goes from 1015 to 1000. In Germany there is now full employment, and the same holds for France. As a result, monetary and fiscal cooperation can achieve full employment in Germany and France.

Second consider inflation in Germany and France. At the start there is overemployment in both Germany and France. For that reason there is inflation in both Germany and France. Let overemployment in Germany exceed overemployment in France. Let initial output in Germany be 1060, and let initial output in France be 1030. The solution can be determined in two logical steps. Step 1 refers to monetary policy. The inflationary gap in the union is 90. The monetary policy multiplier in the union is 4. So what is needed is a reduction in union money supply of 22.5. This policy action lowers German output and French output by 45 each. As a consequence, German output goes from 1060 to 1015, and French output goes from 1030 to 985. In Germany there is still some overemployment left, and in France there is now some unemployment. Strictly speaking, overemployment in Germany and unemployment in France are the same size.

Step 2 refers to fiscal policy. The inflationary gap in Germany is 15, and the inflationary gap in France is −15. What is needed, then, is a reduction in German government purchases of 7.5 and an increase in French government purchases of equally 7.5. The total effect is a decline in German output of 15 and an increase in French output of equally 15. As a consequence, German output goes from 1015 to 1000, and French output goes from 985 to 1000. In Germany there is now full employment and, hence, price stability. And the same applies to France.

As a result, monetary and fiscal cooperation can achieve both price stability and full employment.

3) Comparing monetary and fiscal cooperation with monetary and fiscal competition. Monetary and fiscal competition cannot achieve full employment. By contrast, monetary and fiscal cooperation can indeed achieve full employment. Under monetary and fiscal competition there is a tendency for government purchases to explode. Besides there is a tendency for output to oscillate uniformly. Under monetary and fiscal cooperation there are no such tendencies. Judging from these points of view, monetary and fiscal cooperation seems to be superior to monetary and fiscal competition.

2. The World of Two Monetary Regions

2.1. The Basic Model

The world consists of two monetary regions, say Europe and America. The exchange rate between Europe and America is flexible. European goods and American goods are imperfect substitutes for each other. European output is determined by the demand for European goods. American output is determined by the demand for American goods. European money demand equals European money supply. And American money demand equals American money supply. There is perfect capital mobility between Europe and America, so the European interest rate agrees with the American interest rate. The monetary regions are the same size and have the same behavioural functions. In the short run, nominal wages and prices are rigid.

2.2. Monetary Competition between Europe and America

1) The static model. An increase in European money supply raises European output. On the other hand, it lowers American output. Here the rise in European output exceeds the fall in American output. Correspondingly, an increase in American money supply raises American output. On the other hand, it lowers European output. Here the rise in American output exceeds the fall in European output. In the numerical example, an increase in European money supply of 100 causes an increase in European output of 300 and a decline in American output of 100. Likewise, an increase in American money supply of 100 causes an increase in American output of 300 and a decline in European output of 100. That is to say, the internal effect of monetary policy is very large, and the external effect of monetary policy is large.

2) The dynamic model. At the beginning there is unemployment in both Europe and America. More precisely, unemployment in Europe exceeds unemployment in America. The target of the European central bank is full employment in Europe. The instrument of the European central bank is European money supply. The European central bank raises European money supply so as to close the output gap in Europe. The target of the American central bank is full employment in America. The instrument of the American central bank is American money supply. The American central bank raises American money supply so as to close the output gap in America. We assume that the European central bank and the American central bank decide simultaneously and independently. In addition there is an output lag. As a result, there is a stable steady state of monetary competition. In other words, monetary competition between Europe and America leads to full employment in Europe and America.

3) Some numerical examples. It proves useful to study two distinct cases:
  - unemployment in Europe and America
  - inflation in Europe and America.

First consider unemployment in Europe and America. Let full-employment output in Europe be 1000, and let full-employment output in America be the same. At the beginning there is unemployment in both Europe and America. More precisely, unemployment in Europe exceeds unemployment in America. Let initial output in Europe be 940, and let initial output in America be 970. Step 1 refers to the policy response. The output gap in Europe is 60. The monetary policy multiplier in Europe is 3. So what is needed in Europe is an increase in European money supply of 20. The output gap in America is 30. The monetary policy multiplier in America is 3. So what is needed in America is an increase in American money supply of 10.

Step 2 refers to the output lag. The increase in European money supply of 20 causes an increase in European output of 60. As a side effect, it causes a decline in American output of 20. The increase in American money supply of 10 causes an increase in American output of 30. As a side effect, it causes a decline in European output of 10. The net effect is an increase in European output of 50 and an increase in American output of 10. As a consequence, European output goes from 940 to 990, and American output goes from 970 to 980. Put another way, the output gap in Europe narrows from 60 to 10, and the output gap in America narrows from 30 to 20.

Why does the European central bank not succeed in closing the output gap in Europe? The underlying reason is the negative external effect of the increase in American money supply. And why does the American central bank not succeed in closing the output gap in America? The underlying reason is the negative external effect of the increase in European money supply.

Step 3 refers to the policy response. The output gap in Europe is 10. The monetary policy multiplier in Europe is 3. So what is needed in Europe is an increase in European money supply of 3.3. The output gap in America is 20. The monetary policy multiplier in America is 3. So what is needed in America is an increase in American money supply of 6.7. Step 4 refers to the output lag. The increase in European money supply of 3.3 causes an increase in European output of 10. As a side effect, it causes a decline in American output of 3.3. The increase in American money supply of 6.7 causes an increase in American output of 20. As a side effect, it causes a decline in European output of 6.7. The net effect is an increase in European output of 3.3 and an increase in American output of 16.7. As a consequence, European output goes from 990 to 993.3, and American output goes from 980 to 996.7. And so on. Table 6.2 presents a synopsis.

Table 6.2

Monetary Competition between Europe and America

Unemployment in Europe and America

	Europe	America
Initial Output	940	970
Change in Money Supply	20	10
Output	990	980
Change in Money Supply	3.3	6.7
Output	993.3	996.7
and so on	...	...

What are the dynamic characteristics of this process? There is a continuous increase in European money supply, as there is in American money supply. There is a continuous increase in European output, as there is in American output. As a result, monetary competition leads to full employment.

Second consider inflation in Europe and America. At the start there is overemployment in both Europe and America. For that reason there is inflation in both Europe and America. Let overemployment in Europe exceed overemployment in America. Let initial output in Europe be 1060, and let initial output in America be 1030. Assume that monetary competition is such a fast process that prices do not change during competition. Step 1 refers to the policy response. The inflationary gap in Europe is 60. The target of the European central bank is price stability in Europe. The monetary policy multiplier in Europe is 3. So what is needed in Europe is a reduction in European money supply of 20. The inflationary gap in America is 30. The target of the American central bank is price stability in America. The monetary policy multiplier in America is 3. So what is needed in America is a reduction in American money supply of 10.

Step 2 refers to the output lag. The reduction in European money supply of 20 causes a decline in European output of 60. As a side effect, it causes an increase in American output of 20. The reduction in American money supply of 10 causes a decline in American output of 30. As a side effect, it causes an increase in European output of 10. The net effect is a decline in European output of 50 and a decline in American output of 10. As a consequence, European output goes from 1060 to 1010, and American output goes from 1030 to 1020.

Step 3 refers to the policy response. The inflationary gap in Europe is 10. The monetary policy multiplier in Europe is 3. So what is needed in Europe is a reduction in European money supply of 3.3. The inflationary gap in America is 20. The monetary policy multiplier in America is 3. So what is needed in America is a reduction in American money supply of 6.7. Step 4 refers to the output lag. The reduction in European money supply of 3.3 causes a decline in European output of 10. As a side effect, it causes an increase in American output of 3.3. The reduction in American money supply of 6.7 causes a decline in American output of 20. As a side effect, it causes an increase in European output of 6.7. The net effect is a decline in European output of 3.3 and a decline in

American output of 16.7. As a consequence, European output goes from 1010 to 1006.7, and American output goes from 1020 to 1003.3. And so on.

What are the dynamic characteristics of this process? There is a continuous reduction in European money supply, as there is in American money supply. There is a continuous decline in European output, as there is in American output. As a result, monetary competition leads to both price stability and full employment.

2.3. Monetary Cooperation between Europe and America

1) The model. At the beginning there is unemployment in both Europe and America. More precisely, unemployment in Europe exceeds unemployment in America. The targets of monetary cooperation are full employment in Europe and full employment in America. The instruments of monetary cooperation are European money supply and American money supply. So there are two targets and two instruments. As a result, there is a solution to monetary cooperation. Put another way, monetary cooperation between Europe and America can achieve full employment in Europe and America.

2) Some numerical examples. It proves useful to study two distinct cases. First consider unemployment in Europe and America. Let initial output in Europe be 940, and let initial output in America be 970. The output gap in Europe is 60, and the output gap in America is 30. What is needed, then, is an increase in European money supply of 26.25 and an increase in American money supply of 18.75. The increase in European money supply of 26.25 raises European output by 78.75 and lowers American output by 26.25. The increase in American money supply of 18.75 raises American output by 56.25 and lowers European output by 18.75. The net effect is an increase in European output of 60 and an increase in American output of 30. As a consequence, European output goes from 940 to 1000, and American output goes from 970 to 1000. In Europe there is now full employment, and the same holds for America.

Second consider inflation in Europe and America. At the start there is overemployment in both Europe and America. For that reason there is inflation in both Europe and America. Let overemployment in Europe exceed overemployment in America. Let initial output in Europe be 1060, and let initial output in America be 1030. The inflationary gap in Europe is 60, and the inflationary gap in America is 30. The targets of monetary cooperation are price stability in Europe and price stability in America. What is needed, then, is a reduction in European money supply of 26.25 and a reduction in American money supply of 18.75. As a consequence, European output goes from 1060 to 1000, and American output goes from 1030 to 1000. There is now full employment in both Europe and America. For that reason there is now price stability in both Europe and America. As a result, monetary cooperation can achieve full employment and price stability.

3) Comparing monetary cooperation with monetary competition. Monetary competition can achieve full employment. The same applies to monetary cooperation. Monetary competition is a fast process. The same is true of monetary cooperation. Judging from these points of view, there seems to be no need for monetary cooperation.

2.4. Fiscal Competition between Europe and America

1) The static model. An increase in European government purchases raises both European output and American output. And what is more, the rise in European output is equal to the rise in American output. Similarly, an increase in American government purchases raises both American output and European output. And what is more, the rise in American output is equal to the rise in European output. In the numerical example, an increase in European government purchases of 100 causes an increase in European output of 90 and an increase in American output of equally 90. Likewise, an increase in American government purchases of 100 causes an increase in American output of 90 and an increase in

232

European output of equally 90. In a sense, the internal effect of fiscal policy is rather small, whereas the external effect of fiscal policy is quite large.

2) The dynamic model. At the start there is unemployment in both Europe and America. Let unemployment in Europe exceed unemployment in America. The target of the European government is full employment in Europe, and the instrument is European government purchases. The European government raises European government purchases so as to close the output gap in Europe. The target of the American government is full employment in America, and the instrument is American government purchases. The American government raises American government purchases so as to close the output gap in America. We assume that the European government and the American government decide simultaneously and independently. In addition there is an output lag. As a result, there is no steady state of fiscal competition. In other words, fiscal competition between Europe and America does not lead to full employment in Europe and America. The underlying reason is the large external effect of fiscal policy.

3) A stylized numerical example. An increase in European government purchases of 100 causes an increase in European output of 100 and an increase in American output of equally 100. Correspondingly, an increase in American government purchases of 100 causes an increase in American output of 100 and an increase in European output of equally 100. Let full-employment output in Europe be 1000, and let full-employment output in America be the same. Let initial output in Europe be 940, and let initial output in America be 970. Step 1 refers to the policy response. The output gap in Europe is 60. The fiscal policy multiplier in Europe is 1. So what is needed in Europe is an increase in European government purchases of 60. The output gap in America is 30. The fiscal policy multiplier in America is 1. So what is needed in America is an increase in American government purchases of 30.

Step 2 refers to the output lag. The increase in European government purchases of 60 causes an increase in European output of 60. As a side effect, it causes an increase in American output of equally 60. The increase in American government purchases of 30 causes an increase in American output of 30. As a side effect, it causes an increase in European output of equally 30. The total effect is an increase in European output of 90 and an increase in American output of equally 90. As a consequence, European output goes from 940 to 1030, and

American output goes from 970 to 1060. Put another way, the output gap in Europe of 60 turns into an inflationary gap of 30. And the output gap in America of 30 turns into an inflationary gap of 60.

Why does the European government not succeed in closing the output gap in Europe (or, for that matter, the inflationary gap in Europe)? The underlying reason is the positive external effect of the increase in American government purchases. And why does the American government not succeed in closing the output gap in America (or the inflationary gap in America)? The underlying reason is the positive external effect of the increase in European government purchases.

Step 3 refers to the policy response. The inflationary gap in Europe is 30. The fiscal policy multiplier in Europe is 1. So what is needed in Europe is a reduction in European government purchases of 30. The inflationary gap in America is 60. The fiscal policy multiplier in America is 1. So what is needed in America is a reduction in American government purchases of 60. Step 4 refers to the output lag. The reduction in European government purchases of 30 causes a decline in European output of 30. As a side effect, it causes a decline in American output of equally 30. The reduction in American government purchases of 60 causes a decline in American output of 60. As a side effect, it causes a decline in European output of equally 60. The total effect is a decline in European output of 90 and a decline in American output of equally 90. As a consequence, European output goes from 1030 to 940, and American output goes from 1060 to 970. With this, European output and American output are back at their initial levels. That means, the process will repeat itself step by step.

What are the dynamic characteristics of this process? There is an upward trend in European government purchases. By contrast, there is a downward trend in American government purchases. There are uniform oscillations in European output, as there are in American output. The European economy oscillates between unemployment and overemployment, as does the American economy. There is a continuous appreciation of the euro and a continuous depreciation of the dollar. Accordingly, there is a continuous decline in European exports and a continuous increase in American exports. Moreover, after a certain number of steps, American government purchases are down to zero. Finally compare fiscal competition with monetary competition. Monetary competition can achieve full employment, but fiscal competition cannot do so. Judging from this point of view, monetary competition is superior to fiscal competition.

2.5. Fiscal Cooperation between Europe and America

1) The model. At the beginning there is unemployment in both Europe and America. More precisely, unemployment in Europe exceeds unemployment in America. The targets of fiscal cooperation are full employment in Europe and full employment in America. The instruments of fiscal cooperation are European government purchases and American government purchases. So there are two targets and two instruments. As a result, there is no solution to fiscal cooperation. That is to say, fiscal cooperation between Europe and America cannot achieve full employment in Europe and America. The underlying reason is the large external effect of fiscal policy.

2) A numerical example. Let initial output in Europe be 940, and let initial output in America be 970. In this case, the specific target of fiscal cooperation is full employment in America. Aiming at full employment in Europe would imply overemployment in America and, hence, inflation in America. So what is needed is an increase in American output of 30. What is needed, for instance, is an increase in European government purchases of 15 and an increase in American government purchases of equally 15. The increase in European government purchases of 15 raises European output and American output by 15 each. Similarly, the increase in American government purchases of 15 raises American output and European output by 15 each. The total effect is an increase in European output of 30 and an increase in American output of equally 30. As a consequence, European output goes from 940 to 970, and American output goes from 970 to 1000. In Europe unemployment comes down, but there is still some unemployment left. In America there is now full employment. As a result, in this case, fiscal cooperation can reduce unemployment in Europe and America to a certain extent.

3) Comparing fiscal cooperation with fiscal competition. Fiscal competition cannot achieve full employment. The same is true of fiscal cooperation. Fiscal competition cannot reduce unemployment. Fiscal cooperation can reduce unemployment to a certain extent. Judging from these points of view, fiscal cooperation seems to be superior to fiscal competition.

4) Comparing fiscal cooperation with monetary cooperation. Monetary cooperation can achieve full employment. By contrast, fiscal cooperation cannot achieve full employment. From this perspective, monetary cooperation is superior to fiscal cooperation.

3. The Large Monetary Union of Two Countries

3.1. The Basic Model

The world consists of two monetary regions, say Europe and America. The exchange rate between Europe and America is flexible. Europe in turn consists of two countries, say Germany and France. So Germany and France form a monetary union. German goods, French goods and American goods are imperfect substitutes for each other. German output is determined by the demand for German goods. French output is determined by the demand for French goods. And American output is determined by the demand for American goods. European money demand equals European money supply. And American money demand equals American money supply. There is perfect capital mobility between Germany, France and America. Thus the German interest rate, the French interest rate, and the American interest rate are equalized. The monetary regions are the same size and have the same behavioural functions. The union countries are the same size and have the same behavioural functions. In the short run, nominal wages and prices are rigid.

3.2. Fiscal Competition between Germany and France

1) The static model. An increase in German government purchases raises German output. On the other hand, it lowers French output. Here the rise in German output exceeds the fall in French output. Correspondingly, an increase in French government purchases raises French output. On the other hand, it lowers German output. Here the rise in French output exceeds the fall in German output. In the numerical example, an increase in German government purchases of 100 causes an increase in German output of 141 and a decline in French output of 52. Correspondingly, an increase in French government purchases of 100 causes an increase in French output of 141 and a decline in German output of 52.

2) The dynamic model. At the beginning there is unemployment in both Germany and France. More precisely, unemployment in Germany exceeds unemployment in France. The target of the German government is full employment in Germany, and the instrument is German government purchases. The German government raises German government purchases so as to close the output gap in Germany. The target of the French government is full employment in France, and the instrument is French government purchases. The French government raises French government purchases so as to close the output gap in France. As a result, there is a stable steady state of fiscal competition. In other words, fiscal competition between Germany and France leads to full employment in Germany and France.

3) A stylized numerical example. An increase in German government purchases of 100 causes an increase in German output of 150 and a decline in French output of 50. Correspondingly, an increase in French government purchases of 100 causes an increase in French output of 150 and a decline in German output of 50. Further let full-employment output in Germany be 1000, and let full-employment output in France be the same.

Let initial output in Germany be 940, and let initial output in France be 970. Step 1 refers to the policy response. The output gap in Germany is 60. The fiscal policy multiplier in Germany is 1.5. So what is needed in Germany is an increase in German government purchases of 40. The output gap in France is 30. The fiscal policy multiplier in France is 1.5. So what is needed in France is an increase in French government purchases of 20. Step 2 refers to the output lag. The increase in German government purchases of 40 causes an increase in German output of 60. As a side effect, it causes a decline in French output of 20. The increase in French government purchases of 20 causes an increase in French output of 30. As a side effect, it causes a decline in German output of 10. The net effect is an increase in German output of 50 and an increase in French output of 10. As a consequence, German output goes from 940 to 990, and French output goes from 970 to 980.

Step 3 refers to the policy response. The output gap in Germany is 10. The fiscal policy multiplier in Germany is 1.5. So what is needed in Germany is an increase in German government purchases of 6.7. The output gap in France is 20.

The fiscal policy multiplier in France is 1.5. So what is needed in France is an increase in French government purchases of 13.3. Step 4 refers to the output lag. The increase in German government purchases of 6.7 causes an increase in German output of 10. As a side effect, it causes a decline in French output of 3.3. The increase in French government purchases of 13.3 causes an increase in French output of 20. As a side effect, it causes a decline in German output of 6.7. The net effect is an increase in German output of 3.3 and an increase in French output of 16.7. As a consequence, German output goes from 990 to 993.3, and French output goes from 980 to 996.7. And so on.

What are the dynamic characteristics of this process? There is a continuous increase in German government purchases, as there is in French government purchases. There is a continuous increase in German output, as there is in French output. As a result, fiscal competition leads to full employment. Taking the sum over all periods, the increase in German government purchases is 52.5, and the increase in French government purchases is 37.5. That means, the increase in German government purchases is very large, as compared to the output gap in Germany. And the increase in French government purchases is even larger, as compared to the output gap in France. The effective multiplier in Germany is only 1.1, and the effective multiplier in France is only 0.8.

3.3. Fiscal Cooperation between Germany and France

1) The model. At the beginning there is unemployment in both Germany and France. More precisely, unemployment in Germany exceeds unemployment in France. The targets of fiscal cooperation are full employment in Germany and full employment in France. The instruments of fiscal cooperation are German government purchases and French government purchases. So there are two targets and two instruments. As a result, there is a solution to fiscal cooperation. That means, fiscal cooperation between Germany and France can achieve full employment in Germany and France.

2) A numerical example. Let initial output in Germany be 940, and let initial output in France be 970. The output gap in Germany is 60, and the output gap in France is 30. What is needed, then, is an increase in German government purchases of 52.5 and an increase in French government purchases of 37.5. The increase in German government purchases of 52.5 raises German output by 78.75 and lowers French output by 26.25. The increase in French government purchases of 37.5 raises French output by 56.25 and lowers German output by 18.75. The net effect is an increase in German output of 60 and an increase in French output of 30. As a consequence, German output goes from 940 to 1000, and French output goes from 970 to 1000. In Germany there is now full employment, and the same holds for France. As a result, fiscal cooperation can achieve full employment. But the required increase in government purchases is very large, as compared to the output gap.

3) Comparing fiscal cooperation with fiscal competition. Fiscal competition can achieve full employment. The same applies to fiscal cooperation. Fiscal competition is a slow process. By contrast, fiscal cooperation is a fast process. Judging from these points of view, fiscal cooperation seems to be superior to fiscal competition.

3.4. Competition between the European Central Bank, the German Government, and the French Government

1) The dynamic model. At the start there is unemployment in both Germany and France. Let unemployment in Germany exceed unemployment in France. The primary target of the European central bank is price stability in Europe, and the secondary target is high employment in Germany and France. The instrument of the European central bank is European money supply. The target of the German government is full employment in Germany, and the instrument is German government purchases. The target of the French government is full

employment in France, and the instrument is French government purchases. We assume that the central bank and the governments decide sequentially. First the central bank decides, and then the governments decide. In step 1, the European central bank decides. In step 2, the German government and the French government decide simultaneously and independently. In step 3, the European central bank decides. In step 4, the German government and the French government decide simultaneously and independently. And so on.

2) A numerical example. An increase in European money supply of 100 causes an increase in German output of 150 and an increase in French output of equally 150. An increase in German government purchases of 100 causes an increase in German output of 150 and a decline in French output of 50. Correspondingly, an increase in French government purchases of 100 causes an increase in French output of 150 and a decline in German output of 50. Further let full-employment output in Germany be 1000, and let full-employment output in France be the same.

Let initial output in Germany be 940, and let initial output in France be 970. Step 1 refers to monetary policy. The output gap in Germany is 60, and the output gap in France is 30. In this situation, the specific target of the European central bank is to close the output gap in France. Closing the output gap in Germany would imply overemployment in France and, hence, inflation in France. The output gap in France is 30. The monetary policy multiplier in France is 1.5. So what is needed is an increase in European money supply of 20. Step 2 refers to the output lag. The increase in European money supply of 20 causes an increase in German output of 30 and an increase in French output of equally 30. As a consequence, German output goes from 940 to 970, and French output goes from 970 to 1000.

Step 3 refers to fiscal policy. The output gap in Germany is 30. The fiscal policy multiplier in Germany is 1.5. So what is needed in Germany is an increase in German government purchases of 20. The output gap in France is zero. So there is no need for a change in French government purchases. Step 4 refers to the output lag. The increase in German government purchases of 20 causes an increase in German output of 30. As a side effect, it causes a decline in French output of 10. As a consequence, German output goes from 970 to 1000, and French output goes from 1000 to 990.

Step 5 refers to monetary policy. The output gap in Germany is zero, and the output gap in France is 10. So there is no need for a change in European money supply. Step 6 refers to the output lag. As a consequence, German output stays at 1000, and French output stays at 990. Step 7 refers to fiscal policy. The output gap in Germany is zero. So there is no need for a change in German government purchases. The output gap in France is 10. The fiscal policy multiplier in France is 1.5. So what is needed in France is an increase in French government purchases of 6.7. Step 8 refers to the output lag. The increase in French government purchases of 6.7 causes an increase in French output of 10. As a side effect, it causes a decline in German output of 3.3. As a consequence, French output goes from 990 to 1000, and German output goes from 1000 to 996.7. And so on. Table 6.3 presents a synopsis.

Table 6.3
Competition between the European Central Bank,
the German Government, and the French Government
Unemployment in Germany and France

	Germany	France
Initial Output	940	970
Change in Money Supply	20	
Output	970	1000
Change in Government Purchases	20	0
Output	1000	990
Change in Government Purchases	0	6.7
Output	996.7	1000
and so on	...	...

What are the dynamic characteristics of this process? There is a one-time increase in European money supply. There is an upward trend in German government purchases, as there is in French government purchases. There are damped oscillations in German output, as there are in French output. The German economy oscillates between unemployment and full employment, as does the French economy. Taking the sum over all periods, the increase in German government purchases is 22.5, and the increase in French government purchases is 7.5. As a result, competition between the European central bank, the German government, and the French government leads to full employment in Germany and France. Technically speaking, there is a stable steady state.

3.5. Cooperation between the European Central Bank, the German Government, and the French Government

1) The model. At the beginning there is unemployment in both Germany and France. More precisely, unemployment in Germany exceeds unemployment in France. The targets of policy cooperation are full employment in Germany and full employment in France. The instruments of policy cooperation are European money supply, German government purchases, and French government purchases. There are two targets and three instruments, so there is one degree of freedom. As a result, there is an infinite number of solutions. In other words, cooperation between the European central bank, the German government, and the French government can achieve full employment in Germany and France.

2) A numerical example. Let initial output in Germany be 940, and let initial output in France be 970. The solution can be found in two logical steps. Step 1 refers to monetary policy. The output gap in Europe is 90. The monetary policy multiplier in Europe is 3. So what is needed is an increase in European money supply of 30. This policy action raises German output and French output by 45 each. As a consequence, German output goes from 940 to 985, and French output goes from 970 to 1015. In Germany there is still some unemployment left, and in

France there is now some overemployment. Strictly speaking, unemployment in Germany and overemployment in France are the same size.

Step 2 refers to fiscal policy. The output gap in Germany is 15, and the output gap in France is −15. What is needed, then, is an increase in German government purchases of 7.5 and a reduction in French government purchases of equally 7.5. The increase in German government purchases of 7.5 raises German output by 11.25 and lowers French output by 3.75. The reduction in French government purchases of 7.5 lowers French output by 11.25 and raises German output by 3.75. The total effect is an increase in German output of 15 and a decline in French output of equally 15. As a consequence, German output goes from 985 to 1000, and French output goes from 1015 to 1000. In Germany there is now full employment, and the same holds for France.

3) Comparing monetary and fiscal cooperation with monetary and fiscal competition. Monetary and fiscal competition can achieve full employment. The same is true of monetary and fiscal cooperation. Monetary and fiscal competition is a (relatively) slow process. Monetary and fiscal cooperation is a (relatively) fast process. Monetary and fiscal competition leads to a large change in government purchases. Monetary and fiscal cooperation leads to a small change in government purchases. Judging from these points of view, monetary and fiscal cooperation seems to be superior to monetary and fiscal competition.

Result

1. The Small Monetary Union of Two Countries

1) Monetary policy in the union. The monetary union consists of two identical countries, say Germany and France. An increase in union money supply raises both German output and French output, to the same extent respectively. In the numerical example, an increase in union money supply of 100 causes an increase in German output of 200 and an increase in French output of equally 200. The primary target of the union central bank is price stability in the union, and the secondary target is high employment in Germany and France. The instrument of the union central bank is union money supply.

First consider unemployment in Germany and France. More precisely, let unemployment in Germany exceed unemployment in France. Then the specific target of the union central bank is full employment in France. Aiming at full employment in Germany would imply overemployment in France and, hence, inflation in France. Second consider inflation in Germany and France. Let there be overemployment in Germany and France, and let overemployment in Germany exceed overemployment in France. Then the specific target of the union central bank is full employment in Germany and, thus, price stability in Germany. Aiming at full employment in France would imply overemployment in Germany and, hence, inflation in Germany.

Have a look at some numerical examples. Let full-employment output in Germany be 1000, and let full-employment output in France be the same. First consider unemployment in Germany and France. Let initial output in Germany be 940, and let initial output in France be 970. What is needed, then, is an increase in union money supply of 15. This policy action raises German output and French output by 30 each. As a consequence, German output goes to 970, and French output goes to 1000. As a result, monetary policy in the union can achieve full employment in France. Moreover, it can reduce unemployment in Germany. However, it cannot achieve full employment in Germany and France.

Second consider inflation in Germany and France. Let initial output in Germany be 1060, and let initial output in France be 1030. What is needed, then, is a reduction in union money supply of 30. This policy action lowers German output and French output by 60 each. As a consequence, German output goes to 1000, and French output goes to 970. As a result, monetary policy in the union can achieve price stability in the union. But it cannot achieve full employment in Germany and France.

2) Fiscal competition between Germany and France. First consider the static model. An increase in German government purchases raises German output. On the other hand, it lowers French output. And what is more, the rise in German output is equal to the fall in French output. Similarly, an increase in French government purchases raises French output. On the other hand, it lowers German output. And what is more, the rise in French output is equal to the fall in German output. In the numerical example, an increase in German government purchases of 100 causes an increase in German output of 100 and a decline in French output of equally 100. Likewise, an increase in French government purchases of 100 causes an increase in French output of 100 and a decline in German output of equally 100. In a sense, the internal effect of fiscal policy is small, while the external effect of fiscal policy is large.

Second consider the dynamic model. At the beginning there is unemployment in both Germany and France. More precisely, unemployment in Germany exceeds unemployment in France. The target of the German government is full employment in Germany, and the instrument is German government purchases. The German government raises German government purchases so as to close the output gap in Germany. The target of the French government is full employment in France, and the instrument is French government purchases. The French government raises French government purchases so as to close the output gap in France. We assume that the German government and the French government decide simultaneously and independently. In addition there is an output lag. As a result, the process of fiscal competition is unstable. In other words, fiscal competition does not lead to full employment in Germany and France. The underlying reason is the large external effect of fiscal policy.

Third consider a numerical example. Let full-employment output in Germany be 1000, and let full-employment output in France be the same. Let initial output in Germany be 940, and let initial output in France be 970. Step 1 refers to the policy response. What is needed in Germany is an increase in German government purchases of 60. And what is needed in France is an increase in French government purchases of 30. Step 2 refers to the output lag. The net effect is an increase in German output of 30 and a decline in French output of equally 30. As a consequence, German output goes to 970, and French output goes to 940. In step 3, German government purchases are raised by 30, and French government purchases are raised by 60. In step 4, German output goes to 940, and French output goes to 970. And so on. There is a continuous increase in German government purchases, as there is in French government purchases. There are uniform oscillations in German output, as there are in French output. The German economy oscillates between high and low unemployment, as does the French economy. There is a continuous appreciation of the euro. Accordingly, there is a continuous decline in both German exports and French exports. Moreover, after a certain number of steps, German exports are down to zero. And much the same holds for French exports.

3) Fiscal cooperation between Germany and France. The targets are full employment in Germany and France. The instruments are German and French government purchases. So there are two targets and two instruments. As a result, there is no solution to fiscal cooperation. In other words, fiscal cooperation cannot achieve full employment in Germany and France. The underlying reason is the large external effect of fiscal policy.

4) Competition between the union central bank, the German government, and the French government. At the start there is unemployment in both Germany and France. Let unemployment in Germany exceed unemployment in France. The primary target of the union central bank is price stability in the union, and the secondary target is high employment in Germany and France. The instrument of the union central bank is union money supply. The target of the German government is full employment in Germany, and the instrument is German government purchases. The target of the French government is full employment in France, and the instrument is French government purchases. We assume that the central bank and the governments decide sequentially. First the central bank decides, and then the governments decide. In step 1, the union central bank decides. In step 2, the German government and the French government decide simultaneously and independently. In step 3, the union central bank decides. In

step 4, the German government and the French government decide simultaneously and independently. And so on.

Have a look at a numerical example. Let initial output in Germany be 940, and let initial output in France be 970. Step 1 refers to monetary policy. What is needed, then, is an increase in union money supply of 15. Step 2 refers to the output lag. The policy action raises German output and French output by 30 each. As a consequence, German output goes to 970, and French output goes to 1000. Step 3 refers to fiscal policy. What is needed in Germany is an increase in German government purchases of 30. In France, however, there is no need for a change in French government purchases. Step 4 refers to the output lag. The total effect is an increase in German output of 30 and a decline in French output of equally 30. As a consequence, German output goes to 1000, and French output goes to 970. In step 5, French government purchases are raised by 30. In step 6, French output goes to 1000, and German output goes to 970. And so on. There is a one-time increase in union money supply. There is an upward trend in German government purchases, as there is in French government purchases. There are uniform oscillations in German output, as there are in French output. The German economy oscillates between unemployment and full employment, as does the French economy. As a result, the process of monetary and fiscal competition is unstable. In other words, monetary and fiscal competition does not lead to full employment in Germany and France.

5) Cooperation between the union central bank, the German government, and the French government. The targets are full employment in Germany and France. The instruments are union money supply, German government purchases, and French government purchases. So there are two targets and three instruments. As a result, there is an infinite number of solutions. In other words, monetary and fiscal cooperation can achieve full employment in Germany and France. Have a look at a numerical example. Let initial output in Germany be 940, and let initial output in France be 970. What is needed, for instance, is an increase in union money supply of 22.5, an increase in German government purchases of 7.5, and a reduction in French government purchases of equally 7.5.

2. The World of Two Monetary Regions

1) Monetary competition between Europe and America. The world consists of two identical regions, say Europe and America. First consider the static model. An increase in European money supply raises European output. On the other hand, it lowers American output. Here the rise in European output exceeds the fall in American output, as is well known. Correspondingly, an increase in American money supply raises American output. On the other hand, it lowers European output. Here the rise in American output exceeds the fall in European output. In the numerical example, an increase in European money supply of 100 causes an increase in European output of 300 and a decline in American output of 100. Likewise, an increase in American money supply of 100 causes an increase in American output of 300 and a decline in European output of 100. That is to say, the internal effect of monetary policy is very large, and the external effect of monetary policy is large.

Second consider the dynamic model. At the beginning there is unemployment in both Europe and America. More precisely, unemployment in Europe exceeds unemployment in America. The target of the European central bank is full employment in Europe, and the instrument is European money supply. The European central bank raises European money supply so as to close the output gap in Europe. The target of the American central bank is full employment in America, and the instrument is American money supply. The American central bank raises American money supply so as to close the output gap in America. We assume that the European central bank and the American central bank decide simultaneously and independently. In addition there is an output lag. As a result, the process of monetary competition is stable. In other words, monetary competition leads to full employment in Europe and America.

Third consider a numerical example. Let full-employment output in Europe be 1000, and let full-employment output in America be the same. Let initial output in Europe be 940, and let initial output in America be 970. Step 1 refers to the policy response. What is needed in Europe is an increase in European money supply of 20. And what is needed in America is an increase in American money supply of 10. Step 2 refers to the output lag. The net effect is an increase in

European output of 50 and an increase in American output of 10. As a consequence, European output goes to 990, and American output goes to 980. In step 3, European money supply is raised by 3.3, and American money supply is raised by 6.7. In step 4, European output goes to 993.3, and American output goes to 996.7. And so on. There is a continuous increase in European money supply, as there is in American money supply. And there is a continuous increase in European output, as there is in American output.

2) Monetary cooperation between Europe and America. The targets are full employment in Europe and America. The instruments are European and American money supply. So there are two targets and two instruments. As a result, there is a solution to monetary cooperation. In other words, monetary cooperation can achieve full employment in Europe and America. Have a look at a numerical example. Let initial output in Europe be 940, and let initial output in America be 970. What is needed, then, is an increase in European money supply of 26.25 and an increase in American money supply of 18.75.

3) Fiscal competition between Europe and America. First consider the static model. An increase in European government purchases raises both European output and American output. And what is more, the rise in European output is equal to the rise in American output. Similarly, an increase in American government purchases raises both American output and European output. And what is more, the rise in American output is equal to the rise in European output. In the numerical example, an increase in European government purchases of 100 causes an increase in European output of 100 and an increase in American output of equally 100. Likewise, an increase in American government purchases of 100 causes an increase in American output of 100 and an increase in European output of equally 100. In a sense, the internal effect of fiscal policy is rather small, whereas the external effect of fiscal policy is quite large.

Second consider the dynamic model. At the start there is unemployment in both Europe and America. Let unemployment in Europe exceed unemployment in America. The target of the European government is full employment in Europe, and the instrument is European government purchases. The European government raises European government purchases so as to close the output gap in Europe. The target of the American government is full employment in America, and the instrument is American government purchases. The American government raises American government purchases so as to close the output gap in America. We assume that the European government and the American government decide simultaneously and independently. In addition there is an output lag. As a result, the process of fiscal competition is unstable. In other words, fiscal competition does not lead to full employment in Europe and America. The underlying reason is the large external effect of fiscal policy.

Third consider a numerical example. Let initial output in Europe be 940, and let initial output in America be 970. Step 1 refers to the policy response. What is needed in Europe is an increase in European government purchases of 60. And what is needed in America is an increase in American government purchases of 30. Step 2 refers to the output lag. The total effect is an increase in European output of 90 and an increase in American output of equally 90. As a consequence, European output goes to 1030, and American output goes to 1060. In step 3, European government purchases are lowered by 30, and American government purchases are lowered by 60. In step 4, European output goes to 940, and American output goes to 970. And so on. There is an upward trend in European government purchases. By contrast, there is a downward trend in American government purchases. There are uniform oscillations in European output, as there are in American output. The European economy oscillates between unemployment and overemployment, as does the American economy. There is a continuous appreciation of the euro and a continuous depreciation of the dollar. Accordingly, there is a continuous decline in European exports and a continuous increase in American exports. Moreover, after a certain number of steps, American government purchases are down to zero.

4) Fiscal cooperation between Europe and America. The targets are full employment in Europe and America. The instruments are European and American government purchases. So there are two targets and two instruments. As a result, there is no solution to fiscal cooperation. In other words, fiscal cooperation cannot achieve full employment in Europe and America. The underlying reason is the large external effect of fiscal policy. Have a look at a numerical example. Let initial output in Europe be 940, and let initial output in America be 970. What is needed, for instance, is an increase in European and American government purchases of 15 each. The total effect is an increase in European and American output of 30 each.

Symbols

A	autonomous term
B	autonomous term
C	(private) consumption
G	government purchases
I	(private) investment
L	money demand
M	money supply
P	price level
Q	imports
W	nominal wage rate
X	exports
Y	output, income
$\overline{Y}$	full-employment output

b	interest sensitivity of investment
c	marginal consumption rate
d	differential
e	exchange rate
h	exchange rate sensitivity of exports
j	interest sensitivity of money demand
k	income sensitivity of money demand
m	marginal import rate
q	marginal import rate
r	interest rate
s	$1 - c$
t	time

α	parameter
β	parameter
γ	parameter

δ   parameter
ε   parameter
η   parameter
λ   speed of adjustment

A Brief Survey of the Literature

The focus of this survey is on the macroeconomics of monetary union. It is based on that given in Carlberg (2002). As a starting point take the classic papers by Fleming (1962) and Mundell (1963, 1964, 1968). They discuss monetary and fiscal policy in an open economy characterized by perfect capital mobility. The exchange rate can either be flexible or fixed. They consider both the small open economy and the world economy made up of two large countries.

The seminal papers by Levin (1983) as well as by Rose and Sauernheimer (1983) are natural extensions of the papers by Fleming and Mundell. They deal with stabilization policy in a jointly floating currency area. It turns out, however, that the joint float produces results for the individual countries within the currency area and for the area as a whole that in some cases differ sharply from those in the Fleming and Mundell papers.

The currency area is a small open economy with perfect capital mobility. For the small currency area, the world interest rate is given exogenously. Under perfect capital mobility, the interest rate of the currency area coincides with the world interest rate. Therefore the interest rate of the currency area is constant, too. The currency area consists of two countries. The exchange rate within the currency area is pegged. The exchange rate between the currency area and the rest of the world is floating. Country 1 manufactures good 1, and country 2 manufactures good 2. These goods are imperfect substitutes. The authors examine monetary and fiscal policy by one of the countries in the currency area, paying special attention to the effects on the domestic country and the partner country. Moreover they study demand switches within the currency area as well as a realignment of the exchange rate within the currency area.

The most surprising finding is that a fiscal expansion by one of the countries in the currency area produces a contraction of economic activity in the other country. This beggar-my-neighbour effect can be so strong as to cause a decline in economic activity within the area as a whole. Conversely, a monetary expansion by one of the countries in the currency area produces an expansion of economic activity in the other country as well. Levin concludes his paper with a

256

practical observation. Since the cross effects of fiscal expansion in one currency area country may well be negative because of the joint float, it is crucial for econometric model builders concerned with linkages within a currency area to incorporate the induced exchange rate movements into their models.

Sauernheimer (1984) argues that a depreciation brings up consumer prices. To prevent a loss of purchasing power, trade unions call for higher money wages. On that account, producer prices go up as well. He sums up that the results obtained in the 1983 papers are very robust. Moutos and Scarth (1988) further investigate the supply side and the part played by real wage rigidity. Under markup pricing, there is no beggar-my-neighbour effect of fiscal policy. Under marginal cost pricing, on the other hand, the beggar-my-neighbour effect is a serious possibility. Feuerstein and Siebke (1990) also model the supply side. In addition, they introduce exchange rate expectations. The monograph by Feuerstein (1992) contains a thorough analysis of the supply side. Beyond that the author looks into wage indexation and the role of a lead currency. Over and above that, she develops a portfolio model of a small currency area.

The books by Hansen, Heinrich and Nielsen (1992) as well as by Hansen and Nielsen (1997) are devoted to the economics of the European Community. As far as the macroeconomics of monetary union is concerned, the main topics are policy coordination, exchange rate expectations, and slow prices. In the paper by Wohltmann (1993), prices are a slow variable. Both inflation expectations and exchange rate expectations are rational. He contemplates an economy with or without wage indexation. The paper by Jarchow (1993) has a world economy that consists of three large countries. Two of them share one money. Prices are flexible, and real wages are fixed. A fiscal expansion in union country 1 enhances union income. Unfortunately, it can depress the income of union country 2. It can inflate prices in each of the union countries. A depreciation of the union currency is possible.

The present book by Carlberg is volume five of a series on monetary union. Volume two (2000) studies the scope and limits of macroeconomic policy in a monetary union. The focus is on pure policies, policy mixes, and policy coordination. The leading protagonists are the union central bank, national governments, and national trade unions. Special emphasis is put on wage shocks and wage restraint. This book develops a series of basic, intermediate, and more advanced models. A striking feature is the numerical estimation of policy multipliers. A lot of diagrams serve to illustrate the subject in hand. The monetary union is an open economy with high capital mobility. The exchange rate between the monetary union and the rest of the world is flexible. The world interest rate can be exogenous or endogenous. The union countries may differ in money demand, consumption, imports, openness, or size.

Volume three (2001) explores the new economics of monetary union. It carefully discusses the effects of shocks and policies on output and prices. Shocks and policies are country-specific or common. They occur on the demand or supply side. Countries can differ in behavioural functions. Wages can be fixed, flexible, or slow. In addition, fixed wages and flexible wages can coexist. Take for instance fixed wages in Germany and flexible wages in France. Or take fixed wages in Europe and flexible wages in America. A special feature of this book is the numerical estimation of shock and policy multipliers. Further topics are inflation and disinflation. Take for instance inflation in Germany and price stability in France. Then what policy is needed for disinflation in the union? And what will be the dynamic effects on Germany and France?

Volume four (2002) studies the causes and cures of inflation in a monetary union. It carefully discusses the effects of money growth and output growth on inflation. The focus is on producer inflation, currency depreciation and consumer inflation. For instance, what determines the rate of consumer inflation in Europe, and what in America? Moreover, what determines the rate of consumer inflation in Germany, and what in France? Further topics are real depreciation, nominal and real interest rates, the growth of nominal wages, the growth of producer real wages, and the growth of consumer real wages. Here productivity growth and labour growth play significant roles. Another important issue is target inflation and required money growth. A prominent feature of this book is the numerical estimation of shock and policy multipliers. Further information about these books is given on the web-page:
http://www.unibw-hamburg.de/WWEB/vwl/carlberg/netcarl1.htm

Finally have a look at a list of some recent books:
- Alesina, A., Blanchard, O., Gali, J., Giavazzi, F., Uhlig, H., Defining a Macroeconomic Framework for the Euro Area, London 2001

- Allsopp, C., Vines, D., eds., Macroeconomic Policy after EMU, Oxford 1998
- Begg, D., Canova, F., De Grauwe, P., Fatas, A., Lane, P., Surviving the Slowdown, London 2002
- Brunila, A., Buti, M., Franco, D., eds., The Stability and Growth Pact, Houndmills 2001
- Buti, M., Sapir, A., eds., Economic Policy in EMU, Oxford 1998
- Buti, M., Sapir, A., eds., EMU and Economic Policy in Europe: The Challenge of the Early Years, Cheltenham 2002
- Calmfors, L., et al., EMU – A Swedish Perspective, Dordrecht 1997
- Clausen, V., Asymmetric Monetary Transmission in Europe, Berlin 2000
- De Grauwe, P., The Economics of Monetary Union, Oxford 2000
- Deissenberg, C., Owen, R., Ulph, D., eds., European Economic Integration, Oxford 1998
- Eichengreen, B., European Monetary Unification, Cambridge 1997
- Eijffinger, S., De Haan, J., European Monetary and Fiscal Policy, Oxford 2000
- Gros, D., Thygesen, N., European Monetary Integration, London 1998
- Hughes Hallet, A., Hutchison, M. M., Jensen, S. H., eds., Fiscal Aspects of European Monetary Integration, Cambridge 1999
- Hughes Hallet, A., Mooslechner, P., Schürz, P., eds., Challenges for Economic Policy Coordination within European Monetary Union, Dordrecht 2001
- Issing, O., Gaspar, V., Angeloni, I., Tristani, O., Monetary Policy in the Euro Area, Cambridge 2001
- Masson, P. R., Krueger, T. H., Turtelboom, B. G., eds., EMU and the International Monetary System, Washington 1997
- Mundell, R. A., Clesse, A., eds., The Euro as a Stabilizer in the International Economic System, Dordrecht 2000
- OECD, EMU: One Year On, Paris 2000
- Smets, J., Dombrecht, M., eds., How to Promote Economic Growth in the Euro Area, Cheltenham 2001
- Von Hagen, J., Waller, C. J., eds., Regional Aspects of Monetary Policy in Europe, Dordrecht 2000

References

ALESINA, A., BLANCHARD, O., GALI, J., GIAVAZZI, F., UHLIG, H., Defining a Macroeconomic Framework for the Euro Area, London 2001

ALLSOPP, C., DAVIES, G., McKIBBIN, W., VINES, D., Monetary and Fiscal Stabilization of Demand Shocks within Europe, in: Review of International Economics 5(4), 1997, 55 – 76

ALLSOPP, C., McKIBBIN, W., VINES, D., Fiscal Consolidation in Europe: Some Empirical Issues, in: A. Hughes Hallett, M. M. Hutchison, S.E.H. Jensen, eds., Fiscal Aspects of European Monetary Integration, Cambridge 1999

ALLSOPP, C., VINES, D., eds., Macroeconomic Policy after EMU, Oxford 1998

ALOGOSKOUFIS, G., PORTES, R., The Euro, the Dollar, and the International Monetary System, in: P. R. Masson, T. H. Krueger, B. G. Turtelboom, eds., EMU, Washington 1997

ANDERSEN, T. M., Fiscal Stabilization Policy in a Monetary Union with Inflation Targeting, University of Aarhus 2002

ARTIS, M., NIXSON, F., eds., The Economics of the European Union, Oxford 2001

BAIMBRIDGE, M., WHYMAN, P., eds., Economic and Monetary Union in Europe, Cheltenham 2002

BALDWIN, R. E., On the Microeconomics of the European Monetary Union, in: European Economy, Special Edition No 1, 1991

BAYOUMI, T., Financial Integration and Real Activity, Ann Arbor 1997

BAYOUMI, T., EICHENGREEN, B., Shocking Aspects of European Monetary Integration, in: F. Torres, F. Giavazzi, eds., Adjustment and Growth in the European Monetary Union, Cambridge 1993

BEAN, C., Economic and Monetary Union in Europe, in: Journal of Economic Perspectives 6, 1992, 31 - 52

BEAN, C., Monetary Policy under EMU, in: Oxford Review of Economic Policy 14(3), 1998, 41 - 53

BEETSMA, R., BOVENBERG, A. L., The Interaction of Fiscal and Monetary Policy in a Monetary Union: Credibility and Flexibility, in: A. Razin, E. Sadka, eds., Globalization: Public Economic Perspectives, Cambridge 1997

BEETSMA, R., DEBRUN, X., KLAASSEN, F., Is Fiscal Policy Coordination in EMU Desirable?, CEPR Discussion Paper, 2001

BEGG, D., Alternative Exchange Rate Regimes: The Role of the Exchange Rate and the Implications for Wage-Price Adjustment, in: European Economy, Special Edition No 1, 1991

BEGG, D., CANOVA, F., DE GRAUWE, P., FATAS, A., LANE, P., Surviving the Slowdown, London 2002

BEGG, D., VON HAGEN, J., WYPLOSZ, C., ZIMMERMANN, K. F., eds., EMU: Prospects and Challenges for the Euro, Cambridge 1998

BELKE, A., BAUMGÄRTNER, F., Fiskalische Transfermechanismen und asymmetrische Schocks in Euroland, in: Vierteljahreshefte zur Wirtschaftsforschung, 71. Jahrgang, Heft 3, 2002

BERNANKE, B., LAUBACH, T., MISHKIN, F., POSEN, A., Inflation Targeting, Princeton 1999

BERTOLA, G., BOERI, G., NICOLETTI, G., eds., Welfare and Employment in a United Europe, Cambridge 2000

BINI SMAGHI, L., GROS, D., Open Issues in European Central Banking, London 2000

BLANCHARD, O., Macroeconomics, Upper Saddle River 2003

BLINDER, A. S., Central Banking in Theory and Practice, Cambridge 1998

BOFINGER, P., Monetary Policy, Oxford 2001

BRANSON, H. W., HENDERSON, D. W., GOLDSTEIN, M., eds., International Policy Coordination and Exchange Rate Fluctuations, Chicago 1990

BREUSS, F., Außenwirtschaft, Wien 1998

BREUSS, F., WEBER, A., Economic Policy Coordination in the EMU: Implications for the Stability and Growth Pact, in: A. Hughes Hallet et al., eds., Challenges for Economic Policy Coordination within European Monetary Union, Dordrecht 2001

BRUNILA, A., BUTI, M., FRANCO, D., eds., The Stability and Growth Pact, Houndmills 2001

BRYANT, R., The Coordination of National Stabilization Policies, in: A. Hughes Hallett et al., eds., Challenges for Economic Policy Coordination within European Monetary Union, Dordrecht 2001

BRYANT, R., International Coordination of National Stabilization Policies, Washington 1995

BRYSON, J. H., Fiscal Policy Coordination and Flexibility under European Monetary Union, in: Journal of Policy Modeling 16, 1994, 541 - 557

BRYSON, J. H., Macroeconomic Stabilization Through Monetary and Fiscal Policy Coordination: Implications for European Monetary Union, in: Open Economies Review 5, 1994, 307 - 326

BUITER, W. H., The Economic Case for Monetary Union in the European Union, in: Review of International Economics 5(4), 1997, 10 - 35

BUITER, W., CORSETTI, G., ROUBINI, N., Excessive Deficits: Sense and Nonsense in the Treaty of Maastricht, in: Economic Policy 16, 1993, 57 – 100

BUITER, W. H., MARSTON, R. C., eds., International Economic Policy Coordination, Cambridge 1985

BURDA, M., European Labour Markets and the Euro: How Much Flexibility Do We Really Need?, in: Deutsche Bundesbank, ed., The Monetary Transmission Process, Houndmills 2001

BURDA, M., WYPLOSZ, C., Macroeconomics, Oxford 2001

BUTI, M., SAPIR, A., eds., Economic Policy in EMU, Oxford 1998

BUTI, M., SAPIR, A., eds., EMU and Economic Policy in Europe: The Challenge of the Early Years, Cheltenham 2002

CAESAR, R., SCHARRER, H. E., eds., European Economic and Monetary Union, Baden-Baden 2001

CALMFORS, L., Macroeconomic Policy, Wage Setting, and Employment – What Difference Does the EMU Make?, in: Oxford Review of Economic Policy 14(3), 1998, 125 - 151

CALMFORS, L., et al., EMU - A Swedish Perspective, Dordrecht 1997

CALVO, G. A., DORNBUSCH, R., OBSTFELD, M., eds., Money, Capital Mobility, and Trade, Cambridge 2001

CANZONERI, M. B., DIBA, B. T., The Stability and Growth Pact: A Delicate Balance or an Albatross?, in: A. Hughes Hallett et al., eds., Challenges for Economic Policy Coordination within European Monetary Union, Dordrecht 2001

CANZONERI, M. B., HENDERSON, D. W., Monetary Policy in Interdependent Economies, Cambridge 1991

CARLBERG, M., An Economic Analysis of Monetary Union, Berlin New York 2001

CARLBERG, M., Economic Policy in a Monetary Union, Berlin New York 2000

CARLBERG, M., European Monetary Union, Heidelberg New York 1999

CARLBERG, M., Inflation in a Monetary Union, Berlin New York 2002

CARLBERG, M., International Economic Growth, Heidelberg 1997

CARLBERG, M., Intertemporal Macroeconomics: Deficits, Unemployment, and Growth, Heidelberg New York 1998

CARLBERG, M., Sustainability and Optimality of Public Debt, Heidelberg 1995

CARRARO, C., et al., eds., International Economic Policy Coordination, Oxford 1991

CHOI, J. J., WRASE, J. M., eds., European Monetary Union and Capital Markets, Amsterdam 2001

CLAASSEN, E. M., Global Monetary Economics, Oxford 1996

CLAASSEN, E. M., ed., International and European Monetary Systems, Oxford 1990

CLAUSEN, V., Asymmetric Monetary Transmission in Europe, Berlin 2000

CLAUSEN, V., HAYO, B., Makroökonomische Implikationen der Mitgliedschaft Deutschlands in der Europäischen Währungsunion, in: Vierteljahreshefte zur Wirtschaftsforschung, 71. Jahrgang, Heft 3, 2002

COHEN, D., How Will the Euro Behave?, in: P. R. Masson et al, eds., EMU, Washington 1997

COLLIGNON, S., Monetary Stability in Europe, London 2002

COMMISSION OF THE EC, The Economics of EMU, in: European Economy, Special Edition No 1, 1991

COMMISSION OF THE EC, One Market, One Money, in: European Economy 44, 1990

COMMISSION OF THE EC, Stable Money, Sound Finances, in: European Economy 53, 1993

COMMITTEE FOR THE STUDY OF ECONOMIC AND MONETARY UNION, Report on Economic and Monetary Union in the European Community, Luxembourg 1989

COOPER, R. N., Economic Interdependence and Coordination of Economic Policies, in: R. W. Jones, P. B. Kenen, eds., Handbook of International Economics, Amsterdam 1985

COOPER, R. N., The Economics of Interdependence, New York 1968

DANIELS, J. P., VANHOOSE, D. D., Two-Country Models of Monetary and Fiscal Policy, in: Open Economies Review 9, 1998, 263 – 282

DASEKING, C., Makroökonomische Interdependenzen in einer Wechselkursunion, Frankfurt 1994

DE BONIS, V., Stabilization Policy in an Exchange Rate Union, Heidelberg 1994

DE GRAUWE, P., The Economics of Monetary Union, Oxford 2000

DE GRAUWE, P., Fiscal Policies in the EMS - A Strategic Analysis, in: E.M. Claassen, ed., International and European Monetary Systems, Oxford 1990

DE GRAUWE, P., The Interaction of Monetary Policies in a Group of European Countries, in: Journal of International Economics 5, 1975, 207-228

DEISSENBERG, C., OWEN, R., ULPH, D., eds., European Economic Integration, Oxford 1998

DEMERTZIS, M., HUGHES HALLETT, A., VIEGI, N., Can the ECB be Truly Independent? Should It Be?, in: A. Hughes Hallett et al., eds., Challenges for Economic Policy Coordination within European Monetary Union, Dordrecht 2001

DEUTSCHE BUNDESBANK, ed., The Monetary Transmission Process: Recent Developments and Lessons for Europe, Houndmills 2001

DIXIT, A., Games of Monetary and Fiscal Interactions in the EMU, in: European Economic Review 45, 2001, 589-613

DIXIT, A., LAMBERTINI, L., Monetary-Fiscal Policy Interactions and Commitment versus Discretion in a Monetary Union, in: European Economic Review 45, 2001, 977-987

DORNBUSCH, R., FISCHER, S., STARTZ, R., Macroeconomics, New York 2001

DULLIEN, S., HORN, G. A., Auswirkungen der Europäischen Währungsunion auf die deutsche Wirtschaft, Berlin 1999

DUWENDAG, D., KETTERER, K. H., KÖSTERS, W., POHL, R., SIMMERT, D. B., Geldtheorie und Geldpolitik in Europa, Berlin 1999

DYSON, K., European States and the Euro, Oxford 2002

EICHENGREEN, B., European Monetary Unification, Cambridge 1997

EICHENGREEN, B., Policy Making in an Integrated World: From Surveillance to...?, in: A. Hughes Hallett et al., eds., Challenges for Economic Policy Coordination within European Monetary Union, Dordrecht 2001

EIJFFINGER, S., DE HAAN, J., European Monetary and Fiscal Policy, Oxford 2000

ENGEL, G., RÜHMANN, P., Hg., Geldpolitik und Europäische Währungsunion, Göttingen 2000

EUROPEAN CENTRAL BANK, The Monetary Policy of the ECB, Frankfurt 2001

FAVERO, C., et al., One Money, Many Countries, London 2000

FELDSTEIN, M., The European Central Bank and the Euro: The First Year, in: Journal of Policy Modeling 22, 2000, 345 – 354

FELDSTEIN, M., ed., International Economic Cooperation, Chicago 1988

FEUERSTEIN, S., Studien zur Wechselkursunion, Heidelberg 1992

FEUERSTEIN, S., SIEBKE, J., Wechselkursunion und Stabilitätspolitik, in: Zeitschrift für Wirtschafts- und Sozialwissenschaften 110, 1990, 359 – 379

FISCHER, S., International Macroeconomic Policy Coordination, in: M. Feldstein, ed., International Economic Cooperation, Chicago 1988

FISCHER, S., Roundtable on Lessons of European Monetary Integration for the International Monetary System, in: P. R. Masson et al., eds., EMU, Washington 1997

FLEMING, J. M., Domestic Financial Policies under Fixed and Floating Exchange Rates, in: IMF Staff Papers 9, 1962, 369 - 380

FRATIANNI, M., SALVATORE, D., VON HAGEN, J., eds., Macroeconomic Policy in Open Economies, Westport 1997

FRIEDMAN, B. M., HAHN, F. H., eds., Handbook of Monetary Economics, Amsterdam 1990

GALI, J., GERTLER, M., LOPEZ-SALIDO, J. D., European Inflation Dynamics, in: European Economic Review 45, 2001, 1237 – 1270

GANDOLFO, G., International Finance and Open-Economy Macroeconomics, Berlin 2001

GHOSH, A., MASSON, P., Economic Cooperation in an Uncertain World, Cambridge 1994

GIOVANNINI, A., et al., The Monetary Future of Europe, London 1993

GIOVANNINI, A., MAYER, C., eds., European Financial Integration, Cambridge 1991

GROS, D., THYGESEN, N., European Monetary Integration, London 1998

HAMADA, K., The Political Economy of International Monetary Interdependence, Cambridge 1985

HAMADA, K., KAWAI, M., International Economic Policy Coordination: Theory and Policy Implications, in: M. U. Fratianni, D. Salvatore, J. von Hagen, eds. Macroeconomic Policy in Open Economies, Westport 1997

HANSEN, J. D., ed., European Integration, Oxford 2001

HANSEN, J. D., HEINRICH, H., NIELSEN, J. U., An Economic Analysis of the EC, London 1992

HANSEN, J. D., NIELSEN, J. U., An Economic Analysis of the EU, London 1997

HAYO, B., Empirische und theoretische Studien zur Europäischen Währungsunion, Frankfurt 1998

HEFEKER, C., Lohnpolitik und Geldpolitik in Euroland, in: Vierteljahreshefte zur Wirtschaftsforschung, 71. Jahrgang, Heft 3, 2002

HEISE, A., Hg., Makropolitik zwischen Nationalstaat und Europäischer Union, Marburg 1999

HEISE, A., Theorie optimaler Lohnräume – Zur Tarifpolitik in der Europäischen Währungsunion, in: Vierteljahreshefte zur Wirtschaftsforschung, 71. Jahrgang, Heft 3, 2002

HORN, G. A., SCHEREMET, W., ZWIENER, R., Wages and the Euro, Heidelberg New York 1999

HUART, F., Spillover Effects of Fiscal Policy in EMU: A Misconception behind the Stability Pact, Discussion Paper, Lille 2002

HUGHES HALLET, A., HUTCHISON, M. M., JENSEN, S. H., eds., Fiscal Aspects of European Monetary Integration, Cambridge 1999

HUGHES HALLET, A., McADAM, P., The Stability Pact and the Interdependence of Monetary and Fiscal Policy Rules, in: A. Hughes Hallet et al., eds., Challenges for Economic Policy Coordination within European Monetary Union, Dordrecht 2001

HUGHES HALLET, A., MOOSLECHNER, P., SCHÜRZ, P., eds., Challenges for Economic Policy Coordination within European Monetary Union, Dordrecht 2001

ILLING, G., Theorie der Geldpolitik, Berlin 1997

ISSING, O., Anmerkungen zur Koordinierung der makroökonomischen Politik in der WWU, in: Vierteljahreshefte zur Wirtschaftsforschung, 71. Jahrgang, Heft 3, 2002

ISSING, O., GASPAR, V., ANGELONI, I., TRISTANI, O., Monetary Policy in the Euro Area, Cambridge 2001

ITALIANER, A., The Euro and Internal Economic Policy Coordination, in: A. Hughes Hallett et al., eds., Challenges for Economic Policy Coordination within European Monetary Union, Dordrecht 2001

JARCHOW, H. J., Fiskalpolitik in einer Währungsunion, in: Finanzarchiv 50, 1993, 187 - 203

JARCHOW, H. J., RÜHMANN, P., Monetäre Außenwirtschaft, Göttingen 2003

KEHOE, P. J., Coordination of Fiscal Policies in a World Economy, in: Journal of Monetary Economics 19, 1987, 349-376

KENEN, P. B., Economic and Monetary Union in Europe, Cambridge 1995

KORKMAN, S., Fiscal Policy Coordination in EMU: Should it Go beyond the SGP?, in: A. Brunila et al., eds., The Stability and Growth Pact, Houndmills 2001

KRUGMAN, P., Lessons of Massachusetts for EMU, in: F. Giavazzi, F. Torres, eds., The Transition to Economic and Monetary Union in Europe, Cambridge 1993

KRUGMAN, P., The Return of Depression Economics, New York 1999

KRUGMAN, P. R., OBSTFELD, M., International Economics, New York 2002

LANDMANN, O., JERGER, J., Beschäftigungstheorie, Berlin 1999

LAWLER, P., Monetary Policy and Asymmetrical Fiscal Policy in a Jointly Floating Currency Area, in: Scottish Journal of Political Economy 41, 1994, 142 - 162

LEIDERMAN, L., SVENSSON, L., eds., Inflation Targeting, London 1995

LEVIN, J. H., On the Dynamic Effects of Monetary and Fiscal Policy in a Monetary Union, in: K. V. Maskus et al., eds., Quiet Pioneering, Michigan 1997

LEVIN, J. H., A Model of Stabilization Policy in a Jointly Floating Currency Area, in: J. S. Bhandari, B. H. Putnam, eds., Economic Interdependence and Flexible Exchange Rates, Cambridge 1983

LEVINE, P., Fiscal Policy Coordination under EMU and the Choice of Monetary Instrument, in: Manchester School 61, Supplement, 1993, 1-12

LEVINE, P., BROCINER, A., Fiscal Policy Coordination and EMU, in: Journal of Economic Dynamics and Control 18, 1994, 699-729

MARK, N. C., International Macroeconomics and Finance, Oxford 2001

MASSON, P. R., KRUEGER, T.H., TURTELBOOM, B. G., eds., EMU and the International Monetary System, Washington 1997

MASSON, P. R., TAYLOR, M. P., Fiscal Policy within Common Currency Areas, in: Journal of Common Market Studies 31, 1993, 29 – 44

McCALLUM, B. T., International Monetary Economics, Oxford 1995

McKIBBIN, W. J., Empirical Evidence on International Economic Policy Coordination, in: M. U. Fratianni, D. Salvatore, J. von Hagen, eds., Macroeconomic Policy in Open Economies, Westport 1997

McKIBBIN, W. J., SACHS, J. D., Global Linkages, Washington 1991

McMILLAN, J., Game Theory in International Economics, London 1986

MEADE, J., WEALE, M., Monetary Union and the Assignment Problem, in: Scandinavian Journal of Economics 97, 1995, 201-222

267

MICHAELIS, J., PFLÜGER, M., Euroland: Besser als befürchtet, aber schlechter als erwartet, in: Vierteljahreshefte zur Wirtschaftsforschung, 71. Jahrgang, Heft 3, 2002

MOOSLECHNER, P., SCHUERZ, M., International Macroeconomic Policy Coordination: Any Lessons for EMU? A Selective Survey of the Literature, in: A. Hughes Hallett et al., eds., Challenges for Economic Policy Coordination within European Monetary Union, Dordrecht 2001

MOSER, T., SCHIPS, B., eds., EMU, Financial Markets and the World Economy, Dordrecht 2001

MOUTOS, T., SCARTH, W., Stabilization Policy within a Currency Area, in: Scottish Journal of Political Economy 35, 1988, 387 - 397

MÜCKL, W. J., Hg., Die Europäische Währungsunion, Paderborn 2000

MUNDELL, R. A., EMU and the International Monetary System, in: A. Giovannini et al., eds., The Monetary Future of Europe, London 1993

MUNDELL, R. A., International Economics, New York 1968

MUNDELL, R. A., CLESSE, A., eds., The Euro as a Stabilizer in the International Economic System, Dordrecht 2000

NEUMANN, M. J. M., Internationale Wirtschaftspolitik: Koordination, Kooperation oder Wettbewerb?, in: J. Siebke, Hg., Monetäre Konfliktfelder der Weltwirtschaft, Berlin 1991

NEUMANN, M. J. M., Koordination der Makropolitik in Europa, in: B. Gahlen, H. Hesse, H. J. Ramser, Hg., Europäische Integrationsprobleme, Tübingen 1994

OBSTFELD, M., ROGOFF, K., Foundations of International Macroeconomics, Cambridge 1996

OECD, EMU: Facts, Challenges and Policies, Paris 1999

OECD, EMU: One Year On, Paris 2000

OHR, R., THEURL, T., Hg., Kompendium Europäische Wirtschaftspolitik, München 2000

PADOAN, P. C., ed., Monetary Union, Employment and Growth, Cheltenham 2001

PADOA-SCHIOPPA, T., et al., Efficiency, Stability, and Equity, Oxford 2000

PADOA-SCHIOPPA, T., The Road to Monetary Union in Europe, Oxford 1994

PAPADOPOULOU, D. M., Makroökonomik der Wechselkursunion, Frankfurt 1993

PENTECOST, E. J., VAN POECK, A., eds., European Monetary Integration, Cheltenham 2001

268

PERSSON, T., TABELLINI, G., Political Economics, Cambridge 2000

PFLÜGER, M., FRITSCHE, U., Stabilisierungspolitik in Euroland, in: Vierteljahreshefte zur Wirtschaftsforschung, 71. Jahrgang, Heft 3, 2002

PISANI- FERRY, J., et al., A French Perspective on EMU, Paris 1993

POHL, R., GALLER, H. P., Hg., Implikationen der Währungsunion für makroökonometrische Modelle, Baden-Baden 2001

POHL, R., GALLER, H. P., eds., Macroeconometric Modelling of the German Economy in the Framework of Euroland, Baden-Baden 2002

ROSE, K., SAUERNHEIMER, K., Theorie der Außenwirtschaft, München 1999

ROSE, K., SAUERNHEIMER, K., Zur Theorie eines Mischwechselkurssystems, in: M. Feldsieper, R. Groß, Hg., Wirtschaftspolitik in weltoffener Wirtschaft, Berlin 1983, 15 - 28

RÜBEL, G., Grundlagen der Monetären Außenwirtschaft, München 2001

RÜBEL, G., ed., Real and Monetary Issues of International Economic Integration, Berlin 2000

SALVATORE, D., The Euro, the Dollar, and the International Monetary System, in: Journal of Policy Modeling 22, 2000, 407 – 415

SARNO, L., TAYLOR, M., The Economics of Exchange Rates, Cambridge 2002

SAUERNHEIMER, K., Fiscal Policy in einer Wechselkursunion, in: Finanz-archiv 42, 1984, 143 - 157

SIEBERT, H., ed., Quo Vadis Europe?, Tübingen 1997

SITZ, A., Währungsunion oder Wechselkursflexibilität, Frankfurt 2001

SMETS, J., DOMBRECHT, M., eds., How to Promote Economic Growth in the Euro Area, Cheltenham 2001

SPAHN, H. P., From Gold to Euro, Berlin 2001

STABILISIERUNGSPOLITIK IN EUROLAND, in: Vierteljahreshefte zur Wirtschaftsforschung, 71. Jahrgang, Heft 3, 2002

STAHN, K., Reputation und Kooperation in einer Währungsunion, Frankfurt 2000

STAUDINGER, S., Coordinating Monetary Policy between Ins and Outs, in: G. Rübel, ed., Real and Monetary Issues, Berlin 2000

SVENSSON, L. E. O., Monetary Policy Issues für the Eurosystem, in: Carnegie-Rochester Conference Series on Public Policy 51, 1999, 79 - 136

TAYLOR, J. B., Macroeconomic Policy in a World Economy, New York 1993

TAYLOR, J. B., WOODFORD, M., eds., Handbook of Macroeconomics, Amsterdam 1999

TORRES, F., GIAVAZZI, F., eds., Adjustment and Growth in the European Monetary Union, Cambridge 1993

VAN DER PLOEG, F., Macroeconomic Policy Coordination and Monetary Integration: A European Perspective, The Hague 1989

VIREN, M., Fiscal Policy, Automatic Stabilisers and Coordination, in: A. Brunila et al., eds., The Stability and Growth Pact, Houndmills 2001

VON HAGEN, J., MUNDSCHENK, S., Koordinierung der Geld- und Fiskalpolitik in der EWU, in: Vierteljahreshefte zur Wirtschaftsforschung, 71. Jahrgang, Heft 3, 2002

VON HAGEN, J., WALLER, C. J., eds., Regional Aspects of Monetary Policy in Europe, Dordrecht 2000

VON WEIZSÄCKER, C. C., Logik der Globalisierung, Göttingen 1999

WAGNER, H., Europäische Wirtschaftspolitik, Berlin 1998

WALSH, C., Monetary Theory and Policy, Cambridge 1998

WELFENS, P. J. J., European Monetary Union and Exchange Rate Dynamics, Berlin 2000

WOHLTMANN, H. W., Transmission nationaler Wirtschaftspolitiken in einer Wechselkursunion, in: Jahrbücher für Nationalökonomie und Statistik 211, 1993, 73 - 89

Index

Druck: Strauss Offsetdruck, Mörlenbach
Verarbeitung: Schäffer, Grünstadt